PREFACE

By Sir Harry Secombe

There's nothing quite like coming across a 50-year-old newspaper or magazine – when you're moving house, perhaps, or having a particularly vigorous spring-clean. The shape and size of their yellowing pages may look familiar, but their contents seem to come from another world.

The Bygone Britain series explores our past through the pages of these old newspapers and magazines, which were only ever meant to be bought, read for a day or so and thrown away, but often end up lining people's drawers or wrapped round their crockery.

I find them endlessly fascinating. On the one hand here are events familiar through the reasoned analysis of history – battles, political upheavals – reported with vivid immediacy. Yet news items such as Chamberlain's successful appeasement mission to Berlin can only be viewed through the lens of hindsight. There are also the news stories that took a long time to happen: the earliest of many items about the Channel Tunnel in Bygone Britain is dated 1907!

Quite unselfconsciously, the articles, letters and advertisements reveal completely different priorities from our own. It is quite shocking that a small and ostensibly sentimental item about the discovery of an abandoned baby finishes with the casual disclosure that the infant was then consigned to the workhouse. Conversely, the behaviour of these aliens from another age has the power to amuse us in a way that would make them quite indignant: the excruciating niceties of visiting cards are surely no laughing matter, and what on earth is wrong with attempting to banish grey hair with radium? Likewise, in these knowledgeable days of niche marketing and core business, we find it absurd to see an advertisement urging hairdressers to sell the odd bicycle on the side.

But there are many hints that the people who populate these pages are not such strangers to us after all. Get-rich-quick schemes and dubious books already feature prominently in the small ads, and the slimming advertisements seem as widespread as in our own press. Some of the ideas voiced in the articles are ones that we thought our own generation had come up with: domestic science as a subject for boys, the dangers of too much exposure to the sun. And, needless to say, affairs of the heart loom large across the pages, whatever the decade.

The things that we can recall ourselves exert their own particular attraction. Coverage of events we remember, pictures of celebrities, advertisements for objects we coveted excite a warm glow of recognition and affection. Other pictures may arouse quite opposite emotions: horror and self-loathing to think that we ever went around with lapels like that! Our reactions to our memories are as much a gauge of how we as individuals have changed as of how society has changed.

So what conclusions can we draw from leafing through the pages of the Bygone Britain books? The increasing pace of technological change is evident, as is the growing informality – in manners, in language, and in address to the readers. The problem page letters confirm this. Early in the century, the letters themselves do not appear; all we see are the replies, addressed to a mysterious correspondent with a fanciful name: Heart's Ease or Sapphire. Fifty years later many writers think nothing of revealing their true identities along with their troubles. (In passing, let us be thankful for the demise of the enterprising service offered by the *Hairdressers and Toilet Requisites Gazette*, whereby people sent in samples of falling hair – and worse – for trichological analysis.)

Does the very different look of the articles in the 1900s and those of the 1960s – tiny, dense text with small headlines giving way to more spacious type with *Sun*-style screamers – mean that our powers of concentration are declining? That papers and magazines have to try harder to wrest our attention from television is obvious, but modern technology, availability of newsprint, and more widespread literacy have all played their part in shaping our contemporary press.

Whether you have a serious interest in British history and society, or you're an avid consumer of trivia; whether you can remember most of the first seventy years of this century, or you weren't even born, you will find plenty to wonder at, to mourn and to laugh about in the Bygone Britain series.

BYGONE BRITAIN

IN THE NEWS
1900–1970

LONDON: HMSO

Researched and prepared by Publishing Services, Central Office of Information.

© Selection and introduction Crown copyright 1995

Applications for reproduction should be made to HMSO

First published 1995

ISBN 0 11 701894 5

Published by HMSO and available from:

HMSO Publications Centre
(Mail, fax and telephone orders only)
PO Box 276, London SW8 SDT
Telephone orders 0171 873 9090
General enquiries 0171 873 0011
(queuing system in operation for both numbers)
Fax orders 0171 873 8200

HMSO Bookshops
49 High Holborn, London, WC1V 6HB
(counter service only)
0171 873 0011 Fax 0171 831 1326
68-69 Bull Street, Birmingham, B4 6AD
0121 236 9696 Fax 0121 236 9699
33 Wine Street, Bristol, BS1 2BQ
0117 9264306 Fax 0117 9294515
9-21 Princess Street, Manchester, M60 8AS
0161 834 7201 Fax 0161 833 0634
16 Arthur Street, Belfast, BT1 4GD
01232 238451 Fax 01232 235401
71 Lothian Road, Edinburgh EH3 9AZ
0131 228 4181 Fax 0131 229 2734
The HMSO Oriel Bookshop
The Friary, Cardiff CF1 4AA
01222 395548 Fax 01222 384347

HMSO's Accredited Agents
(see Yellow Pages)

and through good book sellers

Acknowledgments

We would like to thank the staff of the British Library Newspaper Library at Colindale
for their ready and cheerful assistance and co-operation, and for their expertise in problem
solving. The staff at the British Library at Bloomsbury have also helped in turning up rare
and distant journals. We are also indebted to the National Magazine Company, to the
National Federation of Women's Institutes, and to the Thomas Cook archive, who so kindly
allowed us to access to their archives. Copyright in the extracts quoted generally belongs to
the newspapers and the magazines concerned, and to their successors in business. Present
owners have been most kind in granting permission to quote. In spite of all our efforts, it
has not been possible to trace all present copyright owners in the extracts featured.

We would like to thank our colleagues in COI Pictures Section for helping us to choose the
photographs for this book.

The cover photograph of the investiture of the Prince of Wales is by courtesy of Topham
Picturepoint.

INTRODUCTION

In 1900 self-confident Britain, a small group of islands off north-west Europe (with unpredictable weather, draughty houses and no idea of good cooking), was arguably the world's greatest power, and its empire, and its people, reached to the furthest parts of the world. By 1970 the days of empire had gone. Self-doubt and self-criticism had succeeded self-confidence, but British influence still made itself felt in different, less direct, ways.

In the News draws on innumerable newspapers both national and regional, journals, and magazines. Here are some of the serious, not so serious and unusual news stories of the period 1900–70. They form a patchwork of quotes, and reports, about eye-catching incidents – some a part of history, some forgotten. The scene is mainly Britain, but a few overseas events that made an impact at home are also highlighted – for example, the Delhi durbar of 1912, the death of Lenin, the Wall Street crash, and the Soviet invasion of Czechoslovakia. Although the national dailies are featured, many of the events appear as covered by the regional press: thus the death of Queen Victoria is reported by the *Abergavenny Chronicle*, and an awful indictment of crime in London in 1919 comes from the *Tavistock Gazette*.

Causes célèbres, headlines and stories from the gossip columns; coronations, royal weddings, jubilees; careers of celebrated people; the deeds of pioneers and heroes; spy sensations, diplomatic coups, war news and scandals – these are only part of the coverage. The endless to-ings and fro-ings of the peerage and high society were described with reverence throughout the press between 1900 and the 1930s. By the 1950s one senses a change of focus. In 1958 a group of frenzied teenage Scots girls charged and overwhelmed Tommy Steele. ('I have never experienced anything like it', said a steward. 'I thought he was going to be killed.') By the late 1960s we were getting the latest on the Great Train robbers or the stars of swinging London: Simon Dee, for example, or Cilla Black, Lulu, Joe Orton, or Chi Chi the panda. In 1900 papers reported the relief of Mafeking and the Boxer rebellion; much detail and one telling headline after another prefaced these reports. Apart from news from the front, the First World War coverage throws light on the Edith Cavell story ('a pitiable tragedy') and the public's concern about Zeppelin raids. For war's end, the *Lisburn Herald* provides a delightfully scatty report.

British views on Hitler; mass production of gas masks and other harbingers of war; and the Abdication are all featured. Wartime hardship and effort contrast with post-war reconstruction and the fruits of prosperity in the 1950s and 1960s, when North Sea oil was beginning to flow. Burning issues in the 1940s and 1950s were the groundnuts scheme and the endless search for the abominable snowman, as were Piltdown man, and the four-minute mile. There were amazing transformations in the quality of life: according to Harold Macmillan in 1957, the British had 'never had it so good' (he also appears many years earlier, in 1913, when, as an Oxford undergraduate, he speaks as a guest at the Cambridge Union).

By the late 1960s the stories seem so much closer to home, yet it is still a shock to realise that they are a whole generation away. Britain's position in Europe was just as much an issue as it is today. Emotions about the Vietnam war were running high. Vassall, Profumo and Philby underlined the chill of the Cold War, and in 1970 the Leila Khaled affair again focused attention on the Palestinian problem.

The early 1900s see the deaths of Lord Queensberry and Oscar Wilde, Sir Arthur Sullivan, Queen Victoria, Cecil Rhodes, Baroness Burdett-Coutts, Algernon Swinburne and Florence Nightingale. Pity Lord Pirbright in 1903, when *Public Opinion* couldn't really think of anything much to say, the lord in question being rather an upright nonentity. Dr Crippen, George Bernard Shaw, Scott of the Antarctic, Rebecca West and Lawrence of Arabia were among the headline makers of the period 1910–1930; King George V made the first royal Christmas Day broadcast in 1932, establishing himself as an accomplished broadcaster. We have a glimpse of the first marriage in 1933 of the lovely, and wealthy Margaret Whigham, future Duchess of Argyll, first debutante to manage her own publicity, and one of Britain's most consistent social column headline makers. In the musical world 1953 brings the early death of the adored Kathleen Ferrier, among the very greatest singers Britain has ever produced, and an early appearance of the infant Andrew Lloyd Webber.

In the early years there is also much, and at length, about the evils of drink, which throws light on urban misery and deprivation. See *Good Tidings* in 1903, *British Workman* in 1905, or *Scottish Women's Temperance News* in 1908. In 1908 *Vegetarian* sponsored a huge gathering at Central Hall, Westminster, to promote the reward to be gained from clean living. Alas, the wavering tones of the group of over-eighties assembled on the platform could not be heard. Social evils and the dark side of life loom large in accounts of plague in Glasgow and street mugging by 'hooligans' in 1900, the murder of millionaire store-owner William Whiteley in 1907, and the Sidney Street siege in 1911. In 1935, according to the *Dover Express*, magistrates pondered on whether the miners (often in the news) could afford to own a wireless.

Suffragettes are a perennial news item in the early years. In 1914 the mortified mother of two fractious girls had to apologise for the protest they staged at a court at Buckingham Palace. In 1958 the last presentations took place, but by this time debutantes apparently had no axes to grind.

The British obsession (perhaps justified) about the weather emerges from reports of the lightning and snow in December 1906, the great fogs of the 1940s and 1950s, and the subsequent campaign for cleaner air.

We can always be relied upon to enter wholeheartedly into national moments of exaltation and pain. Various are included here: the conquest of Everest coincides with the coronation of Queen Elizabeth II in 1953; and the death of Arkle in June 1970 marked the departure of a great national favourite, perhaps the most extolled racehorse of modern times – an event guaranteed to unite the British in grief and nostalgia.

John Collis
August 1995
Central Office of Information

1900 ■ 1909

LORD QUEENSBERRY CREMATED.

In the grey dawn of Saturday the ashes of the Marquis of Queensberry, whose body was cremated at Woking the previous day, were consigned to their final resting-place at Kinmont, Dumfries, the family estate, which has now passed into the possession of Mr. E. T. Brook, manufacturer, Huddersfield.

The obsequies were of a simple character, prayers being offered up by the parish minister.

Daily Mail **1900**

ANOTHER HOOLIGAN VICTIM.

Addressing a jury at the Bethnal-green Coroner's Court yesterday, Dr. Wynn Westcott, Coroner for North-East London, said, "There seems to be an outbreak of crimes of violence at the present time. You should have had a third case here this morning, but we have been unable to get sufficient evidence on the matter, and therefore had to postpone the inquiry. A man was supposed to have been attacked by roughs in the streets, and so much injured that he died in the Bethnal-green Infirmary. I understand the police of these divisions, Bethnal-green, Hoxton, and Hackney, have been strengthened, with a view of preventing this ruffianism in our streets, which is so prevalent at the present time." The latest victim of Hooliganism was named John Schaefer, a general labourer, aged 33 years, who resided with his father at 9, Baxendale-street, Bethnal-green, and on Sunday night was kicked to death in Gibraltar-walk, a narrow thoroughfare running off Bethnal-green-road.

Evening Standard **1900**

COURT CHRONICLE.

WINDSOR CASTLE.

ON WEDNESDAY morning, the 21st ult., the Queen went out, accompanied by Princess Victoria of Schleswig-Holstein. In the afternoon Her Majesty drove out, accompanied by Princess Victoria of Schleswig-Holstein, and attended by the Hon. Mrs Mallet.

On THURSDAY morning the Queen went out, accompanied by Princess Henry of Battenberg. In the afternoon Her Majesty drove out, accompanied by Princess Henry of Battenberg, with Princess Victoria Eugénie, and attended by Viscountess Downe. Prince Victor Napoleon and Prince Louis Buonaparte visited Her Majesty.

On FRIDAY morning the Queen went out, accompanied by Princess Henry of Battenberg. In the afternoon Her Majesty drove out, accompanied by Princess Christian of Schleswig-Holstein, and attended by the Hon. Aline Majendie.

On SATURDAY morning the Queen went out, accompanied by Princess Henry of Battenberg and Princess Victoria Eugénie. In the afternoon Her Majesty and Princess Henry of Battenberg drove out, attended by Viscountess Downe. The Duchess of Albany and Princess Alice arrived at the Castle.

On SUNDAY morning the Queen and the Royal family, as well as the members of the Royal household, attended Divine service in the private chapel. The Rev. J.H. Ellison, M.A., Chaplain in Ordinary to Her Majesty and vicar of Windsor, officiated. The Bishop of Winchester preached. In the afternoon Her Majesty drove out, accompanied by Princess Henry of Battenberg and the Duchess of Albany.

On MONDAY morning the Queen went out, accompanied by the Princess Alice of Albany. Her Majesty held a Council at half-past one. In the afternoon Her Majesty and Princess Henry of Battenberg drove out, attended by Viscountess Downe.

On TUESDAY morning the Queen went out, accompanied by Princess Alice of Albany.

Queen **1900**

THE LATE SIR ARTHUR SULLIVAN.

FUNERAL ARRANGEMENTS.

By the gracious permission of her Majesty, the funeral service preceding the interment of the remains of Sir Arthur Sullivan in Brompton Cemetery on Tuesday next will take place at noon that day in the Chapel Royal, St. James's.

The service, fully choral in character, will be conducted by the Sub-Dean, the Rev. Dr. Edgar Sheppard, the priests in waiting being the Rev. R. Tahourdin and the Rev. H. G. Daniell-Bainbridge, the last mentioned attending with Sir Frederick Bridge to represent Westminster Abbey. Dr. Cresar has undertaken to be at the organ, and the opening sentences of the Burial Service will be sung to Croft's setting by the full choir of the Chapels Royal. Stainer's music has been chosen for Psalm xxxix., and the Lesson will be read by the Sub-Dean. It has not yet been definitely decided whether the anthem is to be the one from Sir Arthur Sullivan's oratorio *The Light of the World*, based on the words, "Yea, though I walk through the valley of the shadow of death," or his beautiful melody so often impressively rendered in his own presence at the Chapel Royal, St. James's :—

> "Wreaths for our graves the Lord hath given,
>   The tomb with crowns is hung,
> And, blest with music learnt in Heav'n,
>   Our song of praise is sung.
> The gulf of death, now dark with fears,
>   Is bridged by hope and love ;
> The memories we have sown in tears
>   Bloom fair in light above."

The antiphon, "I heard a voice from heaven," will be sung to the music of Sir J. Goss, and the hymn which Sir Arthur Sullivan made so popular, "We are but strangers here," is to follow.

At the conclusion of this part of the service the body of the deceased musician will be removed to Brompton Cemetery, where the interment is fixed to take place, the Rev. Dr. Sheppard, as an old personal friend of Sir Arthur Sullivan, officiating to the close. On the arrival of the *cortège* at the grave, the actual committal will be preceded by the reading of several sentences from the service ordered for the Burial of the Dead ; and after the usual prayer, which is appointed to follow, it is possible that another work of the departed will be heard—namely, the anthem, "Brother, thou art gone before us," which Sir A. Sullivan set to the familiar words of Dean Milman.

The names of the pall bearers cannot yet be definitely announced, but they are being selected from a large circle of old personal friends and gentlemen prominently associated with the musical and dramatic professions.

Owing to the limited amount of accommodation available in the Chapel Royal, it will be impossible to admit thereto more than a tithe of those who have already applied for tickets, and we are requested by the family of Sir Arthur Sullivan to state that all further applications for seats at St. James's must of necessity be regretfully declined.

Evening Standard **1900**

THE PLAGUE AT GLASGOW.

ANOTHER CASE.

It is officially announced to-day that there is another case of plague at Glasgow, a ward-cleaner in Belvidere Hospital having contracted the disease. The woman, however, had been inoculated, and the attack is of the mildest type. The cases now number 17. There is one suspected case, and 115 persons are under observation.

Evening Standard 1900

THE PEKIN LEGATIONS.
ANOTHER REASSURING MESSAGE.
MINISTERS TO BE SENT TO TIEN-TSIN.

A telegram reached the Foreign Office this morning from her Majesty's Consul at Tien-tsin, dated the 21st inst., stating that he had that day received a letter from her Majesty's Minister at Pekin dated the 4th inst. appealing for relief. There were enough provisions to last a fortnight, but the garrison was unequal to hold out against the determined attack for many days. There had been 44 deaths, and about double the number of wounded.

WASHINGTON, JULY 24.

Wu-Ting-Pang, the Chinese Minister, has received a cablegram from Sheng Taotai stating that the Foreign Ministers at Pekin are to be sent under escort to Tien-tsin, and the Imperial Government has not only been protecting them, but has also supplied them with food.—Reuter.

Evening Standard 1900

LONDON'S ROAR OF JUBILATION.

WILD FRENZY THAT SURPASSES DESCRIPTION.

LORD MAYOR SPEAKS TO A VAST SHOUTING MULTITUDE.

THOUSANDS SERENADE MRS. BADEN-POWELL.

Mafeking is free! No more doubt, no more anxiety, no more hours of weary waiting for the glad news. It has come.

At 9.30 last night the announcement came that the Boers had abandoned the siege. It is not possible to gauge the rapidity with which the news spread through the metropolis and throughout the country, for almost immediately, from all parts, came inquiries by telephone asking if it was true.

London simply went wild with delight.

Daily Mail 1900

Winston Churchill (far right) as a prisoner in the Boer War.

CAMEOS AND CURIOS OF COURT LIFE.

By the Author of "An Englishman in Paris."

THE CZAR IN PROVERB.

Kings may be bless'd, but Tam was glorious,
O'er a' the ills o' life victorious.—BURNS.

ONE MAY SAFELY TAKE IT THAT, great poet though he was, the author of "Tam O'Shanter" had but a very vague notion of the inner life of the Russian people, and of their mental and moral attitude towards such an autocrat as Catherine the Great. There was not the remotest reference to them when he wrote the above lines, yet it would be difficult to find any more pertinently describing that attitude. The average Scotsman, however, has that in common with the Slav—and notably is this the case with the peasantry and the humbler classes, that both are unconsciously epigrammatic in their criticism of men and things, and above all of the great ones of the earth.

As a rule, the Russians of the less educated kind leave their rulers alone in normal times. Their submission is almost complete. Next to God, they can think of nothing more majestic, more entitled to reverence, than their Czars. But when illness or death supervenes, they depart from their mutism; they feel, as the American Colton expressed it, that " kings and their subjects, masters and slaves, find a common level in two places—at the foot of the Cross and in the grave." And that feeling finds vent in their proverbs, some of which are very old, others more modern, but all exceedingly pithy.

The rumours about Nicholas II.'s illness were most disquieting at the beginning of last week; as I write they are more reassuring, although it is feared that, owing to his far from robust constitution, the recovery of the young ruler will be very slow. In October, 1894, Russia was equally swayed between hope and dread, and the tongues of the mouchiks became loosened. At that period I took some pains to collect their proverbs, but it is a far cry from London to the nearest European frontier of the mighty Empire, and owing to other duties, and, above all, to a series of papers on the Czars, the opportunity for publishing them at the right moment was lost.

Queen 1900

DEATH OF OSCAR WILDE.

Mr. Oscar Wilde died yesterday afternoon in a small hotel in the Latin Quarter of Paris. The cause of death was meningitis. The verdict that a jury passed upon his conduct at the Old Bailey in 1895, destroyed for ever his reputation, and condemned him, remarks the *Times*, to ignoble obscurity for the remainder of his days. When he had served his sentence of two years' imprisonment, he was broken in health as well as bankrupt in fame and fortune. He was the son of the late Sir William Wilde, an eminent Irish surgeon. His mother was a graceful writer, both in prose and verse. He had a brilliant career at Oxford, and undoubted talents in many directions. He was known as a poet of graceful diction; as an essayist of wit and distinction; later on as a playwright of skill and subtle humour. All his plays, adds our contemporary, had the same qualities—a paradoxical humour and a perverted outlook on life being the most prominent. They were packed with witty sayings, and the author's cleverness gave him at once a position in the dramatic world. The revelations of the criminal trial in 1895 naturally made them impossible for some years. Recently, however, one of them was revived, though not at a West-end theatre. After his release in 1897, Wilde published " The Ballad of Reading Gaol." He also appeared in print as a critic of our prison system, against the results of which he entered a passionate protest. For the last three years he has lived abroad. It is stated on the authority of the *Dublin Evening Mail* that he was recently received into the Roman Catholic Church. Mrs. Oscar Wilde died not long ago, leaving two children.

Pall Mall Gazette 1900

RECONCILED, BUT—

"Notwithstanding the so-called Liberal re-union, Mr. Asquith and others still claim their full right of free speech, and we venture therefore to seriously doubt if the condition of Liberalism has been improved by this surface show of unity. The divergence must, soon or late, come to practical expression."—Daily Paper.

He (Campbell-Bannerman):—"And now, darling, we are quite reconciled again."
She (Asquith):—"Quite, dearest."
He:—"And you will not say any of those unkind things again, will you, dear?"
She:—"Unkind things, dearest? I never said anything unkind."
He:—"Oh, but, darling, I'm sure——"
She:—"Nonsense! I only objected to you flirting so outrageously with that horrid Miss Pro-Boer."
He:—"I? Miss Pro-Boer? Why, I never——"
She:—"Oh, you horrid man! How can you——"
(And so on. And the whole row begins again.)

Daily Express 1901

TRAGEDY AT KEW BRIDGE.

Yesterday evening, between eight and nine o'clock, on the arrival of a City train at Kew Bridge Station, the station master noticed a well-dressed gentleman sitting in the corner of a first-class compartment. He had paid no attention to the cries of "All change," and the official went in and shook him, thinking he was asleep. The man collapsed, and it was then observed that he was bleeding from wounds in the head. Acting-sergeant Clayden, 47 T R, was called, and he sent for Dr. Henshaw, who said the unfortunate man had been dead some time. His death had been caused by a bullet entering the mouth and passing out at the back of the head, and then through his hat. A six-chambered revolver was found on the floor, that had been once discharged. There was nothing to lead to identification. He had a massive ring on, but only 3½d. in money. He had a return ticket from Finsbury Park to Kensal Rise. He is about 40. It is presumed he had been to Doncaster Races, and changed at Finsbury Park and Dalston.

Evening Standard 1900

LONDON GRAIN MARKET.

THE BALTIC.—WHEAT.—Trading to-day in cargoes of wheat of all qualities and in all positions has ruled quiet, but holders are firm, asking yesterday's prices. No sales are reported.

MAIZE steady, but inactive. 21s. 7½d. asked steamers mixed American, shipment within 21 days, and 19s. 6d. for December-January. Plate sellers do not offer, and round qualities are unchanged.

BARLEY quiet. Azoff, shipping or shipped, would come at 19s.

OATS dull, and if anything in buyers' favour.

Parcels to London inactive. Sales:—Maize: Mixed American, September, 20s. 6d.

London Wheat "Futures."—At the first call the official quotations of the London Produce Clearing House were:—September, 6s 8½d ; October, 6s 9½d ; December, 6s 10¾d ; March, 7s 0¾d.

Maize "Futures" opened as follows:—September, 4s. 5¼d. ; December, 4s. 3d. ; February, 4s.

Evening Standard 1900

GROWING SCHOOL RATES.

LIVERPOOL'S STRONG ACTION.

Liverpool City Council yesterday debated for nearly three hours the question of the expenditure of the school board, which has issued a precept for £171,000, a sum £42,000 more than that levied last year, or equal to an increased rate of threepence in the pound. The finance committee of the council proposed that provision should be made for the precept demanded, but an amendment was submitted that a petition be presented to Parliament to give the control of school board work to the borough council and county council. After a long discussion on school board extravagance and the gift of free education to classes of the community for whom it was not originally intended, the amendment was carried by 45 votes to 32. A further amendment was submitted that, "in view of promised legislation on the subject, the council take no action in the matter until the intentions of Parliament are known." This was approved by 41 votes to 38, and when put as a substantive motion it was agreed to. Nothing of a political character was introduced into the discussion.

Daily Express 1901

M.P.'S MEASURING FISH.

In one of the Committee-rooms of the House of Commons yesterday was witnessed the strange sight of a group of honourable and gallant members standing round a trunk of small fish.

Spread out on the floor were hundreds of immature plaice, and Mr. Akers-Douglas, First Commissioner of Works, was busily engaged with a footrule measuring the length of many of them.

Round him were Sir W. Brampton Gurdon, Mr. C. Seale-Hayne, Hon. L. W. Rothschild, Mr. G. Doughty, and Mr. M. Vaughan Davies, all assisting in the novel occupation.

The trunk of fish had been brought straight from the fishing cutter to convince the members of the Committee that a vast quantity of immature and undersized flat-fish are being landed and sold to the detriment of the fish supplies.

There were 400 to 500 plaice in the trunk, but of these only about ten were over the prescribed length of 8in., and Mr. C. Hellyer, of Hull, informed the Committee yesterday that 40,000 trunks of fish of this character had been landed in London this year.

Daily Mail 1900

BARMAID SLAPPED HIS FACE.

Timothy Lane, a billiard-marker employed at the Railway Tavern, New Cross-road, S.E., pulled down a British flag which his employer hoisted in celebration of the relief of Mafeking, and expressed the opinion that the Queen ought to be shot.

His employer summarily dismissed him, and yesterday he asked the Lambeth County Court judge to give him redress.

It was stated that when Lane made use of the treasonable expression the barmaid slapped his face.

"Quite right, too," said the Judge. "A case for summary dismissal has been fully made out."

BREAK OF THE DROUGHT

WATER FAMINE PERIL STAYED, BUT NOT YET PAST.

Rain fell copiously for several hours in the northern counties yesterday, as was predicted in these columns, and leaden skies gave promise of further supplies.

Never was rain more welcome. Villagers and townsfolk, who have been on short water rations, welcomed the downpour joyously, and in many instances stood out of doors bareheaded to experience the unwonted drip of the refreshing showers.

In India, when the hot weather breaks and the first rains fall, everyone rushes out and welcomes the water; but it is an unusual enough proceeding in old England.

The drought has broken, but days of rain are required to avert all danger of the threatened famine. Fortunately, there is every indication of a real change, and a further rainfall may be expected to-day.

At Halifax, for instance, the downpour meant one day's supply roundly, and a week's continuous rain will not bring the reserve to what it was this time last year. Alderman Wade, the chairman of the Water Committee of the Halifax Corporation, has intimated that he cannot again accept such a position of responsibility as supplying 200,000 people with water.

The suggestion that heavy cannon should be fired to bring down rain is receiving much support at Halifax. Restricted supply, by shutting off from six in the evening to six in the morning, will probably continue for some time, and if there is not a lot more rain there will probably have to be more restrictions. Many mills and factories are seriously hampered. In some places old wells long since disused have been resorted to.

MANCHESTER RELIEVED.

In Manchester and district the rains of the past twenty-four hours have given considerable relief. Yesterday the inflow at Longdendale Reservoirs was almost equal to the restricted consumption, while for some time previously it had been practically nil.

Replying to complaints about the quality of the Manchester water, Sir John Harwood states that a great quantity of moss is growing in the mains. In some places it is 3ins. thick. Two years ago, when the pipes were cleaned, 700 tons of moss, shells, and other things were taken out.

The Waterworks Committee have been criticised for not having the second pipe to Thirlmere completed. Sir John now says that if the work had been proceeded with as originally intended the pipes would have cost £80,000 more than now, owing to the state of the market. Fear is expressed in certain quarters that if the present restrictions are not removed there may be a serious epidemic.

A severe thunderstorm raged in Berwickshire yesterday forenoon, accompanied by brilliant lightning and heavy rain. The lightning struck a house in North-road, Berwick, and set the roof on fire. The pipes melted, but the fire was easily extinguished.

The villages in Suffolk and Essex are suffering considerably from the dryness of the season. At Middleton, near Sudbury, ponds are dried up for the first time for many years, and some of the villagers are compelled to purchase water from the fortunate owners of wells. Unless heavy rains fall serious consequences are feared.

Daily Express 1901

Daily Mail 1900

OPEN-AIR TREATMENT FOR CONSUMPTIVES.

The accompanying illustration gives an idea of the new building about to be erected in connection with the well-known hospital at Brompton, which is under the immediate patronage of both the King and Queen, where the open-air treatment will be largely practised, in addition to the convalescent home. There will be accommodation for 100 patients, these being drafted from the parent institution as they may be recommended by the physicians. This departure will involve a large outlay, but it is confidently hoped that the many friends of the charity will rally round, and of their liberality contribute to the establishment of this long-desired addition to the committee's work. The site is an admirable one, situated at Heatherside, near Frimley, Surrey, and is well adapted to the purposes required. The surroundings are delightful, and much practical good is hoped for from the healthful locality, combined with the eminent medical skill which those for whom the place is designed will have in a very large measure. We commend this new country branch of the Hospital for Consumption, Brompton, to the warm sympathy and interest of our readers.

Queen 1901

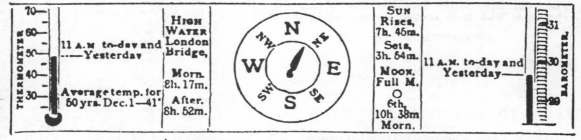

WEATHER FORECAST ISSUED AT 11 A.M. TO-DAY.

South of England (with London and Channel).—Variable breezes, finally easterly; dull, misty, slight rain locally.

Readings by Messrs. NEGRETTI and ZAMBRA's Instruments.

Pall Mall Gazette 1900

LADY WARWICK.

An Italian Organ Grinder Prosecuted on her Complaint.

At the Dunmow Police-court this afternoon an Italian organ grinder, named Carmino Diennunzio, was charged on information laid by the Countess of Warwick with having cruelly treated a monkey on April 28 at her ladyship's Essex residence, Easton Lodge.

Prisoner appeared in the court-yard at the lodge with an accordion and a monkey attached to a string. After playing several tunes and dancing about to the amusement of the servants, the man was about to leave the lodge grounds when Lady Warwick and her maid entered the courtyard, about to go out for a drive in a motor car.

Lady Warwick at once gave the man a shilling and noticing that the monkey squealed, she examined it and found its neck very much cut about. She offered to buy the animal, but the man refused to sell.

Lady Warwick at once wired to the Society for the Prevention of Cruelty to Animals and had the man arrested.

She wired from Warwick Castle that both she and her maid, who saw the alleged cruelty, were unable to leave their apartments to attend the court owing to colds.

The bench dismissed the charge, the chairman remarking that the prisoner had been sufficiently punished by being kept in prison for a week.

Evening News 1902

CRICKHOWELL.

DEATH OF THE QUEEN. – There was quite a crowd opposite the post office on the eventful 22nd January, anxiously awaiting news of the health of Her Majesty. At 7.30 a telegram arrived announcing the peaceful demise of the Queen, and the sad tidings rapidly became common knowledge. The bells of St. Edmunds' Church and St. Cattoes' Church soon sent forth their mournful dirges, and the district was plunged into the deepest sorrow. A number of the inhabitants quickly showed their deep respect for England's greatest ruler by wearing black ties, etc., and there existed everywhere evidence of great grief. Crickhowell, although one of the tiniest little towns in the realm, is most loyal to the throne, and yields to none in affection for its august ruler The neighbourhood had the honour of receiving a visit from royalty in the person of the late and lamented Duke of Clarence some years ago, and a splendid reception he had. On Sunday memorial services were held in the various churches and chapels, special reference being made to the sad event which was uppermost in all minds. The Rev. T. J. Bowen, R.D., paid a glowing tribute to the memory of "one who established herself in the affections of all." At St. Edmund's Church "God save the King" was sung with much pathos and feeling. It is expected that Saturday will be observed as a general holiday here. It is worthy of mention that all social functions have been postponed, and the Crickhowell Harriers did not meet, nor will they meet on the 2nd February.

Abergavenny Chronicle 1901

DEATH OF MR. RHODES.

Millionaire Empire-Builder who was not Sordid.

"When I am dead tread me into my grave and pass on. I shall have done my work."

The death of Mr. Cecil Rhodes occurred at three minutes to six o'clock (Cape time). It was notified in the London newspaper offices by Reuter's cablegram at thirteen minutes past six (English time). Full consciousness remained with Mr. Rhodes until three minutes before he passed away, peacefully and painlessly, in the presence of Dr. Jameson, Sir Charles Metcalfe, Mr. Smartt (Commissioner of Public Works), Colonel Elmhurst Rhodes, and Mr. Walton (member of the House of Assembly for Port Elizabeth). In addition to these close friends by his bedside, there were present all his attendants and "boys." Of all those who had watched and cared for him during his illness, Dr. Stevenson was the only one absent at the end. A few minutes previous to passing away he faintly muttered the names of his brother and some others, evidently meaning to say "good-bye."

The Cause of Death.

Mr. Rhodes's death at the early age of forty-eight, was due, as the daily bulletins indicated would be the case, to heart weakness. The first serious warning he had of this disease came when he was visiting a remote district of Rhodesia in 1897. This attack prevented him attending the opening of the direct railway line to Bulawayo.

The Carlisle Patriot.

FRIDAY, OCTOBER 28, 1904.

THE NORTH SEA OUTRAGE.

The country has been deeply stirred from one end to the other by an outrage so unprecedented, so unwarrantable, and so wholly incompatible with the ways of civilised nations, that it is difficult to believe that it can be countenanced by any responsible Government. Yet up to the time of writing the Russian Government has wholly failed to show any true appreciation of the gravity of the case. Even the message of the Czar, courteous and conciliatory as are its terms, is altogether out of keeping with the offence. For the deliberate attack upon a British fishing fleet by the Russian warships constitutes nothing less than an act of war in time of peace—a wanton insult to the British flag. The Czar expresses his "sincere regret for the sad loss of life that has occurred." He might have used the same words had a visitation of Nature played havoc with British ships.

Evening News 1902

An Alarming Indictment.

THERE is much being written and said at the present time about the demoralizing customs and habits in social life in the form of drunkenness, gambling, and smoking. Prominent ministers have been pointing out excesses in these directions committed by young and old. Observers tell of how the wine cup and the gaming table are luring women votaries to ruin.

Some may regard this charge against society women as too sweeping, yet there is reason to fear there is considerable warrant for it. Those who give themselves up to social functions lead a monotonous life and are exposed to many temptations. They are troubled with *ennui*, and seek relief from it in excitements of the passing hour. They have much time on their hands, and they try to kill it by luring pastimes. They often need stimulants to carry on their entertainments, and it is natural for them to test the effects of the tempting bowl. They come in contact with companions who find a fascination in the convivial smoke and find it hard to resist it. The victims do not mean to go to an excess, but ere they are aware they are bound in the chains of evil habits. The strong may be proof against the snares which beset their pathway, but the weak fall a prey to the temptations of their environment.

Good Tidings 1903

The Late Lord Pirbright.

LORD PIRBRIGHT succumbed, on Friday, to the illness from which he had been suffering during the last six months—an internal malady accentuated recently by a chill. He was about sixty-three years of age, and leaves no heir to his title.

The *Daily News* (Saturday):—" When the door of the House of Lords opens to the new made peer, he, in nine cases out of ten, passes finally from the light of common day. The shadows of the prison close around him, and he is forgotten. The name that he has made familiar to the world ceases to be, and with his name his personality also disappears. LORD PIRBRIGHT was an excellent example of this common-place of political life. As LORD PIRBRIGHT, he was an absolute stranger to the British public. The man in the street, if asked to state what he knew of LORD PIRBRIGHT's career, would have declared his unbelief in the existence of any such person. Yet there was a time when LORD PIRBRIGHT was one of the minor lights of Toryism and was as familiar a figure throughout the country as he was in Parliament. That was in the days when he was known as BARON DE WORMS. His peerage brought him dignity and oblivion. On only one occasion that we can remember did he emerge from the obscurity of his later years. That was when, a few weeks ago, he contributed perhaps the most effective criticism of that much riddled scheme, the Sugar Convention.

Public Opinion 1903

NEWS - OF - THE ... WEEK....

The latest Swedish invention which is being discussed is a portable telephone. With each instrument is a coil of thin copper wire, and it is reckoned that a soldier could easily carry 13,000 feet of this with him. The uses suggested for the portable telephone are innumerable. Outposts, it is declared, could by its aid keep in constant communication with the main force, and it is pointed out that it would furnish a valuable means of keeping in touch with headquarters for police and fire brigades. For use between railway carriages on a moving train, for engineers at work underground or on great public works, for steamers, etc., it would be most desirable.

＊

Crusader 1904

• • •

Mrs. Howard, of Buckingham Gate, informs us that her wire-haired bitch Tasmore Clytie by Venoel—Sting was served on the 9th and 11th of February by Mr. N. A. Louraine's Bob Brittle by Ch. Tipton Slasher—Sting.

• • •

Fox Terrier Chronicle 1905

THE Metropolitan Police number 15,765. During 1900 eighty-one were injured by stopping runaway horses, and twenty-one were hurt by vehicles while regulating the traffic. The property stolen in the twelve months was valued at £112,000, a sum less than has been recorded since 1800. There were 1,768 burglaries against 1,782 in the previous year. The number of ex-convicts let loose from London during the year amounted to 681. The public left in licensed vehicles 17,000 umbrellas and 200 watches.

Gentleman's Journal 1901

Total Abstinence and Commercial Life.

NOTABLE CITY OFFICIALS WHO ARE ABSTAINERS.

Mr. John H. Lile is well known among the Wesleyan body, as a City Guardian, as Chairman of several important Corporation Committees; he has frequently attributed his success in life to the advantages of total abstinence.

British Workman
1905

Mr. John H. Lile, C.C.

Our Octogenarians.

A HIGHLY SUCCESSFUL MEETING AT MEMORIAL HALL.

Admission to the hall was free by ticket, but late in the evening a collection was taken to defray expenses, and during this some pianoforte music was rendered. At the outset a verse was sung of the National Anthem. The front row of the platform was filled by the guests of the evening, who stood and faced the inevitable photographer, who did his work with lightning rapidity.

The octogenarians present were: Mr. C. P. Newcombe, 80; Miss Warlow, 81; Professor Mayer, 81; Mr. T. Wyles, 88; Mr. Joseph Wallace, 84; Mr. T. A. Hanson, 86; Mr. S. Saunders, 91.

The Memorial Hall lacks good accoustic properties and ordinary speakers are poorly heard. All the octogenarians could hardly be expected to be audible at the rear of the building, and indeed, some failed, but the chairman set an excellent example and read an address of more than half-an-hour's length in tones that could be heard everywhere.

Mr. NEWCOMBE has rarely spoken better. His language was chaste and spirited, his line of argument good, and his illustrations well culled. It was a speech of remarkable power and, being in manuscript, will probably, as it deservedly should, see the light.

Vegetarian **1905**

SOCIETY WEDDING.

LADY'S LATE "TRY ON."

Under Sec. 6 of the Factory and Workshops Act of 1901 Madame Jessica Rice, court dressmaker, of 49, Ebury-street, Pimlico, was summoned at Westminster Police Court yesterday for employing five young women for about an hour on a specific night this month beyond the legal limit of eight o'clock.

Miss Mary Sadler, inspector under the Act, said that overtime could be worked thirty times in a year, but notification and an accurate record and registration were essential. A chance visit being paid to defendant's premises found the young women working overtime without notice, and a prosecution was ordered.

A solicitor for the defence said that a wedding order of a lady married to a prominent Government official was the cause of the exceptional stress. The lady did not "try on" till the very latest possible moment, and defendant's young women habitually worked many hours per week less than the Act of Parliament allowed. There was in this instance a technical offence, but it amounted to nothing if a common-sense interpretation of the Act was given.

Mr. Francis: You must not ask me to say what is common-sense in an Act of Parliament. (Laughter.) This Act says that work shall commence at a particular hour in the morning. It does not say that workers "may start work."

One of the workgirls was sworn, and said they usually worked only sixty hours a week out of the sixty-eight allowed by the Act. They were treated with every consideration.

Mr. Francis said very explicit regulations were laid down for overtime exceptions. He was afraid he was not allowed by the Act to take a common-sense view in a case like this, but he had some power as to the fines. He could inflict a penalty of £5 on each summons, but he thought the justice of the case would be met of a fine of one shilling on each and payment of the costs.

Daily News **1905**

LIGHTNING AND SNOW.

A HOUSE STRUCK IN NORFOLK.

An extraordinary medley of weather early yesterday morning startled the inhabitants of some parts of East Yorkshire. A heavy fall of snow was accompanied by a severe thunderstorm, the lightning being very vivid. The storm lasted nearly two hours, and as a high wind blew at the time the snow drifted deeply on the wolds and moors.

Thunder and lightning also visited Yarmouth yesterday morning with a fall of snow.

At East Ruston, Norfolk, a flash passed through a room where a family were at breakfast, smashing glass, crockery, and furniture, tearing down a corner of the house, and slightly injuring a girl, while a man passing near was knocked down by what he described as "a cloud of smoke and fire."

The storm was renewed last night along the Yorkshire coast, and during the height of it the lightning lit up the wild scene most vividly.

From Sunderland, where tramway traffic had yesterday to be carried on with snow ploughs, also come accounts of thunderstorms, while the snowstorm recommenced last night with almost increased fury.

Manchester Guardian 1906

STARTLING ACCIDENT AT COLWYN BAY.

Shortly before four o'clock on Tuesday afternoon as a train for Llandudno was about to leave the Colwyn Bay Station Mr. A. Davies, of Wrexham, ran suddenly across the platform to enter it. Accounts differ as to what occurred, but it appears that in his hurry Mr. Davies collided with another person, who staggered back slightly, and so struck an elderly lady who was passing with her back to the train. The lady overbalanced and fell between two carriages on to the line. The train was then moving, and the stationmaster, Mr. Noble, whistled loudly to stop it. The guard applied at once the vacuum brake. In the meantime Mr. Davies, seeing the imminent peril of the lady, sprang down on to the line without hesitation and at the risk of his life. Seizing the lady he pulled her off the rail next to the platform, and when the train stopped both were under the carriage. Railway officials went to their assistance, and they were helped back on to the platform. The lady sustained no bodily injury, but she suffered considerably from nervous shock. Mr. Davies, who was complimented upon his plucky action, sustained a bruise on the arm. The event caused much excitement in the station.

London Welshman 1906

THE ELECTION CONTEST.
To-day's Declarations appear on Page 9.

Total Number of Members	670
Elected to Date	660

STATE OF PARTIES.		PARTY GAINS.	
LIBERALS AND ALLIES:—		LIBERALS AND ALLIES:—	
Liberals	374	Liberals	194
Labour	49	Labour	38
Nationalists	84	Nationalist	2
	507		234
UNIONISTS	153	UNIONISTS	14
Liberal, &c. Majority	354	Net Liberal, &c. Gain	220
Liberal majority over all others			88

Evening Standard 1906

MURDER OF WILLIAM WHITELEY.

MYSTERY OF THE MOTIVE.

SENSATIONAL THEORY UPHELD.

STRANGE STORY OF RAYNER'S FATHER.

DETAILS OF MURDERER'S DOUBLE LIFE.

Reynolds Newspaper 1907

William Whiteley, the millionaire, famous throughout the world as the "Universal Provider," whose huge emporium in Bayswater is one of the sights of London, was foully murdered on Thursday before the eyes of his shop assistants and customers. The alleged murderer is a young man, whose name is Horace George Rayner, though he has used several aliases. Eyewitnesses state that he fired twice at Mr. Whiteley with a revolver, the second shot taking fatal effect instantaneously. He then placed the revolver to his left temple, and fell dangerously wounded beside the victim.

Subsequently, the following extraordinary statement was found written on a slip of paper in one of Rayner's pockets :—

To all whom it may concern.— William Whiteley is my father, and has brought upon himself and me a double fatality by reason of his own refusal of a request perfectly reasonable.—R.I.P.

Cosmopolitan Financier 1907

The World's Gold Market.

The amount of capital in the United Kingdom—the gold market of the world—seeking profitable investment, is stupendous !

Of the aggregate wealth of the United Kingdom (expressed in a capitalised form, and estimated two or three years back by Sr. R. Giffen, the well-known statistician, to amount to no less than £15,000,000,000, a very large proportion — possibly £5,000,000,000—is on the constant look-out for a "safe thing."

Catholic Times 1908

The Dowager Duchess of Newcastle has been ordered a rest cure, which she is undergoing at 15, Mount-street, Grosvenor-square. According to medical advice she will be confined to her room for a week longer. Her friends have permission to see her for an hour daily in the afternoon. The strenuous life which the Duchess leads working among poor factory girls, attending meetings and classes in the slums, and the various poor charities clothing and needlework societies in which she is interested have told upon her health.

Evening Standard 1906

GREAT OIL BLAZE.

FIREMEN'S HARD FIGHT AT BATTERSEA.

A fine spectacle was presented by a fire which broke out about 2.30 this morning at the oil stores of Messrs. S. Bowley and Son, Wellington-road, Battersea.

A great body of firemen from the land and river stations was quickly concentrated at the outbreak, but for a long time their efforts had little effect. Thousands of spectators were attracted to the neighbourhood by the glare.

The premises run to the riverside, and the burning oil on the surface of the water gave the Thames the appearance of being on fire for about a hundred yards.

Firemen on the Beta had to turn their attention to the floating flames to prevent their drifting down the river.

Several barges were moored at Messrs. Bowley's wharf, and these caught fire, one of them sinking. The heat was intense. A quantity of iron in a yard some distance away was almost red hot, and the walls of an adjacent omnibus stable became scorched to such a degree that the horse-keepers had great difficulty in averting a stampede of the frightened animals.

People living in the vicinity removed their belongings, but the firemen were, in the end, able to confine the flames to the premises in which they broke out. The outbreak was got under by 6.0 a.m.

A portion of the premises in Wellington-road was saved, but the remaining part, stretching to the water's edge, was destroyed.

In the operations a fireman was rather badly injured, and had to be removed.

Altogether there were 140 firemen, with eighteen steamers, river floats, and an immense quantity of apparatus from stations all over London.

The loss, which is very heavy, is covered by insurance in the North British and Mercantile and other companies.

James Cable, Coxswain of the
Aldeburgh lifeboat, won the
Royal National Lifeboat
Institution's silver medal for
gallantry three times.

Scottish National Exhibition.

MORE NOTES FROM THE B.W.T.A. STALL.

With the return of autumn days and shorter nights, the attendance inside the Halls of the Exhibition was greater than in the summer months. In June, July, August, and September the music and other outdoor amusements were greatly patronised. Many a time our helpers were glad to go and listen to the lovely music at the bandstand and in the concert hall, for little was doing at the stall. In October, our last month, we were visited by many friends.

Our introduction to the public was gradual, but when we were known we were appreciated. By the time we had passed our six months in the Exhibition we were acknowledged as very real friends and helpers to all who came in our way

Sales of books and pamphlets were much more frequent.

The petition for the English Licensing Bill needed no one to advertise it; people knew what it meant and gladly gave it a help on by signing.

There were very few exceptions to this. A soldier asked if "we intended to deprive the working man of his only comfort and joy, his glass of beer." We tried to explain it to him, but it was ineffectual—his one glass had been too many for him.

Very different testimony was borne by a stalwart young policeman on the night of the closing. "Can a policeman sign the petition?" was his question. "Isn't a policeman a free man?" was the reply. "I would sign all the public-houses away if I could," he said. 'We don't need to read your phamphlets, we see too much every night." Then his last remark brought a glow of pleasure to all who heard him. "Get them all to become Christians, then we'll have no more trouble."

Scottish Women's Temperance News 1908

"Our Dumb Friends' League."

Many attractions have been arranged for the Garden Party which Mrs. Moss-Cockle is giving on behalf of "Our Dumb Friends' League," (a Society for the Encouragement of Kindness to Animals), on Saturday, September 12th, at Clewer Park, Windsor. The Mysterious Howards have kindly placed their services at the disposal of the League, and are giving an entertainment during the afternoon. Alastor, the celebrated palmist, is also to provide amusement for the guests by means of which he hopes to benefit Funds, whilst military bands will play on the lawns. Miss Lilian Braithwaite has kindly consented to say a few words on behalf of the Society, and will be supported by Mr. Arthur J. Coke, (Secretary), and others. Admission to the Garden, which will be held from 3 to 6 p.m. is by invitation card, which can be obtained through Mr Arthur J. Coke, (Secretary), at the Headquarters of the League, 118, Victoria Street, London, S.W Clewer Park is one mile from Windsor Station.

Advice 1908

The Fatal Shampoo Case.

Unpleasant Sequel.

Police Court Charges.

There has been another unpleasant sequel to the fatal shampoo case at Harrods Stores, reported in our August edition. A charge of manslaughter has been brought by the Public Prosecutor against William Henry Eardley, the manager of the department, and Beatrice Clarke, one of the assistants, in connection with the death of Helenora Catherine Horn-Elphinstone-Dalrymple, who succumbed after a dry shampoo with carbon tetrachloride.

The warrant was granted by Mr. Horace Smith at the Westminster Police Court, and the charge came on for hearing on the 24th ult.

Mr. Leycester and Mr. Francis Humphreys, instructed by Mr. Williamson, of the Treasury, prosecuted, and Mr. Bodkin defended.

Process was granted on sworn informations of Dr. Augustus Pepper, of St. Mary's Hospital, and Dr. John Henry Chaldecott, lecturer on anæsthetics at the same institution, reference also being made to the opinion expressed by the coroner's jury who investigated the circumstances of the young lady's death. The verdict given was "Accidental death, accelerated by the fumes of tetrachloride of carbon," with a rider that "Harrods Stores were not justified in employing unskilled operators to perform this dangerous operation."

Opening the case, Mr. Leycester said that on July 12th Miss Dalrymple went to Harrods for a dry shampoo. In the course of that process she died. The case for the prosecution was that this process was of a most dangerous nature, performed by the use of a most dangerous substance, and one that required skill in the administration of it; that the defendants both knew that it was a dangerous substance; that the defendant Clarke, who used it, had none of the requisite skill or knowledge to use it; and that the defendant Eardley was the person who put her into a position to do what she did.

The Process.

There was no dispute about the process, as the defendants themselves gave evidence at the inquest, and described it. On the 6th inst. Mr. Pepper, who was advising those responsible for this prosecution, and Dr. Chaldecott, an eminent anæsthetic, visited Harrods, and were, as would be expected from such a firm, treated with perfect candour and propriety. They were allowed to inspect the premises, and to witness in actual progress the operation of a dry shampoo performed by one assistant on another. It was performed, of course, in the hairdressing saloon, which was large and well ventilated. The saloon was divided into a number of cubicles—each intended for the use of a separate customer. The cubicles were, for all ordinary purposes, quite well ventilated, but for the purpose now under investigation the ventilation was of very little use.

The way in which it was done was that the customer, sitting facing a window, was operated on by an assistant who held a basin to the back of the head to catch the fluid with which the hair was washed.

Fumes from the Liquid.

About half a pint of this highly volatile fluid was used, and half a crown was charged for the process, as against eighteenpence for an ordinary shampoo. It was good for business, and no doubt customers liked it, and but for its dangerous character there was no reason why it should not be used.

There was an electric fan in each cubicle, so that a forced draught of air could be directed towards the customer's head, fulfilling the double purpose of drying the hair and dissipating the fumes from the liquid. It seemed to be recognised, counsel continued, that the fumes did need dissipating, because they were, in fact, of a most deadly nature—extremely dangerous even if inhaled by perfectly healthy persons, and, of course, still more dangerous if a person had some undetected weakness of the heart.

Immediately Collapsed.

Proceeding to deal with the facts leading up to Miss Elphinstone-Dalrymple's death, Mr. Leycester said the defendant Clarke told her that the shampoo might make her feel faint. When the shampoo had been in progress for two minutes the lady said she did not feel well, and almost immediately collapsed. Miss Clarke, no doubt with the best intention, laid her on the floor of the cubicle, where she died before the arrival of a doctor a few minutes after-

Hairdresser and Toilet Requisites Gazette 1909

The St. Blazey Siege.

Telegraphing last night the Central News Bodmin correspondent stated that Cecil Dench, the armed desperado who has remained barricaded in his house at St. Blazey since Wednesday last, still remained unarrested, but there were signs that he is reaching the end of his food supplies, and it is known that he has had nothing whatever to drink for two days. The police have decided not to make any effort to rush the house, but are keeping a vigilant watch in order to frustrate any attempt on Dench's part to escape, and also to make sure that no food goes into the house. They are convinced that the man's lack of food and water will eventually force him into submission.

Referee 1909

BARONESS BURIED

SCENES IN THE ABBEY.

MOURNERS IN TEARS.

THE QUEEN'S WREATH.

A striking tribute was paid to the memory of the late Baroness Burdett-Coutts yesterday, when great crowds assembled in the streets to witness the funeral procession pass on its way from Stratton House, her famous residence in Piccadilly, to Westminster Abbey, her last resting place.

At ten minutes past eleven the funeral began its solemn journey. During the previous two days Stratton House had been visited by more than twenty thousand people, who wished for one last glance at the great lady, whose life and work were so intimately associated with many of the interesting events and famous personalities of the Victorian era. Amidst respectful silence, the men with bared heads, the women with moist eyes, the plain oak coffin, with its silver fittings, was borne down the steps that lead into Stratton street, and placed in an open hearse. A small bunch of sweet herbs, the choice of Mr. Burdett-Coutts, the husband, and bearing the touching inscription, "To my best and dearest, from the garden on the hill," was laid upon the coffin, and was the only floral tribute of the many hundreds received at Stratton House to be taken to the Abbey.

Reynolds Newspaper 1907

12,000 Miles for £6.

The Farmer's Opportunity.

SETTLERS WANTED

FOR

NEW SOUTH WALES.

A LAND OF REWARD FOR

LABOUR AND INDUSTRY.

Full particulars will be furnished to intending Settlers on application to the Agent-General for New South Wales, 123, Cannon Street, London, E.C.

HEMLOCK POISONING AT LANDKEY.

FARMER LOSES THREE STEERS.

Mr. Owen Dunn, of Newhouse Farm, Landkey, has had the misfortune to lose three steers, value £30 during the past week. The animals are grazing with others in a field adjoining the Venn road, when on Friday morning they were found to be lying ill. Mr. Percy Penhale, veterinary surgeon, was called in, but nothing could be done to save the steers, which were suffering from hemlock poisoning, and they passed away in a few hours. In the fields in which the animals were grazing there is no hemlock growing, but Mr. Dunn thinks that the steers chewed some dry roots of hemlock (which is much more poisonous than the top growth) which possibly were in some dressing placed on the land a few months ago. Hemlock is fairly plentiful in the district, but neither Mr. Dunn nor his predecessors at Newhouse Farm has ever previously lost cattle as the result of eating this deadly poison. At Bishopstawton, about a mile distant, Mr. Prideaux, a dairyman, lost several cows from the same cause, however, about two years ago.

North Devon Journal 1909

IN PARLIAMENT.

[BY MR. SOARES, M.P.]

THE BUDGET.

In a densely crowded House, Mr. Lloyd-George rose to unfold the most dramatic Budget of modern times. With the exception of half an hour's interval at 6 o'clock, his disquisition lasted until close upon 8 o'clock in the evening. The strain imposed on members of the House was somewhat severe, not only because of the length and intricacies of the speech, but also because of the manner in which it was delivered. As a rule it is a pleasure to listen to the speeches of Mr. Lloyd George. Usually he is energetic, witty, and full of nervous vigour, but on Thursday last he displayed none of these qualities. For the first three-quarters of an hour, it is true, he dealt in his usual inspiriting and forcible manner with the social problems of the future, but from that time onwards both his voice and his strength seemed to fail. The remainder of his speech was closely written in type on voluminous sheets of paper, and these sheets were read to the House in a quiet and wearied manner until the whole of them had been disposed of. The House had not assembled, however, for the purpose of listening to oratorical fireworks. The importance lay, not in the manner of the speech, but in its matter. And as to the latter, no one will deny there was sensation both enough and to spare.

Since first it was introduced, the Budget has been called by many names, opprobrious and the reverse, but I think its best definition came from the lips of the Chancellor of the Exchequer himself. "This is a war Budget," said the Chancellor of the Exchequer: "it is for raising money to wage implacable warfare against poverty and squalidness. I cannot help hoping and believing that before this generation has passed away we shall have advanced a great step towards that good time when poverty and wretchedness, and human degradation, which always follow in its camp, will be as remote to the people in this country as the wolves that once infested its forests." No one will deny that it is essentially a Poor Man's Budget. Its distinguishing characteristics are the taxation of wealth and luxuries, and its ultimate haven is found in far-reaching measures of social progress and reform. The working-man will have to pay more for his tobacco and his whisky, but both are articles of luxury, and throughout the whole of the Budget there is not a single tax imposed which is in any way harmful to the efficiency of labour.

North Devon Journal 1909

DEATH OF MR. SWINBURNE.

HIS CAREER AND WORKS.

We deeply regret to announce the death of Mr. Swinburne, the famous poet, which occurred at his residence, the Pines, Putney, yesterday morning.

Mr. Swinburne had been suffering from influenza and pneumonia. Last Tuesday his case became critical. The patient never rallied, and the end came as stated above.

Algernon Charles Swinburne was the son of the late Admiral Charles Henry Swinburne and of Lady Jane Henrietta, daughter of the third Earl of Ashburnham. He was born in Chester-street, Grosvenor-place, on April 5, 1837. He was educated at Eton and Balliol College, Oxford, and left the university without taking a degree. He then spent some time in travelling on the Continent, and in 1864 became acquainted with Walter Savage Landor. On his return to England he became closely associated with Dante Rossetti and William Morris. Henceforth his life was that of a man of letters, and most of his time was spent in London.

Referee 1909

1910–1919

NOTED DEATH ROLL.

MISS FLORENCE NIGHTINGALE.

TWO EARLS AND A JUDGE.

As the result of a remarkable series of deaths the nation has to mourn the loss of a number of noted people. No less than five persons who have served their country nobly and well passed away during the week-end. They were:

Miss Florence Nightingale, one of the greatest women of her age.

Earl Spencer, the Liberal statesman.

Mr. Justice Walton, the distinguished judge.

Earl Amherst, a Crimean veteran.

Sir Fleetwood Edwards, Serjeant-at-Arms, House of Lords.

THE LADY OF THE LAMP.

Miss Florence Nightingale, "the Angel of the Crimea," died somewhat unexpectedly from heart failure on Saturday afternoon at her London home.

Two members of her family were present when she passed away.

Miss Nightingale celebrated her ninetieth birthday on May 12. It is more than half a century since she did her great work of organising the Army nursing service in the Crimea, and it is more than forty years since Miss Harriet Martineau, who predeceased her by thirty-four years, wrote her biography.

A grateful nation presented Miss Nightingale with £50,000, which she devoted to the foundation of the Nightingale Home for the Training of Nurses.

King Edward made her a member of the Order of Merit in 1907, and a year later the City of London gave her its freedom. She was a Lady of Grace of the Order of St. John of Jerusalem.

The "Lady of the Lamp," as she was known to the suffering soldiers of the Crimea, Miss Florence Nightingale, has held undisputed place in the hearts of English men and women as the greatest heroine of modern times.

She was the daughter of a Hampshire gentleman, and was born in Florence, Italy. When quite a girl she commenced the hospital work that relieved the sufferings of thousands, and caused her to stand out as the most romantic figure of the Victorian age.

Soon after the Crimea war had broken out reports came to hand showing how ill-equipped for a severe winter's campaign the English soldiers were. Sickness soon made its appearance in the camps, and the grim shadow of death hovered over the starved soldiers, whose bed of frozen snow was often their winding sheet.

Into this picture of death came the heroic figure of Florence Nightingale, with a band of thirty-eight noble women who had volunteered to accompany her.

Dunstable Borough Journal 1910

OLIVER CROMWELL'S HEAD.

EXHIBITED TO ARCHÆOLOGISTS.

At a meeting of the Royal Archæological Society at Burlington House last night there was exhibited to the members the embalmed head of Oliver Cromwell.

A short description and history was given by the Rev. H. R. WILKINSON, who said that it had been in his family for three generations and had never previously been exhibited, except privately. Notes made by his grandfather stated that the tradition was that the skull was blown off Westminster Hall and picked up by a sentry who hid it and only confessed on his death-bed to his wife that he had it in his possession. Afterwards it passed into the possession of the Cambridgeshire family of Russell and came to Sam Russell, a needy actor. Then it was sold to a Mr. Cox, proprietor of a museum in Spring-gardens, and transferred by him to three persons, who exhibited it in Bond-street. Next it came into the hands of Mr. Wilkinson's grandfather.

In the course of a discussion which followed SIR HENRY HOWORTH said the evidence seemed to him to make it extremely probable that the head shown was really that of the Protector.

PROFESSOR BOYD DAWKINS said he did not think he had heard of a more complete chain of circumstances, and added that he thought that the skull at Oxford, which it was once claimed was that of Cromwell, might be dismissed from their consideration.

THE PASSING OF THE KING.

This year will be known in history as the year in which King Edward VII. died. He had reigned not much more than nine years, but in that time he had won greatness, and was universally acknowledged as the most commanding figure in Europe. The year began for him much in the same way as other years. He went about amongst his people as usual and took his full share of State duties and responsibilities. On February 21 he read his Speech at the opening of Parliament, and on March 6 left for his accustomed sojourn at Biarritz. The news despatched from there gave no cause for disquietude until early in April there was a rumour that the King's health was not all that could be desired. On April 27 his Majesty returned to England, and went to Sandringham, where he caught a chill. No uneasiness was felt by the public, although it was noticed that on his return to Buckingham Palace the King remained indoors. Then, on Thursday, May 5, it was announced that he was unable to go to meet the Queen at Victoria Station. On the following day the nation was startled by the issue of a bulletin stating that his Majesty was suffering from an attack of bronchitis. Public anxiety was at once aroused, and the nation feared the worst. Throughout the day crowds of people, quiet and grave-faced, waited outside the Palace for the bulletins. These only deepened the anxiety, and hope died when at 10.30 a notice was posted on the great gate stating that there was no change in the King's condition. Still the crowds waited until, about midnight, came the sad news that King Edward had breathed his last. He had died at 11.50 p.m. on May 6.

Dunstable Borough Journal 1910

If there are any mothers to-day who leave their children entirely to the care of nurses—and

Royal Mothers as Nurses. we fear this is not improbable—the examples of Queen Victoria, Queen Alexandra, and the Princess of Wales, in looking after their children, should shame them.

The Princess of Wales has never left her children to the exclusive care of nurses; she has always been the real mistress of the nursery.

A story lately published fully emphasizes this.

A lady attending the Princess told her one day that seeing her own little girl looking ill and miserable, she examined the child and found her covered with bruises.

"Covered with bruises! How could that be? Did you not see them when she was bathed in the morning?"

"No, madam; of course her nurse baths her."

"Her nurse? Do you mean to say you leave her to a nurse? I always see to mine myself."

"But, madam! Do I understand that you see your baby bathed each morning?"

The Princess answered with a direct emphasis not unusual to her:

"See! No, I bath him myself; bath him, do you understand, every morning."

This direct motherly care should put many a Society mother to shame.

Babyland 1910

The Times 1911

BLOODSHED.

TROOPS AND CROWD IN CONFLICT.

RAILWAY WAGON BLOWN UP.

AWFUL DEATH ROLL.

SIX KILLED AND MANY INJURED.

HOSPITAL FILLED WITH WOUNDED.

Llanelly County Guardian 1911

A COINCIDENCE.

TO THE EDITOR OF THE MORNING ADVERTISER.

SIR,—As one who has been associated with electrical work since the early days—well, of over half a century or more ago—I wish to draw attention to the coincidence as regards the arrest of Crippen and the apprehension of Müller 46 years ago for the murder of Mr. Briggs, an aged City bank clerk.

One of the earliest uses of electric telegraphy by ocean cable in connection with the criminal law was the transmission to the United States of information which led to Müller's arrest. The Müller case, I may add, caused almost as much excitement at the time as the Crippen case is now arousing, and the employment of the telegraph to aid in Müller's capture earned as much applause for the inventions of science as the use of " wireless " has done in the present case.

Chief-inspector Dew, who, with the aid of Marconi's great invention and a fast mail steamer, has effected Crippen's arrest, is a rising and successful Criminal Investigation officer. I knew him when he was at Bow-street, and his zeal in the discharge of the responsible duties which now devolve upon him is evidenced by his whitening locks.

Of course the discerning officers of the Montrose from the captain down deserve great detective praise.—I am, Sir, yours, &c.,

JNO. J. CALDER.

Noel Park, Wood-green, N., Aug. 2.

Morning Advertiser 1910

Under arrest: 'Dr' Crippen walks down the gangway of the *Montrose* with his mistress, Ethel Le Neve (who had been travelling disguised as a boy), followed by Chief Inspector Dew. After a five-day trial at the Old Bailey, Crippen was found guilty and hanged on 8 October 1910.

STRIKE NEWS.

SCENES IN WEST WALES.

TRADE PARALYSED.

MILITARY RE-INFORCEMENTS AT LLANELLY

RIOT ACT READ.

JOHN JOHN.

Everything is in a state of chaos in West Wales. The blocking of the traffic on the first day of the strike appears to have completely dislocated the down line service.

All sections of the community are now feeling the inconvenience caused by the cessation of traffic, and now begin to realise the importance of railways as an indispensable part of our social system.

The feeling prevails that a dispute of such far-reaching effects cannot last long.

The chief distributing centres of Wales are now in a state of paralysis.

No milk was sent yesterday to the big towns from the rural districts of West Wales.

The Post Office Authorities are bravely contending with their difficulties by chartering motor cars, but the delivery of letters and parcels is entirely dislocated.

Three hundred out of the seven hundred soldiers drafted into Cardiff have responded to calls from other districts, Llanelly in particular, and a large number of policemen have also been "called back."

There is no getting away from the fact that the military were unnecessary at Llanelly, and with their advent the temper of the strikers and their sympathisers was raised.

The Firing on the Crowd
KILLED.
JOHN JOHN (21), tinplate worker, of Railway-terrace, a member of the Llanelly Oriental Stars football team.
LEONARD WORSELL (20), labourer, who lodged at 6 High-street, Llanelly, a native of London.

INJURED.
JOHN FRANCIS (24), tinplate worker, Glanmor-place, bullet wound through neck. Dangerous.
J. HANBURY, Railway-terrace, shot in thumb

Llanelly County Guardian **1911**

Llanelly County Guardian **1911**

VICTIMS OF THE RIOTS.

EXHAUSTIVE CORONER'S INQUIRY.

VERDICT OF "JUSTIFIABLE HOMICIDE" IN THE SHOOTING CASES.

THE JURY BRING IN A RIDER.

MYSTERY OF EXPLOSION CLEARED UP.

Captain Scott's ship, the *Terra Nova*, at McMurdo Sound, January 1911.

The dogs on the deck of the *Terra Nova*, seen from the engine room hatch.

Captain Scott,
April 1911.

Mr Meares and Captain Oates cooking food for the dogs, May 1911.

The Sidney Street siege: Winston Churchill, then Home Secretary, can be seen at the far left of the gateway.

RUSSIAN MURDERERS AT BAY

PROLONGED FIGHT WITH SCOTS GUARDS AND POLICE.

MAXIM & FIELD GUNS READY FOR ACTION.

ASSASSINS' FIERCE RESISTANCE TO THE DEATH.

The Battle of Houndsditch, in which three policemen were killed and two more injured, has been followed by amazing scenes—an orgy of naked Anarchism.

In a commonplace London street, lying between Mile End-rd. and Commercial-rd., East, two desperate Anarchists converted a house into a fort, and for eight hours carried on a pitched battle against nearly 1,000 police and soldiers.

In their search for the murderers who shot down their three comrades, the police tracked down two of the suspected men to a house in Sidney-st., and early in the morning made preparations for their arrest.

A force of police, armed with revolvers, went to the house about three or four o'clock, and, expecting resistance, made it their first care to remove from the building the tenants occupying various rooms.

OFFICIAL REPORT OF THE FIRE

The following official report of the fire was issued at the headquarters of the London Fire Brigade:—"Called at 1.30 p.m. Place, 100, Sidney-st., Mile End, East; name of occupier, unknown; business, private. Supposed cause of fire, unknown; whether insured, unknown. Damage, a house of ten rooms and contents burnt out and roof off, and two men, names and age unknown, burnt to death."

Detective-sergeant Leeson.
Who was injured in the attack.

The People 1911

LOCKED IN CIRCLE OF ICE

CAPTAIN SCOTT REMAINS IN ANTARCTIC ANOTHER YEAR.

Thrilling Adventures.

Yet another thrilling chapter has been added by Britons to the tragic story of polar adventure. From Captain Robert F. Scott has come a spirited narrative of hairbreadth escapes from death through which he passed with his companions in the course of his efforts to reach the South Pole. At the time of forwarding his despatch the goal was still 150 miles off. With four of his companions he was still pressing on, his perseverance making it necessary that he should spend another year in the Antarctic regions. As Capt. Scott has, so far as is known, failed to reach the South Pole, the honour of that great achievement belongs solely at present to Capt. Amundsen, the Norwegian explorer, whose success was recently described in our columns. Capt. Amundsen, according to his own narrative, attained the Pole on Dec. 14-17 last, and it is, of course, clear that Capt. Scott, who on Jan. 3 was still 150 miles from his objective, could not under any circumstances have beaten Amundsen in the great race for supremacy. Captain Scott's narrative was brought to New Zealand by his ship, the Terra Nova, and covers a period of nearly 12 months. It begins on Jan. 25, 1911, and ends on Jan. 3, 1912. Luck was against the explorer from the outset, and in face of many difficulties the final start for the Pole was delayed until late in the season. On Jan. 3 the party of heroes were at lat. 87.32 S., or within 150 miles of the Pole, Shackleton's farthest south lay a few days' march ahead. The explorer sent Lieut. Evans and three men back with the message dated Jan. 3, which we print below. There remained a band of five men about to undergo the supreme trial. They were:

Captain Scott, R.N.
Captain Oates, Inniskilling Dragoons (in charge of transport animals).
Dr. Wilson, chief of the Scientist Staff.
Lieut. Bowers, Royal Indian Marine, commissariat officer.
Petty Officer Evans, R.N.

Captain Scott's ship, it is stated, will return to the south in November next, to be in readiness to bring back Captain Scott and his companions after their two-year Antarctic sojourn. Meanwhile, every man whose heart responds to the story of gallant deeds will wish the prisoners of the ice all good fortune and a safe return to the honours that await them.

News of the World 1912

FRIEND OF RUSKIN.

DEATH OF NOTABLE LADY WORKER AMONG SLUM DWELLERS.

One of the most practical and energetic philanthropists of her time has just passed away by the death of Miss Octavia Hill, of Marylebone-road, London. Born about 1838, Miss Hill was a friend and pupil of Ruskin. In the 'sixties, when slumming has not yet become fashionable, Miss Hill conceived the idea of obtaining possession of some squalid house property, of collecting her own weekly rents, and of exercising what influence she could in securing the transformation alike of dwellings and of tenants. She laid her proposals before Ruskin, who advanced £3,000 for the experiment. Miss Hill then bought three houses, in a state of dirt and neglect, near her home in Marylebone. The tenants were encouraged to keep their houses clean; rents had to be paid promptly; and those whose too-frequent wife-beating and rowdiness made their neighbours miserable were quickly ejected. Her crusade against slums soon grew in strength. Houses in Marylebone were bought by Lady Ducie and another lady and placed under Miss Hill's care. As time went on more and more dwellings in different parts of London came under her control, and a number of women assisted her in her work. In 1887 was formed the Women's University Settlement in Blackfriars-road, whose members co-operated with her in dealing with cottages in Southwark. Dwellings erected by the Ecclesiastical Committee were also put under her control. Miss Hill's work was not confined to the slums. She was an active supporter of the Commons' Preservation Society, and threw herself with zeal into efforts to preserve the amenities of a beautiful landscape.

News of the World 1912

MOTOR TRAFFIC COMMITTEE.

The Select Committee of the House of Commons on motor traffic met on several days this week to consider the draft report submitted by the chairman, Sir George Toulmin, M.P. The report, it is stated, consists of some 50 pages, summarises the large body of evidence laid before the Committee, and makes various recommendations. It is expected that the report will be completed and adopted in a few days, and that it will be issued before the close of the Parliamentary session. Forecasts of the principal recommendations indicate that the Committee will strongly recommend the appointment of a central Traffic Authority, the formation of which, it will be recalled, was urged by the Royal Commission on London Traffic of 1905. In view of the increasing number of fatal accidents due to the motor omnibus it is felt that the Committee must make some recommendations which will tend to increase the safety with which these vehicles are now worked.

Tramway and Railway World 1913

2 35   DISASTER TO SCOTT EXPEDITION

CAPT SCOTT AND SOUTHERN PARTY ALL
DEAD

CENTRAL NEWS AGENCY
TAMARU N Z MON AFTN
CAPT SCOTT REACHED THE SOUTH POLE
ON JAN 18 LAST YEAR THE PARTY WAS
OVERWHELMED IN A BLIZZARD ON THEIR RE
TURN JOURNEY AND CAPT SCOTT AND THE
ENTIRE SOUTHERN PARTY PERISHED

The tape message which told London the terrible news. An earlier message stated that "a serious calamity had overtaken the expedition."

Daily Mirror 1913

WILFUL WILLIE.

NURSE REICHSTAG: "But, Master Willie, you haven't enough money to buy every Dreadnought. Do-come and look at the next window."

News of the World 1912

DRAMATIC DERBY PROTEST
Suffragist Seizes the King's Horse, and is Struck Insensible

WOMEN'S BOMBS TO GET VOTES.

Blowing Up of House Built for Mr. Lloyd George.

"TO WAKE HIM UP."

Mrs. Pankhurst Defiantly Takes All Responsibility.

Suffragettes visited the uncompleted house which was being built for Mr. Lloyd George, at Walton Heath, near Epsom, early yesterday morning and tried to blow it up with two gunpowder bombs. They were partially successful.

One of the bombs exploded and wrecked a considerable part of the upper portion of the house.

The other bomb did not explode, as a lighted candle which would have ignited the fuse was blown out by the force of the first explosion.

Had the outrage happened twenty minutes later six workmen might have been killed or seriously injured.

The damage to the house is considerable. Windows were shattered, ceilings were ripped of lath and plaster, doors were wrenched off their hinges, and two side walls were blown out of the perpendicular and cracked.

A headless hatpin and a hairpin were found in the cupboard by the second bomb, but otherwise there is little to help the police in their investigations, except a golosh dropped by one of the women in their flight.

At the head offices of the W.S.P.U., in Kingsway, official ignorance was professed of the outrage.

In the evening, however, Mrs. Pankhurst defiantly admitted that the outrage was the work of suffragettes. (Photographs on pages 1, 3 and 9.)

Daily Mirror 1913

IN MEMORIAM

Emily Wilding Davison, Died June 8, 1913

"She had the step of the unconquered, brave, not arrogant."
George Meredith.

It is with the deepest regret that we have to record the death of Emily Wilding Davison, who died at Epsom Cottage Hospital, last Sunday afternoon, of the injuries received in consequence of her protest made during the running of the Derby on Wednesday in last week. We gave the facts of what happened on the racecourse in our last issue. Miss Davison never recovered consciousness from the moment that she was knocked down by the King's horse; and although there was hope on Thursday morning that she might do so, her condition became rapidly worse as the day wore on. On Friday, an operation was performed on her by Mr. Mansell-Moullin, F.R.C.S., but it could not save her, and she died two days later. Members of the Women's Social and Political Union, who visited her on those last days, draped the head and foot of her bed in the colours of the Union, that she might die under the flag she had served so unselfishly and with such magnificent courage.

Votes for Women 1913

Last Wednesday afternoon a dramatic protest was made during the running of the Derby by a militant Suffragist—a protest which may have tragic results. As the King's horse, Anmer, was sweeping round the bend at Tattenham Corner a woman suddenly rushed out from the crowd, and, flinging herself in front of the horse, caught hold of the bridle. The horse fell, throwing the jockey and severely kicking the woman, who was flung right under the animal. She lay insensible, and was removed to Epsom Cottage Hospital, where she was at first reported to have died soon after her arrival there. This report, however, proved later to be incorrect; and it was stated by the house-surgeon, in answer to inquiries, that she was alive, though suffering from severe concussion.

She had lain unconscious since her admission to the hospital, and it was impossible to say whether her life would be saved. At nine o'clock on Wednesday evening she had not yet recovered consciousness, and the wound in her head was regarded as exceedingly serious.

The jockey, according to the *Evening News*, was suffering from slight concussion, and his left arm was injured, but no bones were broken. The same paper stated that the doctor reported to the King that it would be possible to remove

MISS EMILY DAVISON

him to London by motor-car the same evening, and to his home at Newmarket the following day.

Votes for Women 1913

Suffragettes with promotional umbrellas selling their newspaper, April 1913.

A deputation of
Cardiff suffragettes.

Mrs Pankhurst is carried away from a demonstration outside Buckingham Palace.

THE GOVERNMENT'S METHODS OF BARBARISM.

FORCIBLE FEEDING IN THE ROWETT RESEARCH INSTITUTE

BERNARD SHAW'S BOLD, BAD WORD SPOKEN.

Mrs. "Pat" Scores Triumph Nevertheless.

EVERYBODY LAUGHED.

Speech That The Author Of "Pygmalion" Didn't Make.

Mrs. Patrick Campbell uttered the Unprintable Swearword at His Majesty's Theatre on Saturday night, and the play stopped for a whole minute till the audience had done laughing.

The Censor did not intervene, and in "Pygmalion" Mr Bernard Shaw has been permitted once again to shock the British public.

"May I see you across the Park, Miss Doolittle?" politely asks a nice-mannered young "nut."

To which she replied "Not —— likely" so unexpectedly, and in such perfectly-bred tones that the effect of incongruity is overwhelming.

The phrase is absolutely appropriate to the moment, and Mrs. Patrick Campbell's consummate comedy acting robs the phrase of all offensiveness, making it only extraordinarily funny.

But when the suburban flapper, imagining that it is the latest slang term of Smart Society, repeats the word a minute or two later, the effect is inartistic and unpleasant. It must be altered.

Though prepared by the *Daily Sketch* for a sensational utterance from the flower-girl turned "lady," when the actual moment arrived it took the large audience entirely by surprise.

They rocked to and fro in their seats and shook with laughter. They roared with laughter. They cried with laughter.

The play had a triumphant reception, which not even the protracted dialogue of the last act could impair.

Daily Sketch 1914

LADY BLOMFIELD APOLOGISES

Daughters Present Against Her Wish.

FAMILY INDIGNANT.

Granddaughters Of A Bishop As Suffragettes.

A humble apology has been tendered to the King, the *Daily Sketch* learns, for the amazing act of ill-breeding by which Thursday night's Court was interrupted.

The two ladies who created the scene were Miss Mary and Miss Eleanor Blomfield, daughters of the late Sir Arthur Blomfield, the architect, and granddaughters of a former Bishop of London.

As they approached the Throne Miss Mary Blomfield cried out to their Majesties, "For God's sake stop forcible feeding." Her sister, Miss Eleanor Blomfield, did not take part in the demonstration, but was at once requested to leave.

Lady Blomfield, the *Daily Sketch* is assured, is the last person in the world to countenance such an outrageous breach of good manners.

Her two daughters went to Court on Thursday night in direct opposition to the wishes of their mother.

Daily Sketch 1914

Mr. Macmillan then dealt with the proposal of a referendum, asking whether it was really seriously proposed that after the Government had been defeated they were still to continue in office. A cynical proposal. At the last Colonial Conference every Prime Minister had expressed his belief that it was a desirable thing. The advantages of Home Rule were hardly denied now. For nearly one hundred years Ireland had been knocking at the gates of England asking for Home Rule. It was now the critical hour when it was for England to decide whether or not a small Protestant ascendancy should rule over the whole of Ireland, or whether there should be a new rule.

Mr. Macmillan combined both the Oxford charm with the logicality of Cambridge.

The Granta 1913

TROOPS LANDED.

NO 'WAR' YET.

Star 1914

THE QUEEN,
The Lady's Newspaper.

RADIUM AND DISEASE.

THE RECENT RESULTS of the uses of radium and researches in its powers as a remedial agent in cancer and other diseases are decidedly encouraging for the present and hopeful for the future. Fortunately for sufferers from this dread scourge of the flesh, while it is too soon to talk of radium as an undoubted cure, it has been proved a curative agent, and efficacious in affording marked relief both by itself and in conjunction with operations. At any rate, we are now entitled to talk of apparent cures, since Dr Lazarus-Barlow, the director of the Middlesex cancer research laboratory, states that, whereas in a given period of 1912 all the inoperable cases admitted into the Middlesex Hospital died, in the corresponding period of 1913 almost half of the patients regained, after treatment with radium, such a favourable state of health as to allow of their being discharged, and that many of them are now going about their daily work. A ratio of even "apparent cures" of nearly 50 per cent. is incomparably better than the death rate of 100 per cent. which occurred in the inoperable cases in the same hospital from June to September, 1912. These thirty-two apparently cured patients, out of sixty-eight inoperable cases, owe a certain debt to the curative power of radium, and their case affords the surest foundation for hope that we have so far received in relation to the cure of cancer.

Queen 1914

WOMEN'S SUFFRAGE.
Conservative and Unionist Women's Franchise Association.

LORD ROBERT CECIL made one of his fine speeches on the 27th ult. at a meeting of the Conservative and Unionist Women's Franchise Association at the Bechstein Hall, Miss Balfour presiding in place of the Countess of Dundonald, who was absent through illness. A point which Lord Robert Cecil urged strongly was that the Conservative and Unionist party would make a mistake if it became associated in the mind of the public with opposition to every change, however desirable. He reminded the large audience that the Labour party was absolutely convinced and pledged to women's suffrage. The Liberal party, on the other hand, was not in that position, but a large majority of its members were in favour of women's enfranchisement, and he was credibly informed that no Liberal candidate was acceptable now who was not in favour of women's suffrage. He thought that Conservative and Unionists ought to ask themselves whether they really were convinced that women's suffrage was so dangerous that they could not support it.

Speaking strongly of the risks at the present time of the introduction of corrupt influences in public affairs, he thought there was no surer safeguard against corruption than the extension of the franchise to women. The Countess of Selborne, president of the association, was among those present at the meeting. Miss Anna Martin delivered an interesting address.

Queen 1914

FATHER OF MODERN CARTOONISTS DEAD.

Sir John Tenniel, Of 'Punch,' Whose "Pilot" Was Never Dropped.

CREATOR OF "ALICE."

Made Politicians' Fortunes, But Had No Politics Himself.

Sir John Tenniel, the famous *Punch* cartoonist, who made politics live for his own time and "Alice in Wonderland" for all time, has died in London at the age of 93.

He was the colleague of Thackeray, drew a cartoon of the Great Exhibition of 1851, worked for *Punch* for 50 years, retired 13 years ago, never caricatured Lloyd George, and had almost completely passed out of the public mind.

But the three most famous of his cartoons, reproduced on Pages 1 and 16, recall to all who remember the days before Marconis what a force his pencil was once.

POLITICS IN PICTURES.

"Dropping the Pilot" has been rather too much talked about. Some people are a little tired of the pilot who never was dropped. The original of it—it showed the German Emperor's dismissal of Bismarck—was bought by Lord Rosebery and presented by him to Bismarck.

The "British Lion's Vengeance on the Bengal Tiger" and "Sink or Swim" show how the nation felt in the height of the Indian Mutiny and the Home Rule crisis. Tenniel had the art of conceiving the national sentiment as a picture and the art to make a picture of it.

This was only one side of his work. The other gave us the immortal illustrations of "Alice in Wonderland" and "Alice Through the Looking Glass."

SIR JOHN TENNIEL.
—(By Himself.)
(From Cassell's "The History of Punch.")

They have been adapted cleverly by "F. C. G.," but the originals of

The Mad Hatter,
The Walrus and the Carpenter,
The March Hare,
Tweedledum and Tweedledee,
The Red Queen, and
The Lion and the Unicorn Fighting for the Crown

were Tenniel's.

Yet people sometimes said that Tenniel had no humour.

"My drawings are sometimes grotesque," he said, "but that is from the sense of fun and humour. Some people declare that I have no humour. Now I believe that I have a very keen sense of humour, and that my drawings are sometimes really funny."

HIS FIRST CARTOON.

His start on *Punch* was due to the withdrawal of Doyle, who objected to the anti-Papal line that the paper was taking on the appointment of Catholic Bishops to English sees. Tenniel's first cartoon shows Lord John Russell as Jack the Giant Killer attacking "Giant Pope." His first double-page cartoon was a picture of the nations of the world flocking to the Great Exhibition of 1851.

In the course of his career he designed over 2,000 full-page cartoons for that journal.

His work, it was said, destroyed Cabinets and precipitated wars, and it most assuredly exerted a great influence in directing public opinion.

But although he made Cabinet Ministers' fortunes he once said: "As for politics, I have none."

Daily Sketch 1914

MURDER OF THE HEIR

Archduke Francis Ferdinand And Duchess Of Hohenberg

SHOT IN THE STREET.

Duchess Dies In Futile Attempt To Save Husband's Life.

The Archduke Francis Ferdinand, heir to the throne of Austria-Hungary, and his wife, the Duchess of Hohenberg, were killed yesterday by an assassin in the streets of Sarajevo, Bosnia.

A bomb was thrown first; but this only injured members of the Royal suite in a carriage following that of the Archduke. Later a student shot the Archduke and the Duchess.

The Duchess was killed in trying to shield her husband.

Archduke Francis Ferdinand drove to the town hall, where he said to the Burgomaster:—

We came to Sarajevo to make a friendly visit, and are greeted by a bomb. This is outrageous.

It was after the Royal party left the town hall that the assassin fired his deadly shots.

The assassin is an 18-years-old Servian student who had been banished from Bosnia.

The Cabinet were immediately summoned to Vienna.

The Archduke and Duchess were very well known in London.

They were here at the end of last November on a visit to the King and Queen, and attended many public events.

Immediately the startling news reached Buckingham Palace the King sent to the Austro-Hungarian Embassy a request that an expression of the deep sympathy of himself and the Queen should be forwarded to the Austrian Court.

Daily Sketch 1914

LODY SHOT.

German Spy Executed in the Tower of London.

COURT-MARTIAL SEQUEL

The German spy, Carl Hans Lody, who was found guilty last week by a Court-martial of war treason by conveying information to Germany, was shot on Friday last at the Tower of London. It will be remembered that the Court-martial found Lody guilty, but the sentence was not announced in public at the close of the proceedings. We are now officially informed that Lody was sentenced to be shot: the sentence was duly confirmed, and was carried out at the Tower.

Star 1914

CHARITABLE POLICEMAN AND THE BELGIAN REFUGEES.

The following appeared in "The Star" of the 25th inst. :—

"Now that it seems clear that for some weeks, at least, the greater part of Belgium will be under the heel of the Prussian army, it is the more necessary that the needs of the unfortunate Belgians who have been harried by the brutal Uhlans of the Kaiser should be vigorously taken up here. In this generous movement we award the palm to that unnamed Metropolitan Police Constable whose story was told in yesterday's 'Star.' He was on duty outside Charing Cross station at midnight on Saturday when the Continental train disgorged thirteen Belgian refugees, two working carpenters from Brussels, their wives and nine children. They had crossed from Ostend, paying 60 francs out of a total of 70 francs which they possessed, and they arrived at Charing Cross without a friend, without a shelter, without a word of English, and less than 10s. in their possession. Then they met that Policeman—a ' man with a dark moustache ' is all that we know of him, but we salute him to-day as a good comrade and a good Englishman. He might have landed them in a Police Station or a casual ward, but he took them to his own house, gave them his bed, made up other beds on the floor, fed them—they had had nothing for 36 hours—gave them breakfast in the morning, and put them on the road to the Belgian Consulate. When they offered him their money he 'only laughed'—a good laugh that to hear, especially when one is a destitute stranger in a foreign land. We hope the example of that Policeman outside Charing Cross at midnight will find many imitators."

Police Review 1914

MR. ROBERT ROSS AS BEST MAN

At To-day's Romantic Wedding Of Oscar Wilde's Son.

One of the most interesting literary and theatrical weddings of recent years will take place to-day at St. Mary's Catholic Church, Cadogan-square, between Mr. Vyvyan B. Holland, the younger son of Oscar Wilde, and Miss Violet Craigie, daughter of the late Lieut. Edmund Warren Craigie.

The wedding is a sequel to a charming romance, in which Sir Herbert Tree took a leading part. It was at a dinner party at his house last July that the young people, both of whom are well known in artistic circles, met for the first time.

They fell in love promptly, and the engagement was announced shortly afterwards.

The best man will be Mr. Robert Ross, the literary executor of Oscar Wilde, and the bride will be given away by her cousin, Mr. Gerard Turner.

The bride will wear a striking dress of silver tissue, embroidered with little green leaves. Her bridesmaids will be Miss Pamela FitzGerald and Miss Heather Roche (who will wear white dresses and black sashes and will carry baskets of violets), and little Miss Ellis, who will distribute favours of violets.

Daily Sketch 1914

Prime Minister Lloyd George with Winston Churchill, then First Lord of the Admiralty.

THE WEDDING
OF THE
SEASON.

MR. NEIL PRIMROSE, M.P., AND LADY VICTORIA STANLEY.

TO-DAY'S CEREMONY.

UNION OF TWO HISTORIC HOUSES

The marriage of the Earl of Derby's only daughter, Lady Victoria Stanley, and the Hon. Neil Primrose, M.P., Under-Secretary of State for Foreign Affairs, and younger son of the Earl of Rosebery, took place this afternoon at St. Margaret's, Westminster.

The event, uniting as it does two famous and historic houses, excited widespread public interest, although much had been done, owing to the circumstances of the war, to make is as quiet as possible. As early as noon Westminster was aglow with primroses, and itinerant vendors reaped a rich harvest.

The crowd which assembled was very large, and when the first of the guests arrived at the church there were thousands of people eagerly anxious to catch a glimpse of the occupants of the carriages.

Pall Mall Gazette 1915

A PITIABLE TRAGEDY.

GERMANS MURDER AN ENGLISH LADY.

CAVELL.—Executed by order of Court-martial in Brussels, on the 12th inst., on a charge of aiding the escape over the frontier of British, French and Belgian soldiers, Edith Louisa, Directrice d'Ecole des Infermieres, Rue de la Culture, Bruxelles, eldest daughter of the late Rev. Fredk. Cavell, of Swardeston, Norfolk, and of Mrs. Cavell, 24, College-road, Norwich, aged 49.

We extract that touching obituary from "The Times" of Monday relative to the affair.

The following statement has been issued by the Press Bureau from the Foreign Office for publication.

The Foreign Office are informed by the United States Ambassador that Miss Edith Cavell, lately head of a large training school for nurses at Brussels, who was arrested on August 5 last by the German authorities at that place, was executed on the 13th inst., after sentence of death had been passed on her.

It is understood that the charge against Miss Cavell was that she harboured fugitive British and French soldiers and Belgians of military age, and had assisted them to escape from Belgium in order to join the colours.

So far as the Foreign Office are aware, no charge of espionage was brought against her.

HOW MISS CAVELL WAS MURDERED.

Details of the execution at Brussels show that it took place in a garden or yard in Brussels, surrounded by a wall (says a "Daily Mail" telegram from Amsterdam).

A German firing party of six men and an officer were drawn up in the garden and awaited their victim. Blindfolded with a black scarf, she was led in by soldiers from a house near by.

Up to this minute the woman, though deadly white, had stepped out bravely to meet her fate. But before the rifle party her strength at last gave out, and she tottered and fell to the ground, thirty yards or more from the spot against the wall where she was to have been shot.

The officer in charge of the execution walked to her. She lay prone on the ground motionless. The officer then drew a large service revolver from his belt, took steady aim from his knee, and shot the woman through the head as she lay on the floor.

Crewe Chronicle 1915

VISITS WITH MOTHER A devoted mother is Lady Mainwaring, who first braved the unwritten law of convention that baby shall not visit with its mother the drawing-rooms of Society.

Lady Mainwaring, however, would have none of it, and took baby Diana right along with her, as the Americans would say. And Diana liked it, too. She is a charming little morsel of youthfulness, just about two years now.

I believe it was her mother, too, who introduced the fashion of a knot of flowers fastened to baby's perambulator coverlet.

Mother and Home 1916

EDITH CAVELL.

A congregation representative of every grade in the community assembled in St. Paul's on Friday for the service held to commemorate the noble life and the glorious death of Miss Edith Cavell. Many atrocious crimes have been committed in this war. None has so deeply moved the whole world as the callous murder in the dead of night of this gracious Englishwoman, who had dedicated her whole life to the service of others and the alleviation of pain, and whose only fault was one that sprang from a tender and compassionate heart. Against the gloomy background of an inexpiable crime, the grandeur of soul, the dignity of mien, and the forgiving spirit exhibited by this heroic woman in her last hours on earth shine out with a glorious effulgence. This death scene in a Belgian prison will rank with the great death scenes of history. There are some crimes that can never be forgotten or forgiven. This is one of them. Germany, in taking the life of Edith Cavell, has shown that she is an outcast among the nations. It is a crime that will cost her dear.—"Daily Chronicle."

Crewe Chronicle 1915

IRISH OUTLOOK TAKES A GRAVER TURN.

TROUBLE SPREADING

Redmond and Carson Support the Government.

ALL IRELAND UNDER MARTIAL LAW

(Official Press Bureau.)

The following announcement has been received from the Chief Secretary for Ireland:—

At noon yesterday (Monday) serious disturbances broke out in Dublin.

A large body of men identified with the Sinn Feiners, mostly armed, occupied Stephen's Green and took possession forcibly of the Post Office, where they cut the telegraphic and telephonic wires.

Houses were also occupied in Stephen's Green, Sackville Street, Abbey Street, and along the quays.

In the course of the day soldiers arrived from The Curragh, and the situation is now well in hand.

So far as is known here

Three military officers,

Four or five soldiers,

Two loyal volunteers, and

Two policemen have been killed, and

Four or five military officers,

Seven or eight soldiers, and

Six loyal volunteers wounded.

No exact information has been received of the casualties on the side of the Sinn Feiners.

Reports received from Cork, Limerick, Ennis, Tralee, and both ridings of Tipperary show that no disturbances of any kind have occurred in these localities.

"The air in Ulster to-day is electric!" says an agency message from Belfast.

Sir Edward Carson has issued a "Don't nail his ears to the pump" manifesto in which he urges his followers to maintain a "dignified attitude of calm and peace."

There are said to be 110,000 enrolled Carsonian Volunteers in Ulster, 27,000 being in Belfast.

So far no blow has been struck.

Destroyers Land Troops.

The two destroyers which left Kingstown last night arrived in Belfast Lough this morning and anchored off Carrickfergus. They landed 150 men of the Yorkshire Light Infantry, who marched to Carrickfergus Castle where a quantity of arms and ammunition is stored, to strengthen the guard of the Norfolk Regiment.

Later a gunboat anchored off Bangor.

Aberdeen Weekly Journal 1916

THE HOUSE OF WINDSOR.

KING ADOPTS A NEW FAMILY NAME.

GERMAN TAINT ELIMINATED.

The King to-day adopted for his house and family the name of Windsor. The Privy Council at which this was done was one of the most important held since the Coronation. It was attended by the Duke of Connaught, the Archbishop of Canterbury, the Lord Chancellor, the Prime Minister, the Lord President, Earl of Rosebery, Mr. Andrew Fisher (Australia), Mr. G. N. Barnes, Lieut.-General Smuts, and the Hon. W. P. Schreiner (South Africa).

The document signed by the King was as follows:

BY THE KING.

A proclamation declaring that the name of Windsor is to be borne by his Royal House and Family and relinquishing the use of all German titles and dignities.—GEORGE, R.I.

Whereas we, having taken into consideration the name and title of our Royal House and Family have determined that henceforth our House and Family shall be styled and known as The House and Family of Windsor, and

Whereas we have further determined for ourselves and for and on behalf of our descendants and all other the descendants of our grandmother Queen Victoria, of blessed and glorious memory, to relinquish and discontinue the use of all German titles and dignities, and

Whereas we have declared these our determinations in our Privy Council.

Now, therefore, we out of our Royal will and authority do hereby declare and announce that as from the date of this our Royal Proclamation our House and Family be styled and known as The House and Family of Windsor, and that all the descendants in the male line of our said grandmother Queen Victoria who are subjects of these realms, other than female descendants who may marry or may have married, shall bear the said name of Windsor, and do hereby further declare and announce that we for ourselves, and for and on behalf of our descendants and all other the descendants of our said grandmother, Queen Victoria, who are subjects of these realms, relinquish and enjoin the discontinuance of the use the decrees, styles, dignities, titles, and honours of Dukes and Duchesses of Saxony and Princes and Princesses of Saxe-Coburg and Gotha, all other German decrees, styles, dignities, titles, honours, and appellations to us or to them heretofore belonging and appertaining.

Given at our Court at Buckingham Palace this Seventeenth day of July, in the year of Our Lord, 1917, and in the Eighth Year of Our Reign.

God Save the King.

Nottingham Evening Post 1917

ZEPPELIN RAID ON ENGLAND.

54 Killed ; 67 Injured.

(Official Press Bureau.)

The following announcement was issued by the War Office at 1.40 on Tuesday morning—

A Zeppelin raid by six or seven airships took place last night over the Eastern, North-Eastern, and Midland Counties.

A number of bombs were dropped, but up to the present no considerable damage has been reported.

A further statement will be issued as soon as practicable.

The following reports on Monday night's Zeppelin raid were issued by the War Office on Tuesday—

The air raid of last night was attempted on an extensive scale, but it appears that the raiders were hampered by the thick mist.

After crossing the coast the Zeppelins steered various courses, and dropped bombs at several towns and in rural districts in Derbyshire, Leicestershire, Lincolnshire, and Staffordshire.

Some damage to property was caused. No accurate reports were received until a very late hour.

The casualties notified up to the time of issuing this statement amount to—

Killed 54
Injured 67

War Office (later).

Further reports of last night's raid show that the evening's air attacks covered a larger area than on any previous occasion.

Bombs were dropped in Norfolk, Suffolk, Lincolnshire, Leicestershire, Staffordshire, and Derbyshire, the number being estimated at 220.

Except in one part of Staffordshire, the material damage was not considerable, and in no case was any military damage caused. No further casualties have been notified, and the figures remain as 54 killed and 67 injured.

Aberdeen Weekly Journal 1916

OTHER PEOPLE'S IDEAS.
The Food Rations.

MADAM,—I see in to-day's *Queen* that you consider the bread allowance ample. Well, in our household of master, mistress, and maid we find it a very "tight fit" indeed to make the six half-quartern loaves do for the week. Neither I nor the maid eat potatoes, nor anything in the way of eggs, bacon, &c., for breakfast, while I eat toast at every meal, so although my husband is a very small bread consumer, I suppose on the whole we do get through more bread than most people. There is absolutely no waste, the few crusts not finished up are made into puddings or baked for "crumbing"; but, as I have said, six loaves in seven days is barely enough even if we have no visitors at tea-time to eat more bread and butter. But I understand that the allowance of flour is to cover not only bread, but puddings, pastry, cakes, &c., and I cannot think that it is enough for this, but I should be glad if you would give your opinion on this point. I note that in nearly all the recipes for "Semi-meatless dishes" given in to-day's *Queen* flour or breadcrumbs play more or less important parts, and this, of course, would have to come out of the 3lb. weekly (I think the allowance is 3lb. flour or 4lb. bread). We usually make all cakes (plain since the war) at home, but both these and all pastry, suet, puddings, &c., will have to be eliminated from our bills of fare if we are to keep within the limit. This is rather a trial, as my husband is very fond of our plain cakes, boiled puddings, and tarts.

I do not think any working-class family will consider the bread allowance nearly sufficient. I have been making enquiries, and I find that a man doing hard manual labour usually eats at least 1lb. of bread per day. This, however, is rather outside the scope of my letter.

The meat allowance I can manage with, and the sugar will be more than enough if I have to give up cake-making "for the period of the war," but I do not see how I can keep within the bounds of the flour limit. And, frankly, why should I be expected to do so when the pastrycooks and confectioners are still allowed to fill their shops with smartly decorated "fancy" cakes of all kinds? Many are still "iced"!　　　　　　　　　　　　MARTHA.

Queen 1917

Three Mothers in Israel.

Three mothers in Israel have recently left us for the Homeland. Mrs. Jones, mother of Mr. W. Caenog Jones, Coedpoeth, died in her eighty-fifth year. She was well known in our North Wales circuits. Of a peculiarly sweet disposition, her visits amongst the people were greatly welcomed. Her interest in God's work never flagged, and the influence of her kindly life is fragrant. Mrs. Richard Edwards, Rhyl, had attained her eighty-eighth year, and was mother of Mrs. R. W. Jones, of Liverpool. She had been connected with Brunswick Chapel, Rhyl, and, with her husband, stood faithful in days of stress. She followed the Ark from Ebenezer, Victoria Road, to Sussex Street, and thence to Brunswick. Mrs. Platt, lately resident at Towyn, but formerly of Dinas Mawddwy, was in her sixty-ninth year, mother to Mrs. T. Gwilym Roberts, and sister to the Rev. John Jones (g). Methodist preachers gladly remember the sagacious, genial, and devoted hostess at Dinas. She abounded in the work of the Lord.　　　　D. D. D.

Methodist Recorder 1917

SOCIAL AND PERSONAL

The Holy Father has been pleased by Apostolic Brief to elevate the Right Rev. Mgr. Parkinson to the rank of Protonotary Apostolic *ad instar participantium*.

Sir William Steuart Dick-Cunyngham, Bart., was received into the Church by the Rev. Father England at Westminster Cathedral on Monday last.

Tablet 1917

The Imperial War Cabinet, 1917: Lloyd George is fourth from the right in the front row, and General Smuts is on the extreme right.

THE "SUSSEX DAILY NEWS."

He was like a King in our midst, and he reigned not only by the privileges of his great hereditary position, but even more graciously, more beneficently, by his own worthiness. In these calamitous times we often say that nothing can ever be the same again, and it is sadly true that Sussex cannot seem quite the same now that the Duke of Norfolk has been taken to his rest. No one could love the county with a purer devotion than he felt for it. No one has ever done more for Sussex than he did. His influence was incalculable, and it was always the high and ennobling influence of a Christian gentleman. With this exalted quality he combined an extraordinary gift for practical affairs. It would hardly be possible to enumerate all the public under-takings, locally and nationally, which have benefited by his munificence and his wisely directed energy. No movement in Sussex seemed complete without the Duke of Norfolk, and he possessed such a happy manner and such an unfeigned forbearance towards those who did not see eye to eye with him, that he could work amicably with the most diverse elements. . . . He had opportunities beyond those of most men, and he lived up to them with a noble sincerity. He was the leader of the Catholic laity in this country, and the Church of St. Francis and of Newman had no more devoted son. His death will be a poignant bereavement to the whole Catholic community, for he never wearied in offering help and comfort to his own household of faith. From the richest and the poorest, the most famous and the most obscure, prayers will go up for him throughout the British Empire, and in many foreign countries where his name was revered. Thousands who belong to other religious bodies, or to none, will feel sorry that his manly and genial presence is no more to be in their midst. He was broad-minded and tolerant. A trivial action was utterly repugnant to his nature. Surely history will know him as the Good Duke.

Tablet 1917

INTERNAL TROUBLE.

The New (Pan German) Chancellor: "Come, a dose of this and you'll soon be yourself again."
Quoth the Eagle "Nevermore!"

Nottingham Evening Post 1917

By the death of Mr. Abraham Crystal, at the age of sixty-six, this synagogue, situated in Walnut Street, has been deprived of one of its best supporters. For some time he acted as Baal Korah. His rendering from time to time of the Sabbath service will be long remembered. He had a kindly greeting for all. His memory will be cherished by all who had the privilege of knowing him. The greatest sympathy will be extended to his widow, soldier sons, and daughters. The funeral took place on Tuesday week at the Rice Lane Cemetery, where a large gathering assembled. The service was conducted by the Rev. M. Myers.—From H. S.

PRIDE OF ISRAEL SYNAGOGUE.

Jewish Chronicle 1918

Blinded by tear gas, men queue at an Advanced Dressing Station near Bethune, April 1918.

THE ZEEBRUGGE RAID.

A Daring Exploit.

HOW IT WAS CARRIED OUT.

Splendid British Bravery.

The Secretary of the Admiralty has issued a long official narrative of the attack on Zeebrugge and Ostend, from which the following extracts are taken:—

Vice-Admiral Keyes, in the destroyer Warwick, commanded the operations, and at some 15 miles off Zeebrugge the ships took up their formation for the attack. The Vindictive which had been towing the Iris and Daffodil, cast them off, to follow under their own steam. The Intrepid, Iphigenia, and Thetis slowed down to give the first three time to get alongside the Mole. The Sirius and Brilliant shifted their course for Ostend, and the great swarm of destroyers and motor craft spread themselves abroad upon their multifarious duties. Ahead of the Vindictive as she drove through the water rolled the smoke screen——her cloak of invisibility, wrapped about her by the small craft. This was a device of Wing-Commander Brock, R.N.A.S., "without which," acknowledges the Admiral in command, "the operation could not have been conducted." It was in a gale of shelling that the Vindictive laid her nose against the 30-foot high concrete side of the Mole, let go an anchor, and signed to the Daffodil to shove her stern in. The Iris went ahead and endeavoured to get alongside likewise. Commander A. F. B Carpenter (now captain) conned the Vindictive from her open bridge till her stern was laid in, when he took up his position in the flame-thrower, but on the port side.

At the mole—thrilling Stories of Bravery.

The men were gathered in readiness on the main and lower decks, while Colonel Elliott, who was to lead the Marines, waited on the false deck just abaft the bridge, and Captain H. C. Halahan, who commanded the blue-jackets, was amidships. The gangways were lowered, and scraped and rebounded upon the high parapet of the Mole as the Vindictive rolled. The word for the assault had not yet been given when both leaders were killed—Colonel Elliot by a shell, and Captain Halahan by the machine-gun fire which swept the docks. The same shell that killed Colonel Elliot also did fearful execution in the forward stoke's mortar battery.

Belfast Weekly News 1918

The Lisburn Herald

AND

Antrim and Down Advertiser.

SATURDAY, NOVEMBER 16, 1918.

LAGAN-SIDE (and other) ECHOES.

It is expected the General Election will be held on 14th December.

As will be seen by our advertising columns special thanksgiving services will be held in Seymour St. Methodist Church on Sunday.

The Seymour St. Methodist Sunday Schools will be closed on Sunday 17th, but will (d.v.) be re-opened on Sunday 24th November.

Mrs. Banks desires to acknowledge 1½ doz. eggs and £2 0s 6d sent to her this week for our wounded soldiers.

It is encouraging to know, on the authority of the doctors, that the influenza is gradually diminishing in this district.

When the recruiting ceased, on the cessation of hostilities, Lisburn only required two men to complete the full quota.

Second-Lieut. Gordon Harvey, Att. 15th Durham L. Infantry, acknowledges, with grateful thanks, 50 pairs socks from Lisburn Women's Work Party (per Mrs. John Silcock).

The replayed tie between the Duffers and the Caddies in the first round of the Junior Cup will take place at Clonevin Park on to-morrow (Saturday). Kick-off at 2-30.

GREY HAIR can be changed at once to a natural shade of Dark or Light Brown, or Black, by the use of Boyd's One Solution Hair Dye, costing 1/6 per Bottle. ALEXANDER BOYD & CO., Ltd., Chemists, Lisburn.

PEACE & VICTORY

How it was celebrated in Central Cornwall.

A GREAT THANKSGIVING DAY.

ENJOYMENT AND YET REMEMBRANCE.

The National Peace Day on Saturday last to celebrate the Victory over Germany was observed with just as much completeness in Cornwall as in other parts of the country.

The celebrations varied to some extent in detail, but in general purpose and design they were pretty much the same in the different localities.

There were sports, processions, bonfires, teas, luncheons, carnivals and countless other forms of rejoicing. In fact the day was a whirl of pleasurable excitement. In some of the places religious services did bring home to the people the more serious side of the great Day but in the main, the day was given over to enjoyment rather than to contemplation and review. And perhaps it was just as well. True, it was a sad day for many; there was no happiness in the heart of the mother or wife who had lost her son or husband. The flickers of the countless bonfires found no answering light in homes where the supreme sacrifice had been made. Yet national emotions are easily banished and transformed. The same men who saluted the memorial to the dead in Whitehall, doubtless with tear-filled eyes, at a later stage were in the procession marching in the full consciousness of triumph. In the former emotion the bereaved may have found comfort. Was there nothing in the latter—in the whole nature of these Peace Celebrations—of a comfortable nature to the parents and relatives of the departed? Was there no message for them in the gay bunting and the many flags? We think there was, and that in meditation on it hostile feelings gave way to a peace of mind founded on pride and thanksgiving in what had been accomplished.

Cornish Guardian 1919

WAR MEMORIALS.

The Committee of the Civic Arts Association have recently been considering two important questions connected with War Memorials, namely, the question of commissions for such memorials in relation to artists now at the front, and the artistic difficulty present by the attachment of any large number of names to any work of art. They have accordingly decided to circulate the following note in the hope that it contains a suggestion which may be useful to the public.

Owing to the absence of nearly all our younger sculptors and craftsmen on active service, it is desirable that the execution of memorials to the fallen should be, as far as possible, postponed until the conclusion of the war, when it is hoped we shall have among us again those artists of genius who have temporarily sacrificed their art for the nation's cause. To such as these, opportunities for resuming the exercise of their profession will be doubly welcome; and, inasmuch as a work of art, consciously or unconsciously, reflects the spirit and experiences of its creator, we may reasonably hope that the artist who has tasted the solemn glory of the battlefield will thence derive noble inspiration for the creation of war memorials. Artists who are, unhappily, over military age will assuredly welcome the reservation of commissions in order to assist their brethren on their return to civil life; and, indeed, the volume of memorials, sadly increasing, is already of such magnitude that the artists still among us are unable satisfactorily to cope with the demand.

Meanwhile the natural desire straightway to commemorate our young men's sacrifice may be met by placing a wreath, with a scroll of honour attached, on the position assigned to the memorial in church or public edifice; or a memorial book containing their names might be written, and either form in itself a sufficient and satisfactory memorial or be auxiliary to any other to be subsequently decided upon.

These suggestions will not hinder the planning of more conspicuous or more permanent memorials. On the contrary, time and opportunity will be afforded for careful estimation of the funds available; for due deliberation in the choice of the location and character of such memorials, to the no small relief of incumbents and others who are already concerned with the menace to the walls of their parish churches of a crowd of hasty and ill-assorted tablets and stained glass.

Queen 1917

The Conscientious Objector and the Free Churches.

Mr. Hughes declared that the Military Service Act had been so framed that it anticipated and allowed for conscientious objection. The Act had been grossly violated in intention by the tribunals, and those men were in prison as a consequence. It was a very bad thing for the nation to try to crush and arrest the free action of men's consciences. Mr. Coltman urged that Free Churchmen, in particular, could not acquiesce in the continued imprisonment of conscientious objectors. The safeguarding of conscience was the supreme charge of nonconformity. The administration of the Military Service Act had meant the revival in this country of religious persecution, as was clearly shown in the case of the Society of Friends. Freechurchmen could not stand by and see a sister-denomination persecuted.

Crusader 1919

AN EPIDEMIC OF OUTLAWRY

CARS STOLEN, BOOKING OFFICE RIFLED, BIG THEFT OF SILKS.

BIZARRE "WILD WEST" HOLD-UPS.

A most remarkable epidemic of outlawry has occurred in London during the past week-end. Masks, motor-cars, and arms have been employed by these modern bandits in their raids, all of which have been characterised by the utmost audacity, and crimes have been swiftly, silently, and successfully committed by methods that conform most exactly with the highest traditions upheld by "Wild West" desperadoes. Motor-cars have been stolen, railway station booking offices have been rifled, and huge quantities of textiles have been appropriated by a gang which seemingly intends to stop at the proverbial nothing.

WELL-ORGANISED GANG.

It is said that the daring gang of armed men are undoubtedly dangerous experts. It is estimated that up to the present they have secured booty, mostly cloth, to the total value of over £40,000. It is probable that one step towards checking them will be the provision of a number of armed motor-cyclist patrols. Other measures will be of a different character, as it is believed that the gangs at work possess not only a fleet of fast cars, but also an extensive spy system.

OFF WITH THE CAR.

One of the latest exploits was the theft of a motor from the Kenley Aerodrome, where Corporal Grigsby, of the R.A.F., saw a man quietly get into a six-seater Crossley car belonging to the R.A.F.

Tavistock Gazette 1919

PEACE: SOME THOUGHTS.

BY MENTOR.

AS I write, there surges from beneath my window a deep, long drawn shout of joy, a roar of gratification at the news that hostilities have ceased and that at last the world is again at peace. If we were to undertake to analyse the sentiment that pervades the crowd, as it swells with gladness, we should not, I believe, find that it is merely satisfaction, because of victory nor the glee of triumph over a fallen foe. It is a sentiment far, far deeper. It is a passion that goes to the root of the humanity which pervades the men and women who "let themselves go," as the maroons sounded Peace. It is thankfulness that the long long night has ended, and that the dawn of other times is shooting athwart the clouds, that are at last dropping back into the horizon of the past. It is the reaction from the pent-up agony of anguish and anxiety, of restraint, disappointment, and of sorrow that have been the fruits of the happenings of the last four years and more. It is joy at the prospect of reunion with those who have borne in these terrible months the cruel heat and burden of battle. It is the sentiment of the relief which men and women nurtured in Freedom experience as they see cast to the dust one of the greatest menaces to Freedom which the modern world has known. That of which the world has rid itself in the crushing of Kaiserism and in the destruction of German militarism, none better than we Jews can estimate. From the first moment when the sword—England's sword—leapt from its scabbard, we perceived that in her fight, she was defending, among others, the true interests of our people. Because, with the triumph of Germany and the victory of the culture for which Germany stood, the predominance of which she had determined to implant upon all the world, there would have been no place on earth for Judaism and Jewish principles; and the life of the Jew everywhere would have been made bitter, by reason of the burden which—sharing it with mankind in general, it is true, but always in larger proportion to the rest of humanity—would have been his lot. The war is at an end. The great work—the ghastly work—is done! Right has triumphed over might! God lives in the Heavens!

Jewish Chronicle 19

Whitley Report.

Every effort was made to bring pressure upon the Government to accept the principles of the Whitley Report in Government Departments. After a long period the Government decided to set up an Inter-Departmental Committee to consider how far the Whitley scheme could be applied to Government Departments, and your Secretary submitted evidence to that Committee, along with representatives of other Civil Service Associations. On April 8 the Government called a Conference at which Associations were invited to adopt the scheme agreed to by the War Cabinet. The principles of the scheme did not find favour with the N.J.C., which body decided to propose to the Conference that the Report be not accepted, but that a Committee be appointed, composed of representatives of the Associations and the Government, to consider the Report and any other schemes and report to another Conference to be held not later than the end of May. This proposal was accepted by Mr. Austen Chamberlain, who presided, on behalf of the Government.

Postman's Gazette 1919

1920–1929

An experimental wireless telephony transmitter at Marconi's Chelmsford works. Marconi inaugurated the world's first broadcast news service in February 1920.

DAY OF TERROR.

Two Killed and Many Injured in Irish Shootings.

A riot broke out in the Old Park district of Belfast yesterday afternoon. Hostile crowds engaged in revolver firing and stone-throwing, and seven persons were injured and taken to hospital, including a police-sergeant and two constables. Armed police and military with an armoured car finally quelled the outbreak.

A policeman and a civilian were reported killed and several persons injured during street shooting in three other Irish cities.

Dublin.—Policeman killed and another wounded in shooting in Parnell Square. Civilian fatally shot in raid by troops on house in Manor Street. William Robinson, an ex-soldier and Dublin footballer, seriously wounded by two armed men in Little Mary Street. Several military raids were made in the city during the morning, and there were several arrests.

Galway.—"Black and Tans" fired on civilians late on Friday night, owing to a soldier being shot in the hand. Several persons were injured, one seriously. A state of panic amongst the inhabitants lasted for some hours.

Londonderry.—Two rival mobs fired revolvers in a crowded thoroughfare on Friday night. Troops were shot at and returned the fire. A confectioner's shop was looted. The "Black and Tans" have arrived in the city.

National News **1920**

QUICK ROBBERY.

The premises of Messrs. Asprey and Co., Ltd., the jewellers of New Bond Street, London, were broken into and £5,000 worth of rings stolen in less than ten minutes before daylight on Saturday morning, January 10th. At 5.55 a.m. one of the three armed watchmen on duty ascertained that everything was in order, but by 6.5 the robbery had been committed and the thieves had gone.

They staked everything on rapidity and the thoroughness of their plans. In order to baffle the watchmen in case of an alarm they chained and padlocked the street door.

A circumstance which renders so swift a theft so remarkable is that a very heavy iron shutter—too heavy for one man to lift unaided—had to be raised before the window which was robbed could be reached. It is supposed that it was lifted by a crow-bar. The window was then noiselessly broken by the old trick of placing a treacled sheet of brown paper against the glass.

Jewellers and Watchmakers Trade Advertiser **1920**

POPLAR PRISONERS.

"NO CONFERENCE UNTIL RELEASED.

Mr. George Lansbury, one of the Poplar Councillors in Brixton Prison, in a letter issued yesterday, states that all the "municipal prisoners" are in excellent spirits, and are determined to see "the fight for justice to the poor ratepayers and the unemployed through to the end." The authorities who released Mrs. Cressall, at least in part for their own convenience," he adds, "can just as easily set us all free."

The Deputy Mayor of Poplar, Mr. W. Key, visited the imprisoned women members of the Council, and received a message from them affirming their determination "to take part in no conference or negotiations until we can do so as free women."

The National Administrative Council of the Independent Labour Party, in a statement issued yesterday, calls upon the branches to protest against the imprisoned representatives "being treated as ordinary felons."

Sunday Times **1921**

Photo, London Ster swo, ic.
Sir John Martin Harvey as Sydney Carton.

4,000 TIMES AS SYDNEY CARTON

BY SIR JOHN MARTIN HARVEY.

Sir John Martin Harvey will this month perform, for the four thousandth time, as Sydney Carton in "The Only Way," an event that is unique in the annals of the stage. He here tells "Pearson's Magazine" readers how the play came to be written and many interesting stories of his stage career.

Pearson's Magazine
1921

Evening News 1922

THE LATE F. CULLEN.

INQUEST AND FUNERAL.

A verdict of "Accidental death" was returned at the inquest at East Molesey yesterday morning on Francis Richard Talbot Cullen, the jockey, who succumbed to injuries received on being thrown from his mount, Hilarious, at the big jump on the Steeple-chase Course at Hurst Park on Friday last.

Police-sergeant Smith, who was standing near the jump, said that Hilarious was in with a bunch in the Novices' Steeple-chase, and seemed to take the jump rather badly, breaking his fetlock against a pole in the front of the jump. This appeared to send the horse off its balance, and the jockey shot out of the saddle and fell on his neck.

Mr William Nightingall, the trainer of the horse, said that he saw the accident from the stand. It seemed to him that the horse got too near the guard-rail and could not recover himself. Witness had every confidence in Cullen as a jockey of ability, and the horse had been well schooled and had been ridden in several "schools" by Cullen, who was a first-class jockey, and he had ridden several winners.

Dr Knox stated that the jockey was conscious and described his fall, saying that he fell on his head and felt his neck snap.

Mr Oherihy, brother-in-law of the deceased, stated that Cullen was twenty-eight years of age, was married, and had one child. He had suffered from an injury to the neck some years previously, and in consequence of this the military authorities would not accept him for overseas service, and he served at the Remount Depot at Redhill during the war.

Mr Nightingall, following expressions of sympathy, said the Hurst Park Executive had been most kind in every way, and were taking great interest in a fund which, he understood, was being raised for the widow of the deceased.

The funeral took place at Epsom yesterday afternoon. The coffin was brought in a motor-hearse from Hurst Park, and from Epsom Town to the Cemetery. The hearse was followed by a large number of lads employed at the stables of Messrs Wm. Nightingall and Arthur Nightingall. At the graveside there were other trainers and several jockeys, including C. Hawkins (who was on crutches as a result of a riding accident last year). Among those who sent wreaths were Mr Walen (the owner of the horse Cullen was riding when he met with his accident), the Marchioness of Queensberry, Lady Eame Gordon (whose wreath was in her racing colours), the directors of Hurst Park, Messrs William, Arthur, and J. N. Nightingall, fellow employees of the deceased, and the Epsom Conservative Club, of which the deceased was a member.

The Sportsman 1920

IRISH MINISTRY APPOINTED.

'FINAL' RATIFICATION BY SOUTHERN HOUSE.

GRIFFITH'S PLEA.

"ALL DIFFERENCES MUST BE SUNK."

The House of Commons for Southern Ireland met to-day in the Mansion House, Dublin, and unanimously agreed to final ratification of the Peace Treaty. Mr. de Valera's supporters were absent.

A PROVISIONAL Government composed as follows was elected to act in the interval before the setting up of the Free State Constitution:—

Michael Collins.
William Cosgrave.
Edmund Duggan.
Patrick Hogan.
Fionan Lynch.
Joseph Macgrath.
John Macneill.
Kevin O'Higgins,

and such other persons (if any) as may from time to time be determined by the Ministers for the time being.

SMUTS'S WISE WORDS TO DE VALERA.

General Smuts's letter to Mr. de Valera was sent on the eve of the South African Premier's recent departure from England, and followed his fruitless efforts to bring the Sinn Fein leader and Sir James Craig, the Ulster Premier, together in conference.

The following are main points in the letter:—

For the present no solution based on Ulster coming into the Irish State will succeed.

Force is out of the question.

My strong advice to you is to leave Ulster alone, to concentrate on a free constitution for the remaining 26 counties, and through a successful running of the Irish State . . . eventually to bring Ulster into that State.

The British Prime Minister has made you an offer of freedom—of Dominion status.

For Irishmen to say to the world that they will not be satisfied with the status of the great British Dominions would be to alienate all that sympathy which has so far been the main support of the Irish cause.

If you accept (the Premier's offer) you will become a sister Dominion in a great circle of equal States.

I am satisfied that from the constitutional point of view a fair settlement of the Irish question is now possible and practicable.

Illustrated Sunday Herald **1921**

LONDON'S NEW £4,000,000 PALACE.

ROYAL PAGEANT IN A BRILLIANT SETTING.

CHEERING CROWDS.

PRINCESS MARY'S SIMPLE ACT OF DEVOTION.

The opening of the new £4,000,000 London County Hall by the King and Queen to-day was marked by scenes of great enthusiasm. Crowds lined the route from the Palace and heartily cheered their Majesties.

Evening News **1922**

Evening News **1922**

BOTTOMLEY IN CONVICT CLOTHES.

In Wormwood Scrubs Hospital Pending Appeal.

BUSY WITH ADVISERS.

Horatio Bottomley, following his sentence of seven years' penal servitude, is now in the prison hospital at Wormwood Scrubs.

This course is usual in the case of prisoners awaiting the result of their notice of appeal, and from the hospital he will be able to consult his advisers more easily.

On his arrival at the gaol he had, like all new prisoners, to submit to the routine of entrance — being weighed, measured, and given a bath.

He was stripped of his own clothes and put into convict's garb—khaki jacket and knickerbockers and striped stockings.

For many days he will be engaged in consulting with his solicitors and the friends who have been with him in court throughout the hearing of the case.

MISS ASHLEY'S WEDDING.

THE KING AND THE QUEEN TO BE PRESENT.

TO-MORROW'S CEREMONY.

WONDERFUL SPECTACLE AT ST. MARGARET'S.

"*The Evening News*" is in a position to state that the King and the Queen have decided to be present to-morrow at the wedding of Lord Louis Mountbatten, a second cousin of the King, and Miss Edwina Ashley, the heiress grand-daughter of the late Sir Ernest Cassel.

Evening News **1922**

MOTHER WINS HER CHILD

Father Charged with Abduction : Little Cecelia's Trip to America : "Baa Lamb" for Happy Mamma.

By the direction of Sir Chartres Biron little Cecelia Joy Gibbs has been given into the custody of her mother, and the child's father, Sidney David Benabu, a rich produce broker, of London and New York, is on remand for a week. The charge against him is of unlawfully abducting the child.

Benabu was well dressed in a dark grey suit with a striped stiff collar and black knitted tie. He has a wealth of black hair parted in the centre.

Standing calmly in the dock, leaning one elbow on the dock rails and his head on his hand, Benabu listened attentively to what was said, and after a moment threw his bowler hat and light grey coat on to the seat behind him.

The court was crowded. Mr. John Keeves prosecuted, and Mr. Travers Humphreys and Mr. Bown were for the defence

Allowed to See Cecelia.

Mr. Keeves said that the mother of the little child was a woman named Dollie Lawley Gibbs. From 1913 to the year 1917 she lived with Benabu as his wife. On July 5, 1916, the little girl Cecelia was born, Benabu being the father.

Owing to the man's violent temper Miss Gibbs was forced to cease to live with him in March, 1917. After this she always had, all the time, the custody of the child, at the same time, by arrangement, allowing the father access to see the child when he wanted to.

On Wednesday, March 1, Benabu went to see Miss Gibbs at her London address and asked if he could take charge of the child for exactly six days till the following Tuesday. He also told Miss Gibbs, who was not in the best of health at the time, that it would be in her interests if he took the child, and that he would return it.

On that understanding, and on that understanding alone, Miss Gibbs acceded to the request. On the day that the child should have been restored to its mother Benabu failed to restore it, and on March 7 she received a telegram from Eastbourne from the defendant stating that he proposed to return the child on the 14th. When the 14th came defendant did not arrive, nor did he send back the child.

Illustrated Sunday Herald 1922

"STEPS TO HELL."

More Dress Needed in the Ballroom.

" If people can jazz themselves to hell, they can also reverse and fox-trot to Heaven," said Father Degen, of Coalville, yesterday.

Many of our after-the-war dances, he said, were calculated to produce supple contortionists rather than graceful dancers.

It was to meet the exigencies of quick, vigorous, syncopated movements that dance frocks were so startlingly loose, airy and short. Shoulder straps of stout leather would look safer.

Fancy dress balls were not to be condemned, but there ought to be less fancy and more dress.

Illustrated Sunday Herald 1922

WIFE OR FERRETS ?

A Man's Choice that May Cancel a Wedding.

A well-dressed girl, who said she was about to be married, told the Willesden magistrate to-day that, while her landlady was willing to take her future husband, she refused to take his two ferrets.

The landlady in question asked for an ejectment order against the girl to be applied in the event of the man marrying and bringing his ferrets.

" I have pleaded with my fiancé to give up the ferrets," said the girl, " but he declines to do so—and things are now at a deadlock."

The landlady persisted in her attitude towards the ferrets and the magistrate made an order for ejectment in three weeks time when the wedding is arranged to take place.

Evening News 1922

A MAGIC WORD.

Dog Gives Bench a Lesson in Summary Jurisdiction.

The business at the local police court at Fishguard was pursuing its normal course when a witness mentioned the word "rat."

The magic word reached the cute ears of a dog which had followed its master to the court. The animal set up a penetrating bark which scared a rat from its hiding place.

There was pandemonium for a few moments, but justice was swift; oath, evidence and cross-examination were cut out, and no prison doctor was called in to certify that death was instantaneous.

Illustrated Sunday Herald 1922

PUNCH, OR THE LONDON CHARIVARI.—July 26, 1922.

"I COULD NOT LOVE THEE, DEAR, SO MUCH,
LOVED I NOT HONOURS MORE."

Punch 1922

ESSENCE OF PARLIAMENT.

Monday, July 17th.—The Peers present, or, at any rate, most of them, listened with keen interest as the Duke of NORTHUMBERLAND read letter after letter from touts offering to procure titles at what appeared to be a regular tariff. A Knighthood, for example, was priced at ten thousand pounds, payable on the hire-purchase system.

Punch 1922

Scents and Success.

I saw Miss Irene Vanbrugh wearing one of the new big barbaric pendants the other day. It was in a bluish tint but it may have been jade. I don't know if hers was scented, but they are despatching these from the East now impregnated with wonderful scents that last a lifetime and are reputed to have curious occult qualities. Sounds a bit "sixteenth-centuryish," eh?

Some of the scents are reputed to keep one out of accidents, others kill germs, while a third is magnetic and draws friends. In Paris these are more sought after than here for it is barbaric ornaments that lead. They can be worn when precious stones cannot and with almost any costume. With sports clothes they are just "it."

Everywoman's Weekly 1922

BRAIN WAVES
FROM ELECTRICITY.

Backward Students Pass Examinations.

NEW SCIENCE TEST.

By the application of galvanism to certain regions of the head, a London medical scientist has found a method of increasing one's brain power and capacity for work.

Electric treatment tests were made on a number of backward and indolent students who, after treatment, succeeded in examinations in which they had previously failed.

This statement was made at the annual congress of the British Phrenological Society in London last night by Dr. Bernard Hollander, who said the cry of "quackery" and a dust-storm of prejudice is hindering science in its efforts to grasp and interpret the great problem of the human brain.

DR. HOLLANDER.

Experiments on the Head.

Dr. Hollander said he had tried the experiment of applying galvanism to certain regions of the head for the improvement of mental power.

He found the method so successful that he had since treated a large number of patients deficient in nervous energy, as shown by lack of concentration, application, self-confidence and self-assertion.

That their power for work and their mental efficiency was really increased thereby was proved by the cases of backward and indolent students who succeeded in examinations in which they had previously failed.

"Empty Warehouses."

It was acknowledged by the leading anatomists that "the skull is moulded upon the brain and grows with it," so that it could no longer be denied that the size and shape of the head conformed, for all practical purposes, to the size and shape of the brain.

"Of course," he said, "size of head is not a measure of intellect, because the brain has other functions as well, and even a capacious forehead does not signify superior intellectual attainments, for it may be merely an empty warehouse which has never been stocked with knowledge."

Illustrated Sunday Herald
1922

HOW TO READ A NEWSPAPER.

PROFESSOR COCK'S LECTURE AT WINCHESTER.

Professor A. A. Cock, of Southampton University College, addressed a meeting of the Winchester Women Citizens' Association at the Winchester School for Girls, on Monday evening, on "How to read a Newspaper," this being the second of a short series of lectures on this subject.

The lecturer recalled to his hearers the proposition he had advanced at his first lecture, namely, that interest progressed in waves; the interest being at its intensest at the top of the wave; and further, that when interest flagged and fell into a kind of trough, then the individual was most open to suggestions from outside. Dealing then with the customary "make-up" of a large London daily newspaper, such as *The Times*, the Professor showed how a "mixed grill" of news was offered to readers, and in such a way that readers could choose which to read and which to leave out, according to taste, sympathy and interest. Reading some general paragraphs, the lecturer showed how a writer would sometimes make statements for which there was possibly no foundation. The danger was that many readers, not having their critical faculty sufficiently alert, would accept these doubtful assertions as true. Very frequently headings and sub-headings to news made subtle assertions which were not entirely correct, and there was a great danger that readers should accept these as accurate. To get somewhere near the truth when out for facts, it was wise to take two papers, of opposite views; it was most unwise to be the slave of one newspaper, because an editor often used his skill to build a great structure of argument upon a very few facts, and so to induce many of his readers to be of his own ways of thinking. Let them search for the evidence backing up assertions in the newspapers. They should be on their guard to avoid reading morbid news, such as law court news, unless they were searching for facts for a particular and useful purpose; they ought not to read such morbid news merely from curiosity. One portion of the financial news was always worth looking at, and that was the portion which dealt with foreign exchanges.

Hampshire Herald 1922

THE LAST TOUR.
Michael Collins's Visit to Cork Military Posts.

(FROM OUR OWN CORRESPONDENT.)
DUBLIN, Wednesday.

DUBLIN was shocked beyond measure to-day to learn that General Michael Collins, Commander-in-Chief of the Free State Army, had been killed.

The report reached the city at a very late hour last night, and was at first received with incredulity.

Inquiries at G.H.Q. elicited the fact, early to-day, that it was unfortunately true.

It is known that Collins, who arrived in Cork on Sunday, had visited a number of military posts in the county in the interval before his death.

Evening News
1922

"BELLA DONNA" PLOT ANALYSIS.

"I Was Never Anxious To Poison My Husband," Says Mrs. Thompson.

WEEPING DENIALS IN THE BOX.

MRS. THOMPSON & BYWATERS.

Bywaters' Counsel Puts Forward Theory Of Self Defence.

The essence of Mr. Whiteley's speech on behalf of Frederick Bywaters, charged at the Old Bailey—along with Mrs. Thompson—with the murder of Percy Thompson at Ilford on the night of October 3-4, was that the fatal blows were struck in self defence.

MRS. THOMPSON went into the witness-box as soon as the trial was reopened at the Old Bailey to-day for the continuance of cross-examination by the Solicitor-General, Mr. Inskip, K.C.

She looked very ill, and walked as if she had barely sufficient strength to stand. A wardress helped her across the court into the witness-box.

Arrived at the top of the little flight of steps which leads to the place where witnesses give their evidence, she grabbed at the woodwork in order to steady herself, and almost dropped into the chair provided for her.

Her Letters.

For some moments she gazed on the floor, and seemed as if wakened out of a deep sleep when Sir Henry Curtis Bennett rose and asked in a rather loud voice if she had the typewritten copies of her letters.

She shook her head faintly. An usher walked across the court and handed her a fat bundle running into many pages

Star 1922

Capital Punishment

DURING the past year the public has been shocked out of apathy by a rapid series of executions to which an unhealthy publicity has been given in the Press. There are signs of a popular revolt against the death penalty, and although much of this may spring from morbid sentimentality, yet there is also evidence of a more fundamental opposition based alike upon reason and true sentiment.

This newly aroused interest in the subject offers a splendid opportunity for action by those who wish to see the total abolition of this crude survival of barbarism. There is reason to fear that during recent years the Society has allowed its "testimony" on Capital Punishment to be a substitute for action, but we are glad to know that during the past month, the question has been raised at three of our Quarterly Meetings, and that at each, strong minutes condemning it have been passed and forwarded to the Press, and in two cases to Yearly Meeting.

All the so-called "practical arguments" supposed to justify the retention of Capital Punishment are fallacious. It is said to be a deterrent, yet its abolition in other countries[1] has actually led to a decrease in murder.[2] It is said to be necessary "in order to protect Society," and yet no country that has abolished it has found it so. In any case we are suspicious of this latter argument when we recall that it has been used in precisely the same way to justify most of the revolting punishments of the past.[3]

Young Quaker 1923

The People 1923

ABBEY CEREMONY DETAILS.

LONDON PREPARES FOR A GREAT WELCOME.

DAY OF FESTIVAL.

BIG DEMAND FOR SEATS ALONG THE ROUTE.

On Thursday the hearts of the nation will join in wishing health, wealth and happiness to H.R.H. the Duke of York, when, under the sacred roof of Westminster Abbey, he will meet the Lady Elizabeth at the altar and make her his bride.

The people's Duke has chosen a beautiful Scottish maiden to be his partner in life, and with his characteristic fellowship he has extended the invitations to his wedding feast to the workers of various industries with whom he has been closely associated.

THE LATEST PORTRAITS OF THE DUKE AND HIS BRIDE.

DEATH OF LENIN.

PARALYSING BLOW TO THE SOVIET.

THE GREATEST RED.

WHO WILL SUCCEED HIM?

"Daily Express" Correspondent.

MOSCOW, Tuesday, Jan. 22.

LENIN died at 5.50 p.m. yesterday at his country villa near Moscow.

The news, which was not generally known until this afternoon, has had a paralysing effect on the Bolsheviks. Although it was

LENIN.

known that he was doomed, recent reports of improvement in his condition suggested that the end was not to be expected yet.

Every one feels that the disappearance of the greatest Soviet leader may have tremendous consequences for Russia; especially as the other great apostle of Bolshevism, Trotsky, is out of politics for two months owing to illness, and is at loggerheads with the remaining leaders of the party.

Daily Express **1924**

PARLIAMENT IN SESSION.

LADY ASTOR'S BILL.

WESTMINSTER, Friday.

AFTER many disappointments Lady Astor, with facilities from the Government, succeeded to-day in securing the third reading of her Bill to prevent the sale of intoxicating liquors to young persons under the age of eighteen years. Only ten members voted against it, much of the opposition having been removed in the Committee stage by the insertion of the word " knowingly," a qualification which relieved publicans of what might otherwise have been an onerous responsibility. In the eyes of some members this qualification took the " sting " out of the Bill, and it was left to Sir Frederick Banbury, Colonel M. Archer Shee, Sir Frederick Hall, and a few others to maintain the obstruction that for many weeks had delayed the passage of the Bill. The member for the City is either tiring in his old pastime or he, too, has succumbed to the charms of the other sex, for which he blamed Ministers, for his speeches were short and his efforts at delay half-hearted. He did his best to provoke Lady Astor, but she wisely stopped her ears with her fingers and avoided an explosion. When she came to speak on the third reading she was cooler than usual, as well as more effective, and husband and schoolboy son sitting in the gallery had every reason to be pleased. Between her and Sir Frederick Banbury there was no enmity, though she told the member for the City that the only chance of reformation for a man of his age was to be born again. Letters from Sir James Crichton Browne accusing her of wilful misquotation to " bolster up her silly Bill " were discreetly passed over, and the day passed in pleasant raillery. Only Mr Scrymgeour was excited and serious. Other opponents of the Bill regarded it as a stepping-stone to Prohibition— " the foundation stone of an American statue of Liberty "—but the Dundee member thought it rank treachery to the cause, and only a safety valve for continuing the trade. Two hours sufficed for the report stage and third reading, and Lady Astor as she announced contemptuously but triumphantly that the voting had been 10 against 257 was loudly cheered. The Labour members were all in favour of the Bill, and showed a peculiar anxiety to save Government time.

The Scotsman **1923**

FAMOUS MODEL ILL

Dolores Poisoned By Food: Crab Sandwiches Suspected

As a result, it is suspected, of eating crab sandwiches, Dolores, the famous model, is lying ill at her home in Chelsea. She was stated last night to be in no immediate danger.

About fifteen minutes after eating the meal of which the sandwiches formed part, Dolores complained that she was feeling ill. She went to bed and became quickly worse.

After severe attacks of sickness she had frequent lapses into delirium. A doctor was called and said that probably she may have been poisoned by the crab sandwiches.

Dolores' father ate some of the sandwiches at the same time and felt no evil effects.

Dolores is probably the best known and most beautiful model of modern times. She has posed for Mr. Jacob Epstein, the sculptor, and Mr. C. R. W. Nevinson.

Daily Sketch **1924**

BROADCASTING TRIUMPH.

EVEN THE AEROPLANES HEARD.

The wonder of the King's speech broadcast by wireless from the Stadium amazed and delighted millions. Every word the King spoke could be heard with distinctness, and even the inflections and emphasis of his voice as he stressed a particular passage in his oration were caught.

It was possible to visualise by imagination the whole spectacle at the Stadium. There was the undercurrent of noise as the visitors assembled. The buzz of aeroplane engines flying above Wembley could be heard.

TUMULT OF SOUND.

The notes of the National Anthem turning into a tumult of sound as the people cheered the coming of the King and Queen were plain. All the music came through distinctly, the military orders rang out sharply, and even the little asides of officials and scraps of private conversations were discernible with ease.

Thousands listened to the broadcasting made possible by the special arrangements of the "Daily Express." The open spaces of Regent's Park, the Green Park, and Shepherd's Bush Green were crowded, and so, too, were the assembly rooms of the London stores in which the King's speech was reproduced through loud speakers. At Messrs. Waring and Gillow's, Oxford-street, every member of the audience stood when the music of "God Save the King" came into the room from Wembley.

Every city and town and most villages throughout the whole of Britain had their broadcast centre where local throngs gathered to share in the ceremony.

Owing to atmospheric conditions the speech was not heard well outside the United Kingdom. The United States and Germany failed to hear anything.

Daily Express **1924**

MANNERS AND MODES.

THE RENDEZVOUS (CLOCHE HAT PERIOD).

Punch **1924**

THE JUVENILE SUPPLEMENT.

To the Editor of THE GRANTA.

SIR,

A Man's past is his past. It is passée. Let sleeping doggerels lie, we maintain. Yet in the most recent number of *The Cambridge Mercury* astonishing revelations have been made of our youth. Sir, it is scandalous.

We beg to protest, in the hope that no one will read or buy that infamous periodical, which—absolutely and entirely unknown to us—has made us blush before the Public Gaze. How could the four editors of that journal be so heartless as to lay our immature mentalities stark naked to the vulgar. They evidently believe that indiscertion is the better part of valour.

We are, sir, yours most indignant,
CECIL BEATON.
R. A. BUTLER.

The Granta **1924**

RECOGNITION OF RUSSIA.

THE PREMIER TAKES THE RIGHT COURSE.

Mr. Ramsay MacDonald has lost no time in recognising the Soviet Government as the de jure Government of Russia. He has, in our view, taken the wise and statesmanlike course. The hands of Great Britain are in no way tied and her vital interests are unimpaired. Nothing in the communication made to Moscow prejudices the interests which a British Government has the right and duty to maintain. The plan pursued is recognition first, discussion and adjustment afterwards. If Russia wishes to obtain the full advantage of recognition, her representatives must show good faith and common sense in arranging a new treaty to cover the question of debts and such effective guarantees as may enable trade and commerce to flow once more between the two countries. The fact that Italy has taken a similar step at the same time is of excellent augury. It cannot fail to have its due effect on French policy and French public opinion.

Daily Express 1924

Industrial Concrete Construction.

The history of concrete as applied to building for industrial purposes leaves no doubt at all of its place in that class of building. Buildings in industry to-day have to be far larger than was ever the case before; and they have to reach heights which were never known before. The strains thus involved have given the student of mechanics furiously to think; and only re-inforced concrete has solved his problems for him.

Concrete, as most people know, possesses enormous compressive strength, but no tensile strength at all. That means to say that forces which might tend to compress it out of form can be resisted to the utmost; but those forces which tend to tear it to pieces would rapidly make an end of it were it used alone. Steel, on the other hand, possesses enormous tensile strength; and thus there is an ideality of combination between steel and concrete.

Westminster Illustrated 1925

The maintenance of the Voluntary Hospitals is a question of simple facts and figures. Income must equal expenditure, and free treatment cannot be given except in cases of the helpless poor for whom the public are always ready to subscribe generously. The settled policy of the Hospitals is to require payment from each and every patient according to means—and enquiries as to means are therefore a regular item of hospital routine.

The avoidance of these enquiries and the substitution of honourable, individual payment for a request for charity, is the object of the H.S.A.

Contributor 1926

Figures of the World of Science

There is perhaps no name so well known to the public, and especially those who have any connection or interest in things mechanical, as that of Mr. G. Constantinesco, the famous inventor of the Torque Converter, which, brought to the notice of the world about two years ago, is regarded as the most revolutionary device ever introduced into locomotive and motor car practice and the mechanical industry of power transmission in general.

Mr. George Constantinesco was born in Roumania in 1881, and became a naturalised British subject in 1916. It is scarcely any exaggeration to say that he is one of the greatest mathematicians of the times (his father was a Professor of Mathematics). At the age of fifteen he possessed a thorough knowledge of the differential and integral calculus, which reflects, of course, capacity amounting to genius.

Imperial Trade Journal 1925

What Women Want Most

*D*EAR *women who read these articles! I want you to study every word of them, for if you follow the advice contained therein you need never grow old, and however much kind friends may tell us that old age is beautiful, and that we ought to sit down under it, we know that it is hateful, and means the end of many of the simple joys of life. I have spent ten years in working out this system of facial exercises, and I have great faith in them. I do them every day, and I am not such a bad-looking person of "The Usual Age," so I have a right to talk! It is all very well to feel young, but if your neck is scrawny, and your cheeks dropped, and a network of wrinkles is round your eyes, you must look old. Get the attitude of mind that old age is not necessary. The argument against this idea is, "Look at the animals and the trees and flowers." Yes, but man can use his brain to combat the forces which rule the other kingdoms. He has controlled electricity and steam; he has discovered the radio— all things seemingly just as impossible as keeping the body young. So do not, please, accept old age as inevitable, or, at least believe me when I say that age can be immensely postponed*

Modern Woman 1926

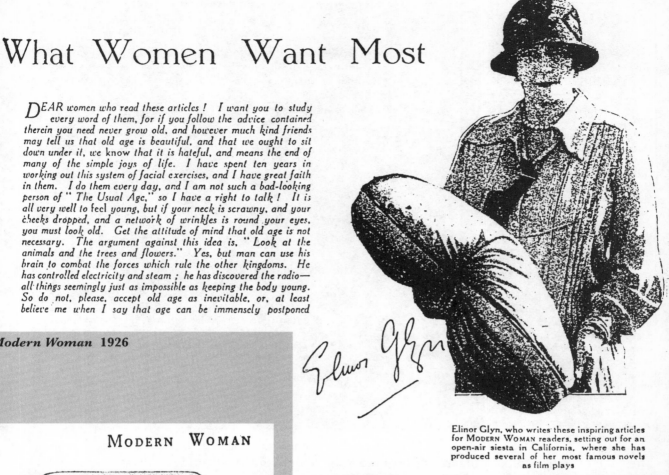

Elinor Glyn, who writes these inspiring articles for MODERN WOMAN readers, setting out for an open-air siesta in California, where she has produced several of her most famous novels as film plays

MODERN WOMAN

Sybil Thorndike as Katharine of Aragon in the fine production of "Henry VIII.," at the Empire

Modern Woman 1926

Northern Daily Telegraph 1925

NATION'S SORROW.

PASSING OF QUEEN ALEXANDRA.

The nation, and with it all the Empire, has been plunged into sorrow by the death of Queen Alexandra, at her home at Sandringham, where she passed quietly away last evening, in the presence of the King and Queen, and other members of the Royal Family.

The news was communicated in the following official bulletin, issued at 5.45 p.m. :—

Her Majesty Queen Alexandra passed away peacefully at 5.25 p.m. to-day. The King and Queen and the members of the Royal Family at Sandringham were present.

(Signed) F. J. WILLANS.

THOMAS HORDER.

The pathos of the last moments was deepened by the fact that the Queen Mother's two grandsons—the Prince of Wales and the Duke of York—although hurrying to her bedside did not arrive until after she had passed away. Their train was delayed by fog.

The General Strike, 1926: workers arrive at the Bank of England by steam lorry and trailer instead of by bus.

An armoured car leads a food convoy from the docks along the East India Dock Road, towards the food depot in Hyde Park.

THE GREAT ARCH OF YPRES.

MEMORIAL TO BRITAIN'S MISSING 58,600.

Britain's war memorial to the 58,600 men who fell in the Ypres salient and who have no known graves, and were therefore officially stated to be "missing," is nearing completion at the Menin Gate, Ypres, Belgium.

It is hoped that the memorial, which takes the form of a great archway over the main road out of Ypres, with the 17th-century ramparts of Old Ypres on either side, will be un-

Menin Gate Memorial.

veiled by the King some time next year. The memorial, which was designed by Sir Reginald Blomfield, R.A., was begun three years ago. It is 130ft. in length, weighs 20,000 tons, and the pediment of the arch is 69ft. from the ground. Beneath the massive stone lion, gazing towards Ypres, is the inscription :

"To the Armies of the British Empire who stood here from 1914-1918, and to those of their dead who have no known grave."

In Delville Wood, near Longueval, in the Somme country, in which one of their fiercest battles of the war was fought in July 1916, the memorial to the South African troops who died in the war is to be unveiled on Sunday, October 3, by the Prime Minister of South Africa, General Hertzog, who will be in Europe in connection with the Imperial Conference.

Daily Mail **1926**

MR. BERNARD SHAW.

£6,500 PRIZE DECLINED.

Mr. George Bernard Shaw, who was last week awarded the 1925 Nobel Prize (£6,500) for literature, yesterday, says Reuter, handed the following communication to the Swedish Minister in London, who immediately forwarded it to the Swedish Royal Academy, Stockholm :

TO THE PERMANENT SECRETARY OF THE ROYAL SWEDISH ACADEMY.

The award of the Nobel Prize for the year 1925 to an English work is a very welcome reinforcement of the cordial understanding between British and Swedish culture established by the famous bequest of Alfred Nobel. It will not be lost on my native country, Ireland, which already claims one distinguished Nobel prizeman [Mr. W. B. Yeats]. It is naturally very gratifying to me personally that it has fallen to my lot to furnish the occasion for such an act of international appreciation.

I must, however, discriminate between the award and the prize. For the award I have nothing but my best thanks. But after the most careful consideration I cannot persuade myself to accept the money.

Daily Mail **1926**

FAISAL'S WOMAN ADVISER.

DEATH OF MISS GERTRUDE BELL.

BRITISH FRIEND OF THE ARABS.

BAGHDAD Monday.

Miss Gertrude Lowthian Bell, Oriental Secretary to Sir Henry Dobbs, High Commissioner of Mesopotamia, died suddenly during her sleep last night.—Reuter.

By SIR PERCIVAL PHILLIPS.

Miss Gertrude Bell was one of the greatest authorities on the Arab tribes and their customs in Mesopotamia and the Middle East. Before the war she travelled extensively over the desert routes, and her knowledge was of great value to the British military authorities during subsequent operations in the Great War.

When Great Britain accepted the mandate for Mesopotamia and established King

Miss Gertrude Bell

Faisal at Baghdad, Miss Bell became a powerful influence in native affairs. The King relied on her advice, and the leading Arab chiefs invariably saw Miss Bell first when they went to Baghdad to talk over political questions with the British High Commissioner.

At her house in one of the residential suburbs of Baghdad she entertained all important visitors, and through her they were brought into contact with the leading figures in King Faisal's Government. At a luncheon party attended by Mesopotamian Cabinet Ministers, British advisers, and guests from abroad, she would carry on an animated discussion in English, French, and Arabic, selecting the language best fitted for the topic of the moment.

TRUSTED BY THE ARABS.

Undoubtedly the Arabs trusted her far more than they trusted any other European. She was capable of dealing with the subtle Oriental mind, and she never hesitated to speak frankly when more devious Oriental methods of advice were insufficient. Her dominant desire was the progress of the Arab race.

A prominent Arab official in the Mesopotamian Government once described her to me as " the uncrowned Queen of Mesopotamia."

Miss Bell was the eldest daughter of Sir Hugh Bell, the North of England ironmaster and colliery owner. She was educated at Queen's College, London, and Lady Margaret Hall, Oxford, taking a first-class in History in 1887. During the war she acted as Political Officer in the Middle East and was mentioned in despatches four times.

Daily Mail **1926**

Evening Standard
1928

SUDDEN ILLNESS OF DAME ELLEN TERRY.

Some Anxiety.

The "Evening Standard" learns that Dame Ellen Terry had a seizure yesterday morning. There is no improvement to-day

DAME ELLEN TERRY—a recent portrait.

in her condition, which gives rise to some anxiety.

Her son, Mr. Gordon Craig, and her daughter Miss Edith Craig, are with her at her home, The Farm, Small Hythe, Kent.

Dame Ellen celebrated her 80th birthday on February 27 while she was staying at Wateringbury. At that time she was suffering from bronchitis, and was unable to receive any but intimate friends.

Her health improved so much afterwards that she was able to motor to Small Hythe, and she has been particularly well all the summer until yesterday.

She was so well last week-end that her daughter left her with her companions and friends to come up to town.

While in London Miss Craig received an urgent message from Small Hythe. At once she got into touch with Mr. Gordon Craig, and they went down to The Farm together.

ONE OF THE 600.

THE LAST OF THE LIGHT BRIGADE.

DUKE OF CONNAUGHT'S REFERENCE.

"I regret to say that the last beneficiary on the fund, Troop Sergt.-Major Edwin Hughes, late 18th Hussars, died on May 18th in his 97th year. There seems to be no doubt that he was the last survivor of those under commissioned rank who took part in the famous charge."

In these simple words, addressed to the Royal Patriotic Fund Corporation in London to-day the Duke of Connaught announced the passing of the last hero of the misguided but epic charge at Balaclava in 1854

Thus the Light Brigade (Balaclava) fund has come to an end although Tennyson's famous poem, known by every schoolboy, will go down to posterity as an historical record of probably the outstanding episode of the Crimean War.

The Duke of Connaught said Sergt.-Major Hughes had outlived the resources of the original fund, but various Societies had come forward with funds which permitted the allowance of this last veteran being continued up to the day of his death.

Bath and Wilts Chronicle 1927

MRS. CHRISTIE FOUND.

AT HARROGATE HYDRO UNDER ASSUMED NAME.

IDENTIFIED BY HUSBAND.

"She does not know me and she does not know where she is."

Mrs. Agatha Christie, the writer of sensational detective stories, who vanished from her home, Styles, Sunningdale, Berkshire, 12 days ago, was found last night at the Hydropathic, a leading hotel at Harrogate, Yorkshire, where she has been staying under an assumed name since the day following her disappearance.

She was identified by her husband, Colonel Christie, who, with police officers, visited the hydro after receiving information that a woman staying there resembled a photograph of Mrs. Christie published in *The Daily Mail*.

SINGING AND DANCING

As to the details of the meeting the reports are conflicting. A statement by the manager of the hydro appears to indicate that Mrs. Christie was quite composed at seeing her husband, but Colonel Christie says that "she has suffered from complete loss of memory," and that "she does not know me and does not know where she is."

Accounts of Mrs. Christie's life at the hotel state that she seemed normal and happy; that she sang, danced, played billiards, read the newspaper reports of the disappearance, chatted with her fellow-guests, and went for walks. She is said to have represented herself as coming from South Africa.

STUDENTS RAID GLASGOW.

Out to Beat £16,000 Collected Last Year.

Glasgow was in carnival mood to-day when 6,000 undergraduates out on their annual charities parade brought a Dickensian touch to Clydeside with their slogan "more" and their mascot Oliver Twist.

Throughout the city they ranged bent on filling their collecting boxes and beating last year's record collection of £16,500.

To help the funds they sold this week 100,000 copies of a special magazine. 6,000 Oliver Twist mascot dolls, one of which has been graciously accepted by the Duchess of York for the little Princess Elizabeth, and several thousand immunity badges for one of which Mr. Baldwin, as Lord Rector sent £1.

A monster procession through the City opened the proceedings and great originality was shown in the 100 processionists.

Oxford Mail 1929

Daily Mail 1926

The lifeboat is squeezed along a narrow street at Port Isaac, 1927.

—:o:—

Rapidly our countryside is disappearing. Field and woodland everywhere have to make way for building purposes, and Belper is no exception. How the aspect of the town has changed may be seen from our hillsides. Nowhere is the change so conspicuous as from the Hunger Hill side overlooking the old Windmill area and Spencer Road, where a new suburb appears to have arisen. In this instance, howeevr, it must be said that the numerous red-tiled houses have rather added to the view than detracted from it. But within this area practically no trees existed and the green fields alone have disappeared. The same cannot be said of other sites acquired, as in Gibfield Lane, where a considerable amount of timber is threatened with destruction to create building sites. How to preserve such sylvan spots will be a difficult problem.

—:o:—

Belper News 1927

ARGENTINE PRESS AND BRITISH IMMIGRATION.

The well-known Buenos Aires newspaper *La Prensa* in an editorial urges British to emigrate to Argentina, and lays stress on the unemployment in Great Britain. "Britain's surplus is the Argentine's lack," says the article. Argentina's need of immigrants is not so peremptory that it must sacrifice quality for quantity. While the incorporation of British into Argentine society has always had excellent results, British in Argentina have never played collective politics, have always had an ingrained respect for the law, and, while conserving a deep affection for the homeland, have never been morbidly or noisily patriotic." *La Prensa* adds that it deplores the lack of initiative shown by the Argentine Government in bringing in British immigrants.

Coloniser 1928

MISS REBECCA WEST.

REBECCA WEST HITS BACK.

Mr. Arnold Bennett Styled "A Funny Old Chap."

"UNCLE" ANALYSED

"The Virtues of a Very Good Solicitor's Clerk."

" She (Miss Rebecca West) is courageous, brutal, acid, very witty, and extremely independent."—Arnold Bennett.

" Mr. Bennett suffers very unhappily from the defect of his virtues, which are, of course, those of a very good solicitor's clerk."—Miss Rebecca West.

From Our Special Correspondent.

CROMER, Tuesday.

MISS REBECCA WEST, whose book ": The Strange Necessity " has drawn from Mr. Arnold Bennett, in his book causerie in the "Evening Standard," a frank review of Miss West's literary qualities and vices, responded piquantly when I interviewed her at Cromer to-day.

Miss West is visiting Cromer to get some sea air and to see a sick relative near here.

"Miss West," wrote Mr. Bennett, "has an agile and acrobatic mind, clever and resourceful enough to enable her to emerge without discredit from the innumerable glorious scrapes which it gets her into."

"UNCLE" EXPLAINED.

And to-day Miss West proved that in that at least her literary uncle is perfectly right. "Uncle," I should say, is derived from a passage in her book when Miss West, without the least idolatry, discusses the four "uncles" of letters of her earlier days—Shaw, Bennett, Galsworthy and Wells.

"Mind you," she said, as we sat on a seat overlooking the sea, " I believe the old fellow is honest. I think I ought to give him credit for meaning what he says. But now is the time when I realise how glorious it is to be alive.

Evening Standard
1928

Evening Standard
1928

SIR G. WILLS'S DAUGHTERS.

One the Wife of a Bishop : Three Unmarried.

MILLIONS LEFT TO THEM.

From Our Own Correspondent.

BRISTOL, Saturday.

The four daughters of the late Sir George Wills, Bart., president of the Imperial Tobacco Company, who has left £10,000,000, while showing the keenest interest in the many benevolent institutions with which their father was associated, have lived very retiring lives, and have figured little in the public life of Bristol.

Sir George, who died on June 11, settled certain trusts for the benefit of his daughters, and left the residuary estate between his children —his son, Sir George Vernon Proctor Wills, and his daughters. It is estimated that, after the deduction of legacies and death duty, they will share several million pounds.

The eldest daughter, Miss Hilda Proctor Wills (one of the executors), is a woman of high educational attainments and great capacity. For many years since the death of her mother she has been her father's right hand.

Upon her devolved the main burden of caring for her father during his long illness, while the responsibilities of maintaining the home at Burwalls, and the country households at Blagdon, Somerset, in Scotland and in Norway, and controlling their staffs, have been very heavy. Miss Wills has been a keen worker as a member of the Peter Hervé Benevolent Institution.

AT BRISTOL CATHEDRAL.

The second daughter, Alice Lilian, is the wife of the Bishop of Bath and Wells. It was when Dr. Wynne Willson went from the headmastership of Marlborough to Bristol Cathedral as Dean that he met his wife. She was much interested in the cathedral work, and their many mutual interests led to marriage.

Since they have been at Wells the Bishop's Palace has been repaired and a vast amount of work done to preserve the beautiful old cathedral, which still retains its moat and many mediæval features of note.

Miss Vera Wills, like her sisters, does a good deal of committee work in connection with benevolent objects in Bristol, and is a most valued member of the Bristol Cripple Children's Society. The youngest daughter, Miss Margaret Wills, also shares in these interests.

Coalville Times
1929

DEATH OF GENERAL BOOTH.

EX-LEADER OF THE SALVATION ARMY.

A SPLENDID ORGANISER.

General Bramwell Booth, the 73-year-old ex-leader of the Salvation Army, died at his residence, The Homestead, Hadley Wood, near Barnet, on Sunday night.

The end came with dramatic suddenness, for though the General had been ill since April of last year, it was not anticipated that there was any need for immediate concern.

Bramwell Booth was born in 1856 at Halifax when his father at the time was a minister in the Methodist New Connexion. He was a delicate child afflicted with deafness which never left him, but he proved himself an indefatigable worker and a splendid organiser with a grasp of detail which once caused it to be said that he would be worth £4,000 a year to any business firm, and he has left the Salvation Army a much larger and influential body than it was when he became its chief.

WALL STREET CRASH

Mr. Graham Expects "Shake Out" to Lead to Easier Conditions Here

AMERICAN BANKS' HELP STEMS TIDE OF RUIN

£200,000,000 Spent in a Day to Save Market After Wild Selling Panic

Wall Street's sensational collapse may lead to easier conditions and the lowering of the Bank Rate in Britain.

This opinion was expressed last night by Mr. William Graham, President of the Board of Trade, at Hendon. Within recent times, he said, it had been stated that we had been dragged in this country at the tail of American speculation. He described the Wall Street collapse as a "vast shake out."

Wall Street's panic showed signs of subsiding yesterday and prices began to rise. The banks, it is believed, have saved the situation, at least for the time being, although thousands of speculators have been ruined.

The colossal sum of £200,000,000 (a billion dollars) is said to have been used by the banks in a day to stem the tide of forced selling.

Daily Mirror 1929

Oxford Mail 1929

RUINED MEN GIVE WAY TO TEARS

Tape Machines Kicked Over in Rage at Collapse

BANKS TO RESCUE

NEW YORK, Friday.

The Stock Exchange closed irregular and easier in tone after the bankers had again halted the definite downward trend, which started during the last two hours as a result of the liquidation of accounts.

It is estimated that the bankers again used millions of dollars to prevent the decline attaining a momentum. The sales to-day totalled 5,923,220 shares.

It is revealed that the bankers who conferred yesterday at Mr. J. P. Morgan's office had worked out a programme for the protection of the stock market to prevent the needless sacrifice of security values.

The *Wall Street Journal* points out that the combined resources of the interested banks amount to six billion dollars, and says that it is generally estimated that they utilised one billion to halt the decline.

TATTOOED PEERS ON SHOW!

Duke of Montrose Takes His Coat Off.

BARED ARMS.

Lord Lonsdale, the Duke of Montrose and Sir Iain Colquhoun, Bart., caused a diversion at a Glasgow dinner last night by taking off their jackets, pulling up their shirt-sleeves and displaying their tattooed arms. The dinner was given by Sir Iain to enable Lord Lonsdale to meet the Lonsdale Belt holders of Scotland.

The Duke of Montrose said that many years ago, when he was in Australia, he was interested in how tattooing was effected, and he went into a tatoo shop out of curiosity to see how it was done.

Lord Lonsdale.

When got to the top of the stairs he saw behind him two heavy-weight boxers, and he decided there and then that the only way that he could see tattooing was by having it done on himself.

Lord Lonsdale remarked later, amid laughter, that he could boast of a similar experience, and to the delight of the company he bared his arms, which were tattooed from armpit to wrist.

The Duke of Montrose and Sir Iain Colquhoun got up then and showed similar tattoo marks.

NURSE CHARGED.

"Known as Doctor" Reference by Police Inspector.

May Sheedy (26), a nurse, of St. Albans-road, Woodford Green, was remanded at Stratford Police Court to-day charged with being the bailee of a quantity of furniture valued at £99 and converting it to her own use.

Detective-inspector F. Cobley said that he saw Sheedy at her address and said:—

"I have every reason to believe you have been known in the district as Dr. Mack, Dr. Mackey and Nurse Sheedy." He cautioned her and told her:—

"You answer the description of a woman who for some time past has been obtaining furniture from tradesmen and disposing of it after you have only paid one or two small instalments." She said: "Everyone has had their furniture back."

Evening Standard 1928

P.D.C.

Carol Lombard, the graceful film star, wears a beautifully draped model.

Are You *a* Greyhound Woman?

TO-DAY is the day of the greyhound woman. The lithe, slender-hipped girl who never ages and shows no sign of a matronly figure as she nears the thirties and forties. Some few of us are born to be slim: others, through frequent dancing and taking much exercise, become slim, and others, again, thrust slimness upon themselves.

These are the women who are most to be admired. When they see unhealthy fat forming upon their bodies, perhaps through lack of exercise, perhaps through over-feeding, they have resolution enough to remedy matters. Women who sit all day at their work, instead of spending the evening in an arm-chair, go out for a brisk walk or do special reducing exercises and diet.

Almost anyone can be slim and healthy these days. There are so many, many methods of reducing and few of them are difficult or tiresome.

And the advantages of a slim figure! Youth, attractiveness, economy. The slender woman usually looks younger and more attractive than the woman who is, as Goldsmith has it, " a little in flesh." And undoubtedly it is far easier and more economical to dress when you are slim than when you are " outsize."

Each day, the number of women who are determined to keep their youth and beauty grows greater. Each day, more women are paying attention to diet and taking exercise. Each day, the band of greyhound women grows greater.

Chic 1929

1930 – 1939

Screen Lovers Contest

Enter this easy Competition now

Ideal

Ideal

John Boles and Bébé Daniels star in the popular colour talkie film " Rio Rita."

A splendid Boncilla Beauty Box with an attractive orange cover will be given to the winner of this easy competition. The Beauty Box contains a large jar of cold cream, face cream, powder and a Boncilla classmic pack. All you have to do is to place the screen lovers on this page and the next two pages in order of preference. For instance, if you prefer John Boles and Bébé Daniels you place them first on the coupon on page 33. Send the Order Form on page 33 to your newsagent or bookstall and then send the Entrance Form and the Contest Form to CHIC, 14 Gordon Street, W.C.1, by January 19th, 1930. The reader whose choice most nearly agrees with the popular vote will be awarded the prize. The fact of entry implies acceptance of the conditions and decisions of the judges.

Starring in the new Ideal-Radio all-talking film " The Very Idea " : Hugh Trevor and Sally Blane.

Chic **1930**

Beauty News from ABROAD

Leni Riefenstahl, the beautiful Austrian dancer, is caught by the camera man, in serious mood.

Chic 1930

FALL OF THE SOCIALISTS.

NATIONAL GOVERNMENT FORMED.

Mr. MacDonald and Mr. Baldwin Join Forces.

The Socialist Government resigned on Monday. Their place has been taken by an Emergency Three-Party National Government.

Mr. Ramsay MacDonald will remain Prime Minister, and Mr. Baldwin has agreed to take office under him as President of the Council.

The following communication was issued from 10, Downing Street, on Monday evening :—

"The Prime Minister, since kissing hands on appointment by his Majesty this afternoon, has been in consultation with Mr. Baldwin, Sir Herbert Samuel, and Mr. Snowden, as to the names to be submitted to the King for inclusion as Ministers in the new Government. Considerable progress has been made.

"The specific object for which the new Government is being formed is to deal with the national emergency that now exists. It will not be a Coalition Government in the usual sense of the term, but a Government of co-operation for this one purpose. When that purpose is achieved the political parties will resume their respective positions.

"In order to correct without delay the excess of national expenditure over revenue, it is anticipated that Parliament will be summoned to meet on September 8th, and proposals will be submitted to the House of Commons for a very large reduction of expenditure and for the provision on an equitable basis of the further funds required to balance the Budget.

"As the commerce and well-being, not only of the British nation but of a large part of the civilised world, has been built up and rests upon a well-founded confidence in sterling, the new Government will take whatever steps may be deemed by them to be necessary to justify the maintenance of that confidence unimpaired."

MRS. LAURENCE OLIVIER

Who was formerly Miss Jill Esmond Moore, the daughter of Miss Eva Moore, the well-known actress, was married to Mr. Laurence Olivier on July 25

Tatler 1930

Norfolk Chronicle 1931

"Box, Wrestle or Speak."

"NATIONAL" CHALLENGES "NATIONAL."

An exciting election is probable at South-West St. Pancras, where two National candidates refuse to give way. The Liberal candidate, Mr. Cecil Hayes, a barrister, who fought Stockton at the last election, challenged Mr. George Mitcheson, the Conservative nominee, to box, wrestle, shoot, ride or speak, the winner to be nominated as the National candidate.

Mr. Mitcheson replied that he weighs about 17st, and is an old amateur boxer and Rugby footballer. As the subject to be debated he chose "The Protection and Safeguarding of our industries and the economic unity of our Empire."

MR. CECIL HAYES.

"I don't care if Mr. Mitcheson weighs 27st." was Mr. Hayes's rejoinder. "If he likes he can make it a fight to a finish instead of three rounds. As I weigh only 12st. I would substitute in the boxing contest 2oz. gloves for 8oz. ones, as a knock-out would take too long with the heavier gloves.

"I take it Mr. Mitcheson has accepted my challenge to a debate. I agree as to the subject. All that remains is to take a large hall and fix the date."

Mr. Mitcheson told a Northern Echo reporter, "I don't care what Mr. Hayes says. This is my seat and I am going to win it. I will bet anyone £10 to £1 that I win the seat."

Northern Echo 1931

TRIBUTE TO A BRILLIANT ARTISTE.

WEE GEORGIE WOOD'S RECEPTION.

For over ten minutes on Monday evening Wee Georgie Wood, the world famous child impersonator, and an artiste in every sense of the word, had to stand on the stage at the Rhyl Pavilion while the audience in their enthusiasm clapped and stamped in the hope that he would be persuaded to prolong his performance. Mr. Wood was greatly touched by the warmth of his reception, and conveyed his thanks to the audience for their kindness to what he was pleased to describe as his other self, "that little boy behind this curtain." He explained how it was that he decided to take a holiday in North Wales and took the opportunity of playing at the Rhyl Pavilion. He hoped that the other performers to follow him would be similarly treated.

Rhyl Journal 1932

TO THE ELECTORS OF NORTH NORFOLK

What is wrong with the Socialist Party's campaign in their stronghold for so many years? Where are the accustomed enthusiasm, the jubilant faces, and the cocksure confidence of previous contests? Gone! and in its place the growing knowledge that they are fighting a losing fight, with the people accustomed to applaud strangely silent.

The electors are thinking, thinking of the broken promises of 1929; where is that work for the unemployed and prosperity for agriculture so glibly foretold by Socialist speakers then? Not realised, and the electors know why. Socialist promises are made to be broken; given to catch votes without heed of the consequences.

What is the alternative? A vote for the National Government, and sure and certain endeavour to do everything possible to bring the country back from the ruin which awaits the nation if the Socialists are returned.

Mr. Ramsay MacDonald, the head of the National Government, expects the electors of North Norfolk to send a Member to Parliament who will support him; see to it that he is not disappointed, and do not relax your efforts until 9 o'clock on Tuesday next.

Norfolk Chronicle 1931

HITLER'S POWER ON THE WANE

ELECTIONS REVEAL BOLSHEVIST PROGRESS

Gloucestershire Echo 1932

FIGURES of the German elections, which took place yesterday, revealed, states Reuter, that while the general political situation is unchanged,

Hitler's power is waning;

Bolshevism is making headway among the discontented workers;

Berlin may be said to be definitely "Red."

President Von Hindenburg is faced with the question whether to retain the Reichstag, in which no majority is likely, or to support the dictatorship of Van Papen.

The poll was 79 per cent, of the electorate as against 84 last July, but this does not account for a drop of two millions in the Nazi vote.

The German Nationals, who support the Junker Government of Von Papen, have increased their strength by 800,000, and the Communists advanced by 700,000.

The provisional final official result shows that regarding the principal parties, the Nazis have 195 seats, compared with 230 in July; Socialists 121, compared with 133; Communists 100 compared with 89; Centre 75, compared with 75; German Nationals 51, compared with 40; Bavarian People's Party 18, compared with 22; German People's Party 11, compared with seven.

NEW MOVE IN THE FAR EAST.

Suggested Restoration of Chinese Empire.

"MANCHUKUO ONLY A PRELIMINARY STEP."

TOKIO, Wednesday—(Reuter).

That the time is coming when the Monarchy will be restored in China, and that the recent setting up of an independent regime in Manchuria under the Chinese ex-Emperor Pu Yi is merely a preliminary step to such a restoration, is the suggestion attributed here to Ting Shi-Yuan, the private representative of Pu Yi.

Ting Shi-Yuan is at present passing through Tokio en route for Geneva, where the Lytton report on the Manchurian question is shortly to come before the League Council for Action.

In connection with significant statement it is recalled here the influential Chinese emissaries from a number of provinces south of the Great Wall are reported to have visited Pu Yi recently, and to have intimated to him the belief that Hopeh, Shantung, Shansi and other provinces were prepared to join Manchukuo, as the new State of Manchuria is called.

Pu Yi's advisers are reported to be convinced that the only way to combat the spread of Communism and restore the unity and stability of China is a return to the Monarchy. They are hopeful that the whole of China will respond if Pu Yi succeeds in aligning the northern provinces of China proper with Manchukuo.

Bournemouth Evening Echo 1932

Miss Muriel Tart, engaged to Mr. Robert FitzGibbon Carse, grandson of the late Dr. Henry FitzGibbon, president of the R.C.S.

Daily Mirror 1932

HITLER SEES VON HINDENBURG.

New Bid for the Chancellorship.

PRESIDENT AGAIN REFUSES?

Efforts to Bring About a Coalition.

BERLIN, Saturday (Reuter.)

A considerable crowd collected outside the Chancellor's office to await the arrival of Adolf Hitler, who met President von Hindenburg at noon. Among the crowd were many Nazis in uniform, and police paraded up and down the street to maintain order. Intense interest was taken generally in the meeting.

AN HOUR'S INTERVIEW.

Hitler's interview with President Hindenburg lasted one hour. The Nazi leader, as he entered and left the Presidential Palace, was enthusiastically cheered. When he came out of the Palace the crowd surged towards the gates. The Nazi leader returned his supporters' greetings by raising his hat before entering his car to return at once to confer with his lieutenants.

Nothing of what occurred at the interview has officially been allowed to leak out. Nevertheless, there is good reason to believe that Hitler outlined to the President his party's political programme, and declared that the majority of the German peoples wanted him as Chancellor, and he therefore should be given a chance to conduct the affairs of the country.

Hindenburg reserved his decision and made no promises.

Bournemouth Evening Echo 1932

New Age 1930

Mr. Leslie Runciman spoke as principal guest at the Bristol Steamship Owners' Association banquet last week. The report says: "There was no shortage of anything in the world to-day. He was not at all sure it would not be a good thing to fill all the ships with these commodities and scuttle them in the Atlantic. . . . The people on whom their censure must firmly and vigorously fall were the bankers. He had it on the authority of Sir Josiah Stamp that . . . the principal cause [of the trouble] was gold."— *Lloyd's List and Shipping Gazette*, December 2.

"PUT THROUGH IT" BY SOVIET.

Ambassador's Report on Treatment of Arrested Englishmen in Russia.

The White Paper containing correspondence relating to the arrest of employees of the Metropolitan-Vickers Company at Moscow was issued at ten o'clock last night.

Sir E. Ovey, in a dispatch dated March 12th, said conditions under the present reign of terror in this country (Russia) are without parallel in Great Britain. It is inconceivable that the Soviet Government can produce credible evidence of any criminal malpractice on the part of the company.

In a dispatch dated March 14th, Sir E. Ovey gives account of Mr. Monkhouse's examination by Soviet officials, who called upon him to make complete confession. Mr. Monkhouse was told that if he continued to refuse to confess he would be treated as a criminal. Subsequently he was told that he had given his evidence like an honest man, and that he was to be released. His first examination began at 8 a.m., and continued without interruption for 19 hours.

On March 14th Sir R. Vansittart, Permanent Under Secretary of State for Foreign Affairs, telegraphed to Sir E. Ovey: "You have no doubt emphasised to M. Litvinoff impossible position for Anglo-Soviet relations if British subjects are used for spectacular treason trials staged for reasons of internal politics."

"Obviously Terrified."

Sir E. Ovey describes in dispatches on March 14th his visit to the prisoners. He says: While the prisoners seemed generally in good health the drawn expressions of Messrs. Thornton and Cushny gave me definite impressions of their having been "put through it." They were all obviously terrified of speaking, and confined themselves to the minimum of replies.

Sheffield Daily Telegraph **1933**

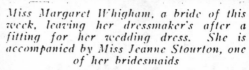

The Lady **1933**

Miss Margaret Whigham, a bride of this week, leaving her dressmaker's after a fitting for her wedding dress. She is accompanied by Miss Jeanne Stourton, one of her bridesmaids

The Hartlepool motor lifeboat *Elizabeth Newton* returning from exercise, 1932.

As Told To
Dr. NANDOR FODOR
The Psychical Researcher

PEERING into the future has ever been a fascinating pursuit of mankind.

On the threshold of this brave New Year 1933 I have obtained for the *Sunday Dispatch* the New Year forecasts of a famous astrologer and an eminent numerologist, together with a message in automatic writing from a so-called spirit control who claims to have lived in the year 200 B.C.

The astrologer is Dr. Francis Rolt-Wheeler, F.R.G.S., director of the Institut Astrologique de Carthage (Tunis). Dr. Rolt-Wheeler, who is in Holy Orders, and is also a Doctor of Philosophy, has written more than 60 books on scientific subjects.

"Before I give my forecast I must preface it by stating causes and reasons," he told me.

We Shall Recover

"The basis of international astrology is that races and nations, like individuals, appertain to certain cycles of rhythm—cosmic, racial, historical, political, and economic.

"Millikan, in strict academic science, has shown that the rays of inter-stellar space affect human character. Eddington has shown that cosmic vibrations touch the mentality.

"It is well known that world religions follow the inverse succession of zodiacal signs, following the Precession of the Equinoxes. Tchichewsky has proved that popular revolutions link to solar cycles. Earth rhythms, such as tides, follow lunar rhythms.

"International astrology is based on the establishment of the rhythms to occur during the coming year, judged by charts of Solar Ingresses, planetary conjunctions, and lunations. On these are superimposed the 'natal' charts of nations and the charts of monarchs, dictators, or determinative statesmen.

"Weal follows concord; woe is indicated by discord. These conclusions are then compared with those of rival countries, and political common sense is applied to the final result.

"My predictive comments on the probabilities for 1933 are:

"**Britain** will recover commercially. The control of the world's finance will leave New York and return to London

Sunday Dispatch 1933

WE have had reminiscences and memoirs of famous generals, admirals, politicians, statesmen and diplomats, but no one has hitherto attempted to relate from within the story of the British Revolutionary Movement.

I propose to do so now. In this series of articles I shall trace its origin and development, showing how a band of revolutionaries endeavoured to form Soviets in Britain and establish the Dictatorship of the Proletariat, even before the Bolshevik Revolution of November 1917.

There are few more fitted than I to tell the story from behind the scenes.

I was a revolutionary before the war, and was actively associated with every agitation and strike from 1914 to 1919. I was leader of the Workers' Committee Movement, which was so powerful during that period; I helped to form the Hands Off Russia Committee, and the People's Russian Information Bureau.

I was president of the former throughout its exotic career, and I became the central figure in the amazing plot to overthrow the Government in 1919, and to establish Soviet rule in Great Britain.

Amazing? It was fantastic! But we did not then think so; indeed, the circumstances seemed very favourable to a revolution.

Sunday Dispatch 1933

AUSTRALIA AND THE
M.C.C. REPLY

Control Board to Meet on Monday

PRESS & THE "SNUB"

Protest "Unhappily Phrased"

MELBOURNE, WEDNESDAY.

The Australian Board of Control will meet on Monday to consider the M.C.C. cable in reply to the Australian cable of protest on "body-line" bowling.

TUESDAY.

The dignified wording of the cable has greatly impressed thoughtful Australians. It is considered that the reply was in sharp contrast to the Board of Control cable, which, even among the strongest antagonists of "body-line" bowling, was thought to be blundering and hastily worded. It is not unlikely that the board may split on the subject, as it is well known that some members objected to the placing of the gun at the heads of the M.C.C.

Manchester Guardian 1933

AGITATOR AMONG THE TROOPS

PLOT TO MARCH ON PARLIAMENT FOILED

A COMMERCIAL traveller visited the Manchester office of the *Sunday Dispatch* last week and asked, almost diffidently, if he might amplify a part of the story told by Mr. W. F. Watson in his "Confessions of a Red."

He established his identity, but his name, for business reasons, is withheld.

Here is his story:

In January 1919 I was a private in the R.A.S.C. (Mechanical Transport). On the first of the month I arrived at Kempton Park depot from France.

DISCONTENT

There were roughly 2,000 men in the camp, and they were waiting for demobilisation.

It had been the rule to give first release to men for whom jobs were waiting, and this created much discontent.

Those kept back felt that all the jobs would be filled before they were released, and, particularly among the older soldiers, it was thought that men should be demobilised in the order in which they had joined the Colours.

There had been an agreement one evening among the men that after parade the following morning they would do no further work.

TO THE WAR OFFICE

Finally a number of delegates were appointed with the idea that they should go to Whitehall and lay their grievances before the authorities.

Then one day we learned that the men who had formed the delegation were to be demobilised at once and drafted home!

This astute move of depriving the men of their leaders might have succeeded but for the presence in the background of a real agitator.

He was a private soldier and an orator, able to appeal to the passions of the men. The day the demobilised leaders left the camp this agitator jumped on the table of the canteen and urged the men to continue the strike.

ARMED MEN MARCH

Later I found that the delegates had already been talked into agreeing to a scheme for taking twenty lorry "loads" of troops the following morning to join a demonstration on the Embankment under the leadership of an ex-sergeant major from outside the camp.

This obviously was to have been the march of the 1,500 armed men referred to by W. F. Watson.

They were to go in procession from the Embankment to the Houses of Parliament, there to present a "Soldiers' Charter."

And, the agitator added, "The Guards are with us!"

At these words I saw my chance.

I said: "Gentlemen, we are being misled. When our friend tells me the Guards are with us, I reply, 'Don't believe it.' The Guards are *soldiers!*

I turned in at midnight with the problem still unsolved of how to stop that march but determined that I must find some means.

If I slept at all it must have been fitfully. I was brought to my senses with a start at about four a.m. There was the sound outside the building of marching men, the tramping of feet on the gravel path, and the hoarse command "Halt!"

IN POSSESSION

We found that a detachment of the Inniskilling Fusiliers and a detachment from another infantry regiment had taken possession of the camp.

The march was definitely off—but the strike continued. Our agitator disappeared from the camp.

Very soon the demobilisation plans we had asked for came into operation. That morning my company, as a lead to the whole camp, paraded for duty. The others followed and the strike was over.

Sunday Dispatch 1933

PACIFISM AT OXFORD

SIR,—When I read of the motion in the Oxford Union " that this House will in no circumstance fight for its King and Country " being carried by 275 votes to 153, I found myself underlining the words " for its King and Country " ; for I realised simultaneously two things : first, that there can be no question for me any more of fighting in a national war ; secondly, that if a war arose because the Covenant of the League of Nations required the use of the ultimate, military sanctions against an aggressor country, I would have to fight.

I believe that a complete reorientation of loyalty has been going on in large sections of the post-war generation. We owe a new allegiance—an allegiance not to any national State, but to the world. I give my own reactions because I believe many people must find themselves now thinking on these lines.

65 Portland Place, W.1.　　　　　　　　JONATHAN GRIFFIN

New Statesman 1933

Exeter Western Mail
1934

Death of Viscount Grey

BRITAIN LOSES GREAT WAR-TIME MINISTER

Vital 1914 Speech Recalled

Viscount Grey of Fallodon, the great Liberal Statesman, and the man whose speech settled the issue whether the British Cabinet could go into the Great War with a united nation behind it, died yesterday at Fallodon, the home he loved, set in the wild border moors of Northumbria.

The end came peacefully at five minutes past six. For nearly seventy hours Lord Grey had lain unconscious, with only his slight breathing to show that he was still alive.

Hour after hour his sister and her daughter Joan watched by the bed-side, while his last remaining reserves of strength ebbed gradually away.

But Lord Grey died without regaining consciousness—without a last smile of recognition for the two devoted women who for 12 days had fought ceaselessly, but without avail, for his life.

Death came to Lord Grey as he would most have wished it—in a setting of perfect peace, amid the quiet countryside that he knew, and loved so well, far from the hurly-burly of political life, and remote from the busy world where for so long he played so great a part.

DAWN CHORUS OF BIRDS.

The dawn chorus of wild birds (the music that he loved) was echoing across the woods as he breathed his last. A flight of wild duck winged their way across the lightening sky, and their harsh cry and the whirr of their fast-beating wings sounded like a last lament for the dead man who was the friend of birds.

South London Press 1933

MAN WANTS TO BE A LANDLORD

"Better to be a Protected Tenant" Says Judge

COURT CATECHISM

When Arthur Percy Humphrey, builder, of 2, Weybridge-st., Battersea, sought possession of the house from George Vallance, a pensioner, he told the Judge at Wandsworth County Court he was the owner of the house.

Defendant, he said, was a weekly tenant at a rent of 14s. 5d.

Judge: How much is in arrear?

Mr. Humphrey: None.

Judge: Then on what ground do you seek possession?—I'm paying 7s. 3d. a week as tenant of Mrs. Vallance.

Judge: Rather a mix-up. You're a tenant of hers and you're suing her for possession?—Yes. I wish to be landlord of my own house.

Judge: How are you a tenant?—Her son has three rooms and I have one room sub-let by her son. They kept giving me notice, so I bought the house.

Solicitor: He wants to have the advantage of being a landlord.

Judge: In these days it is a much greater advantage to be a protected tenant.

An order was made.

A RIVERSIDE "MOLOCH" THAT BECAME AN AUSTERE BEAUTY: THE IMPRESSIVE CHIMNEYS OF BATTERSEA POWER-STATION, WITH PLUMES OF "WASHED SMOKE."
One of the marvels of the great power-station at Battersea is the system by which it consumes its own smoke. The white wreath of vapour from each of its chimneys represents the entire gaseous effluent from something approaching 1000 tons of coal a day. By means of the complicated washing apparatus, practically the whole of the dangerous sulphur fumes are eliminated. It is claimed that Battersea is the first power-station to be so equipped.

Illustrated London News
1934

FOREIGN.

Mary Pickford, the actress, will file a suit for divorce from Douglas Fairbanks in Juarez, Mexico, in a fortnight's time. The ground for her suit will be incompatibility.

Mrs. Elvira Barney has been divorced in New York by her husband, Mr. John Barney, the American singer.

A lonely missionary, who built an aeroplane landing stage on the Island of Bathurst, in the Timor Sea, against possible emergencies, was able to save a British air liner caught in a heavy monsoon.

Shrewsbury Chronicle
1933

Queen
1933

Birmingham Mail
1934

Miss E. H. Glen, O.B.E., buyer for a famous drapery firm.

THE John Lewis Partnership, which includes the shops John Lewis & Co., Ltd., of Oxford Street, and Peter Jones, Ltd., of Sloane Square, London, and Jessop & Son, at Nottingham, was, I believe, one of the first groups of big departmental stores to employ educated women, and to-day a considerable number of secondary school girls as well as a smaller number of College graduates are working in various branches of these well-known drapery emporiums.

But when the other day I went to see Miss Glen, the buyer in the Linen Department, I confess I was somewhat surprised to find that she was a Newnham College student and had taken the Economics Tripos. She is an unusual woman, and occupies an unusual position, and her career is full of interest to those who, like myself, believe that there are many excellent openings in business for the educated and intelligent woman who can adapt herself to " all sorts and conditions " of persons and circumstances.

My talk with Miss Glen confirmed this view : here was a highly educated woman, who might well have been the headmistress of a high school but had chosen to devote her talents to business, and had not only been successful in it but had found a zest and interest in her work which she says she feels she could not have enjoyed elsewhere.

BRITISH FASCISTS.

AIMS EXPLAINED BY SIR OSWALD MOSLEY.

BIRMINGHAM MEETING.

Sir Oswald Mosley, the British Fascist leader, addressed a public meeting at Bingley Hall, Birmingham, last night. He was saluted by a body of 2,000 blackshirts, drawn from all parts of the Midlands, with contingents of several hundreds from London and other centres, and the general audience numbered some thousands.

Sir Oswald spoke for nearly an hour and three-quarters in attacking the present system and outlining the Fascist policy. After this he answered questions, and was thus occupied altogether for two hours and a half.

He said Fascism was nothing less than the creation of a new civilisation. Fascists held that the old world in which they were born and grew up had come to an end for ever, and that little enough time was allowed them to build up the new civilisation. Fascism on the one hand was a revolutionary movement, and on the other was one of patriotism in which love of country was first and foremost.

Blackpool's Oldest Cabman

Celebrates His Diamond Wedding— Held a Licence for 64 Years

HAVING been a cabman for 64 years, holding a licence since he was 13, Mr. Richard Walsh, of St. Annes-road, South Shore, will celebrate his diamond wedding on Saturday.

Both Mr. and Mrs. Walsh are well-known in South Shore, particularly in the St. Annes-road district, where they have lived for over 49 years.

Mr. Walsh is a "sand grown 'un," being born in Preston New-road, and both he and his wife come of farming stock.

Mr. R. Walsh   Mrs. Walsh

* * *

Farming Stock

Mr. Walsh is a grand old man, and celebrated his 81st birthday on Tuesday. He is clean-shaven but has white "side-boards," and a pair of shrewd, twinkling eyes.

Both he and his wife, who is a charming woman, have enjoyed very good health up to the past few years. Mrs. Walsh, however, had a severe illness last year and this has greatly taxed her strength.

The Walsh family, after leaving Marton, farmed at the corner of Shaw-road and Lytham-road for many years, and Mr. Walsh met his wife when she came from Manchester to live in a house opposite. She is a native of Nottingham and her father and grandfather were also farmers.

* * *

For Sixty-four Years

Mr. Walsh wanted to do something else in addition to farming, and when he was thirteen years of age obtained his first licence to drive a cab or landau, which he held for 64 years.

His first vehicle cost £1 and was not dignified by the name of a cab. It was a two-wheeled affair with a detachable wooden top, which he plied for hire near the Bridge of Peace, which probably only the elder local residents will remember, opposite West-street.

He recalls that there was no promenade in those days, and if it were necessary for him to take a passenger from the old Lane Ends, now the County Hotel, to the Royal Hotel, he had to make a detour up Church-street, along Bank Hey-street into Adelaide-place.

* *

Blackpool Gazette and Herald
1934

Belfast Telegraph
1934

GRAND OPERA DISCORD

"SHUT UP, YOU" SHOUTED TO GALLERY

CHATTERERS SILENCED

SIR T. BEECHAM'S OUTBURST

"BARBARISM": "SAVAGERY"

In scathing phrases and stinging epithets Sir Thomas Beecham, the conductor, spoke to-day of the reasons for his outburst on Monday night during one of the most memorable "first nights" of Covent Garden opera.

SIR THOMAS BEECHAM.

In the midst of the overture a background of chattering in the auditorium caused Sir Thomas to turn on his heel, and, facing the audience, call out: "Stop talking."

Then the piece went on —a prelude to Beethoven's "Fidelio."

Worse was to come, however —ill-timed applause from the gallery.

"Shut up, you," cried Sir Thomas, and the offenders, amazed at the conductor's outburst, were silenced.

To-day Sir Thomas, far from having any regrets, was planning what to do if the "chatterboxes" again threaten to spoil the opera.

"I was told," he said to a reporter, "that the audience was stupefied by what I did. They were astonished at being asked to stop talking. I am glad, and what I said had the desired effect.

Simple Funeral

IN a plain coffin, draped in a Union Jack, the body of Mr. T. E. Shaw ("Lawrence of Arabia") will be taken from the little mortuary chapel tomorrow for burial in the village cemetery of Moreton.

The body, which throughout today is lying in simple state before the altar in the little slate mortuary chapel, will be placed in a private motor hearse. There will be no flowers on the coffin, and no inscription. The coffin is of plain elm. It has no breast plates.

Dorset Daily Echo 1935

THE POTEEN EVIL.

DERRY PRESBYTERY REPORT.

ROMAN CATHOLIC EFFORTS TO STAMP IT OUT.

The efforts of the Roman Catholic Church authorities to stamp out the poteen traffic was referred to at a meeting of the Derry Presbytery on Tuesday, when Rev. W. M. Kennedy, B.A., presenting a report on temperance, said the Presbytery of Londonderry had a considerable number of congregations in the Free State. He supposed their concern there in a report like that was mainly with their own people. Their sobriety was beyond reproach, and in the main they commended the Church of their allegiance. But he was sure they would like him, basing himself on some of the query sheets returned to him from the Free State, to express their admiration as a Presbytery of the drastic steps taken by the authorities of the Roman Catholic Church, and with considerable success, to stamp out illicit distillation amongst their own people. "They have our moral support," proceeded Rev. Mr. Kennedy, "in this good work. I have no knowledge of any of our Presbyterian people taking part in this nefarious and illegal business, or in any way aiding and abetting it. I hope none of them have sunk so low as to be associated in any way with poteen. Such a Presbyterian would be regarded by our Presbytery as an outlaw to respectability and religion, justly deserving the contempt of his fellows and the lash of the law." They had reason, however, the report concluded, for gratitude to God that on the whole their people were sober and law-abiding and the future bright with hope, he added.

On the motion of Mr. A. W. Perry, J.P., seconded by Rev James Colhoun, the report was adopted, and Rev. Mr. Kennedy was congratulated on his interest in the work.

Londonderry Sentinel 1935

WARSHIP BUILDING

DISTRIBUTION OF NAVAL CONTRACTS

FROM OUR NAVAL CORRESPONDENT

Now that the contracts involved in the 1933 naval construction programme have all been placed by the Admiralty, with the orders for the two largest ships therein, the 9,000-ton cruisers Minotaur and Polyphemus, 11 firms have received contracts for the hulls or machinery of ships, or both, in this programme. Seventeen firms are now at work upon Admiralty contracts. Twelve received orders under the 1932 programme, and a similar number (although not the same firms in every case) under the programme of 1931.

The benefit to the shipbuilding and engineering firms of the work involved in these three naval programmes may be realized when it is recalled that under the 1929 programme only three firms received orders. Only one cruiser, the Leander, was authorized that year, and was built at Devonport, her machinery being manufactured by Messrs. Vickers-Armstrongs, who also built the destroyers Cygnet and Crescent and the submarine Thames, and engined the submarines Swordfish and Sturgeon, built at Chatham Dockyard. Messrs. Hawthorn Leslie and Co. provided the machinery for the destroyers Crusader and Comet, built at Portsmouth. This was the only time destroyers had been built in one of the public yards, and it was significant that whereas the Cygnet and Crescent, built throughout by Messrs. Vickers-Armstrongs, cost £564,000, the Crusader and Comet, built in a public yard and engined by contract, cost £641,000. The only other firm to benefit under the 1929 programme, Messrs. J. Samuel White and Co., built at Cowes the flotilla leader Kempenfelt and also provided machinery for four sloops of the Shoreham class.

Times Trade and Engineering Supplement 1934

LAWRENCE'S LIFE IN THE TANK CORPS

"Perfect Tommy Atkins" Says Captain Under Whom He Served

TODAY, for the first time the story of "Lawrence of Arabia's" life as a private soldier in the Army was disclosed to a "Dorset Daily Echo" representative by Captain G. E. Kirby, who is in charge of the quartermaster's stores at the camp.

Captain Kirby was Mr. Shaw's superior officer when he joined the Royal Tank Corps at Bovington in 1923.

"It was just as an ordinary recruit that Shaw came to the depot," he said. "He signed the necessary Army forms, as all other recruits must, and was drilled with other newcomers for two months.

"His aptitude for clerical work resulted in the camp authorities drafting him to the quartermaster's depot, where he acted as storeman. There his daily duties were to hand out clothing and equipment to the men.

"That was his position during the two years he was at Bovington.

"He received no favours and asked none. He was very amenable to discipline, much more so than the ordinary soldier, and the fact that he had once been a Colonel was never displayed in his behaviour

"In fact, he was a perfect Tommy Atkins.

Dorset Daily Echo
1935

Dover Express 1935

CAN MINERS AFFORD WIRELESS SETS P

JUDGE GIVES A WARNING.

Comments regarding selling costly wireless sets to miners were made by his Honour Judge Clements at Canterbury County Court on Tuesday, when William Taylor, of Burgess Road, Aylesham, was summoned by Kolster Brandes, Ltd., of Sidcup, for £2 15s.

His Honour said that wireless firms could ascertain a man's wages, and also his circumstances before letting him have a 13 guinea set. He (his Honour) would not assist such firms by giving a committal order.

Mr. A. K. Mowll (for plaintiffs): It means that no miner will get a wireless set.

His Honour: A miner cannot afford to buy a 13 guinea set if he is getting £2 10s. wages and has a young family to support. They must take a risk, and I am not going to send persons to prison.

An order for payment of the amount claimed at the rate of 2s. a month was made.

CITY GOSSIP.

Cardiff and Suburban
News 1935

"A MAN—GOD BLESS HIM"

G.B.S.'s Tribute to Late King

SINCERITY REVEALED THROUGH MICROPHONE

Tribute to King George V. was paid by Mr. George Bernard Shaw, who sailed from Southampton for a West Indies cruise in the Blue Star Line's Arandora Star late this afternoon.

"King George V." he declared, "has left the monarchy in England at a higher standard of respectability and popularity than ever before. We have had popular Kings, without them always being respectable. George V., however, was both respectable and popular, and was one of the finest broadcasters in the country."

Mr. Shaw went on to say that the late King had been correct in utilising the microphone to carry his message to his people, and then, after a brief pause, he added: "I have always said that the microphone is a very wonderful detector of any sort of insincerity. When politicians try to broadcast ordinary electioneering bunk, well, you can tell it is bunk through the microphone, although it may sound all right from the platform when everyone is drunk with excitement.

LATE KING'S SINCERITY

"The unquestionable sincerity with which the late King spoke, the sincere humility of the man; in fact his whole attitude, was such that it made us all say 'A man. God bless him.'"

Mr. Shaw said that very few people could have won the great personal popularity which the King had done by his use of the microphone.

"It is, in fact," he remarked, "fortunate for some that the microphone did not exist in the past, otherwise they might have given themselves away rather badly."

The Heroes and Heroines of the Railway Disaster.

Cardiff citizens were awakened on Sunday morning by the cry of "A Railway Disaster!" Those of us who learned the tragic news on Saturday night awaited with anxiety for the details of the dreadful catastrophe. The one bright spot in this devastating disaster is the heroism of our men and women. The work of the nurses, until bourne down by exhaustion; one private nurse, although herself injured, working on until she fainted; the youth, who tore the wreckage to pieces, in a frantic endeavour to find his mother, until he fell unconscious - all these heroic sacrifices give the lie to those who are constantly asserting that modern civilisation has gone awry. These acts of heroism are typical of those recurring after every accident in this brave old country of ours.

* * * *

The accident itself reminds one of the inevitability of human fragility. One moment everyone happy and joyous; the next the place a shambles- with death and disaster in its train. Even in this most scientific age we have to turn to the warning "In the midst of life we are in death"! It is, however, a blessing to know that in England, at any rate, the slogan still goes "Safety First!"

The Safest Place is "Off the Earth"

Do not think that we are "all at sea" when we point out that the safest place in the world to-day is "on the sea." The grave tragedy of this railway disaster reminds one of the safety there is in travelling on board ship. Statistics prove that, for many years we are safer on the water than on the earth! The old hymn and prayer, "O! hear us, when we cry to Thee, for those in peril on the sea," like many other medieval prayers, has almost lost its meaning.

Southern Daily Echo
1936

West London and
Chelsea Gazette
1934

QUEEN AMONG THE ROSES.

Long Visit To Show At Chelsea.

The Queen, whose love of flowers is well known, spent Friday morning at the summer exhibition of the National Rose Society, in the grounds of the Royal Hospital, Chelsea.

Her Majesty spent well over an hour among the roses. Her first remark, on entering one of the marquees, was, "What a beautiful scent!"

On leaving, the Queen stated that she intended to present the society with a silver challenge cup for competition next year.

The roses were displayed on a black background, which gave emphasis to their fine tints.

Dr. A. H. Williams, the president, and Miss Willmott, a member of the Council, conducted the Queen round the exhibition. Her Majesty frequently stooped to smell the flowers.

She particularly admired a display of deep red roses which had won a first prize, and she asked if she could take some away.

Just before leaving the show the Queen noticed a small tent, at the side of which were a number of Chelsea pensioners, who gave her a smart salute. She entered the tent, and found that it contained an exhibition of flowers and fruit grown by the pensioners.

Sergt. C. Relf, late of the Queen's Own Royal West Kent Regiment, the winner of the Pensioners' Silver Cup, was presented to the Queen, and she congratulated him on his success. She also congratulated Pensioner M. Harrison on his gooseberries and black currants, and before leaving accepted from Pensioner Robert McAllister two carved models—a tiger's head and a parrot.

Mr. KIPLING'S ABBEY BURIAL

Ashes in Poets' Corner

DISTINGUISHED PALL BEARERS

MR. RUDYARD KIPLING, Poet of Empire, was buried in Westminster Abbey today. The urn containing his ashes was placed in that quiet corner in the South Transept consecrated to the memory of those who excelled in the written word—the great masters of verse and prose.

Mr. Baldwin, the Prime Minister and cousin of Mr. Kipling, was one of the pall-bearers. Admiral of the Fleet Sir Roger Keyes and Field-Marshal Sir Archibald Montgomery-Massingberd, Chief of the Imperial General Staff, represented the Services which Kipling so dearly loved, and whose praises he had sung in noble verse and prose.

Southern Daily Echo
1936

DAME CLARA BUTT, the world famous singer, died to-day at her home at North Stoke, Oxford. She was born on February 1, 1873.

Clara Butt possessed a contralto voice of exceptional power and wide range. King Edward the Seventh used to claim a share in her discovery.

As Prince of Wales he attended a performance of Gluck's "Orfeo" by the Royal College of Music at the Lyceum, in which the principal role was taken by Clara Butt, then a girl newly arrived in London.

INVITED TO PALACE

He was so pleased with her singing that he had her presented to him.

Afterwards he spoke of the new singer to Queen Victoria, who invited her to Buckingham Palace. This soon became known, and Clara Butt rapidly rose to fame.

Southern Daily Echo
1936

Cardiff and Suburban News
1935

CITY GOSSIP.

As the King was returning to Buckingham Palace on Thursday after presenting new colours to the Brigade of Guards a man pushed his way to the front of the crowd near the Wellington Arch in Constitution Hill. A revolver fell in the roadway near the King and the troops following him. No shot was fired, but the revolver was found to be loaded in four of its five chambers. The man was arrested, and charged with being in possession of a revolver with intent to endanger life. At subsequent proceedings at Bow Street his solicitor stated that the prisoner wished him to say that there was no attempt at assassination and no intention of assassination, and it appeared that the man was harbouring some grievance against the Home Secretary. The King himself was quite unperturbed by the incident, and with characteristic devotion to duty after his return to the Palace he proceeded to York House to transact State business. The King has received hundreds of messages from all parts of the world expressing relief at his safe return after the incident. The man who was arrested and charged formerly belonged to the Govan district of Glasgow. His name is George Andrew M'Mahon, otherwise Jerome Bannigan, and, it is understood, he is the adopted son of an Irish family named Bannigan, who stay in Govan. He was educated at St. Anthony's Roman Catholic School, Govan, and left the city 11 years ago. Since then not much has been heard of him by his relatives. He appears again at Bow Street Police Court this week.

Home and Country 1936

Mines, Roads and Education.

At the moment of writing there seem to be hopes that the threatened coal strike may not take place. A number of big businesses in this country have agreed to pay more for their coal on condition that a better wage is paid to the miners and negotiations are still going on.

Lord Nuffield, still better known to most of us as Morris of Morris cars, has given £125,000 for the care of crippled children and for research into the causes that produce cripples. One of these causes is sometimes a Morris car! It is interesting to learn that the big Safety Campaign of the Government is really having an effect and that the number of road accidents was " down " last year, though the number of cars in use on the roads was " up."

At the time of the General Election the National Government promised improvements in education. The Government has already begun to fulfil this promise. The Board of Education has written to local authorities about developments in such things as nursery schools, secondary schools and about the raising of the school leaving age.

Lord Rutherford, who won the Nobel Prize for chemistry in 1908, seen here in the Cavendish Laboratory, Cambridge, in 1936, the year before his death. His research established that radioactivity is produced by the disintegration of atoms, which demonstrated the nuclear nature of the atom.

DUKE OF WINDSOR MARRIED

The Duke of Windsor was married to Mrs. Wallis Warfield (Mrs. Simpson) on Thursday at the Chateau de Cande, near Monts, France.

It was exactly at 11.45 that Dr. Mercier, the Mayor of Monts, pronounced the words: "In the name of the law we declare you united in the bonds of matrimony."

The civil ceremony, which began at 11.35, a few minutes late, was very brief.

To the Mayor's ritual question, "Do you consent to take Mrs. Wallis Warfield as your wife?" the Duke replied "Oui" (yes) in a firm voice.

His bride's voice shook unsteadily as she gave her response.

The Mayor then delivered a brief, striking address, in which he expressed his cordial good wishes for the couple's happiness.

A moment later and they were kneeling before the Rev. Anderson Jardine, Vicar of St. Paul's, Darlington, on two white satin cushions before the altar, made of an old oak chest.

Here Mr. Jardine conducted a Church of England service, despite the protest which the Bishop of Fulham telegraphed to him.

The religious service was completed at 12.50 p.m., both ceremonies having taken just over an hour.

Strabane Journal **1937**

Where It First Stood.

FOR those of my readers who feel like shedding a regretful tear over the—at the moment of writing—still sizzling remains of this most startling of all Victorian relics, I would suggest that they take a 'bus ride towards Kensington. If they will get off just west of Knightsbridge Barracks they will see just inside the railings of Hyde Park, where the football pitches now are, the original site of the Crystal Palace when it was set up there for the Great Exhibition of 1851. It was greatly enlarged on its removal to Sydenham.

B.B.C.'s Exciting Broadcast.

BEFORE writing "Finis" to this sad story, I must really congratulate the B.B.C. on its smart work on this occasion. Unwittingly through its 9 p.m. news bulletin it sent thousands of people to the fire and blocked the roads for miles around. But it amply atoned for this at 11 p.m., when there was broadcast a fine eye-witness's account on the spot (with fire-engine bells in the background) and later on another witness's account from the studio.

Church of England Newspaper
1936

Ex-Rector Dies of Wounds

MR. HAROLD DAVIDSON, ex-rector of Stiffkey, died in Skegness Hospital yesterday from injuries received when he was mauled by a lion while speaking to holidaymakers from a cage in a showground. He was 65.

Mr. Davidson was an actor before his ordination 35 years ago.

He once said that he gave up a stage income of £1,000 a year to become a curate at £3 a week. He served at the Guards' Church, Holy Trinity, Windsor, and at St. Martin-in-the-Fields before going to Stiffkey.

Here, for 25 years, he was a country parson. The living at Stiffkey is worth £461 (gross) and a house.

The trial of charges brought against him by the Bishop of Norwich, Dr. Bertram Pollock, opened in the Norwich Consistory Court in March 1932.

GUILTY OF IMMORALITY

The charges were that during five years he habitually associated with women of loose character for immoral purposes.

He was found guilty. Twice he applied for leave to appeal and it was refused. He was then unfrocked.

Mr. Davidson appeared in a number of shows at fairs afterwards, principally at Blackpool, where he was on show at a fair in a barrel.

A barrel show he planned to give in London was stopped by the police, but he appeared in a tent at Mitcham Fair.

AWARDED DAMAGES

He also applied for the post of manager to Blackpool Football Club. At Blackpool he announced his intention of sitting in a barrel in a peep-show and starving himself to death or until the bishop reinstated him.

After a ten-day fast he was arrested and charged with attempted suicide, but subsequently obtained damages from Blackpool Corporation for wrongful arrest and detention.

Early this month he began preaching from the lion's den at Skegness. His address was interrupted by police officers, who arrested him for non-payment of a fine.

News Chronicle
1937

THE CHANGE ON THE THRONE.

Great events moved rapidly in the course of a few short days last week. Everyone is familiar with what has taken place—broadcasting science brought the uttermost parts of the earth into immediate association with the grave occurrences that were passing—and the happenings of these days, charged with high circumstance as they have been may be spoken of more or less in a summarised form. On Thursday King Edward abdicated the most august and proudest position that the world has to offer. On Friday there was passed through all its stages a Bill giving effect to his firm and irrevocable decision to abdicate. When he gave his assent to that measure King Edward performed his last official act. On Saturday morning there was held the Accession meeting of the Privy Council. It was attended by the new monarch, the Duke of York, who took the customary oaths, and later in the day the new Sovereign was proclaimed in London. That day and yesterday members of the Houses of Parliament met and took the oath of allegiance. To-day normal Parliamentary business will be resumed. In these few sentences are comprised fateful happenings that are among the most painful and distressing that have ever occurred in the history of this country.

Banffshire Journal
1936

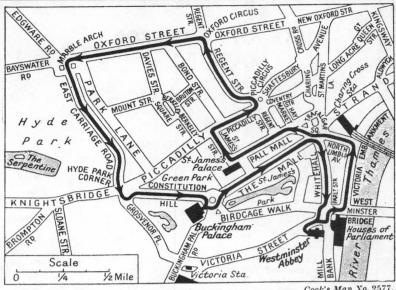

Cook's Map No. 2577.

MAP OF THE ROUTE WHICH WILL BE FOLLOWED BY THE CORONATION PROCESSION ON MAY 12, 1937, STARTING FROM AND ENDING AT BUCKINGHAM PALACE.

Traveller's Gazette 1936

DAYLIGHT AIR RAID TESTS NEXT

EXTENDING PRECAUTIONS

Anti-air raid exercises in daylight will be the next step taken by Wing-Commander E. J. Hodsoll, Inspector-General of the Air Raids Precautions department of the Home Office. The first will be held during the early summer. The town has not yet been selected.

Wing-Commander Hodsoll said yesterday: "We have learned a great deal from exercises under conditions of darkness. We do not wish to form definite conclusions till after a try-out in daylight."

"Black out" tests were carried out at Leicester on Thursday night. On Friday the Home Office issued instructions to local authorities charging them with direct responsibility for fire fighting, recruiting of air wardens, surveying of bombing shelters, and arrangements for evacuating the population of large industrial centres during an air raid.

Sunday Times
1938

A Novelist's Engagement

Mr. Evelyn Waugh, novelist and traveller, son of Mr. and Mrs. Arthur Waugh, and Miss Laura Herbert, twenty-year-old daughter of the late Hon. Aubrey Herbert and the Hon. Mrs. Herbert, and cousin of Lord Carnarvon, announced their engagement last week. The marriage will take place fairly soon

Bystander
1937

UNDEGRADUATE FOUND DEAD IN BATH.

ST. CATHARINE'S has lost a well-known figure in the death of Philip Brunning, a member of the exclusive Anomalies Club.

He was found dead in a bath at his London home one morning shortly after Christmas, as a result of gas poisoning from the geyser. The coroner returned a verdict of " Accidental Death."

Brunning had come home in the small hours of the morning, and having gone to his bath had apparently got into difficulties with the gas-tap of the geyser.

Varsity Weekly
1938

Fashions Committee

Mr. CATTOLICO made a short report on the activities of the Fashions Committee, which until then had worked more or less *sub rosa* and was now coming into the open. There was not the slightest wish or intention to interefere with the Fashions Committees of other bodies, and, in fact, their assistance and co-operation would be most welcome if offered, as he was sure their wish was to work for the good of the Trade at large as earnestly as they did.

Their view was that hairdressing fashions were being evolved mostly in the United States by film companies, and were not always suitable for British conditions. It was intended to create British hair fashions, and with this object in view Mr. Cattolico had approached the Editress of the Woman's Page of the *Daily Mail*, who had consented to publish and broadcast through its pages the fashions to be created by his Committee. No monopoly had been given to that paper, and other papers might be also invited to take an interest in that scheme. It had been agreed to have the first model published very shortly, and the *Daily Mail* photographer had made an appointment with him for that purpose for the following week, when the first coiffure would be presented.

Coiffures would be created either by a member of the Committee or even by an outsider. The creators of these dressings would be quite anonymous and would not be allowed to make capital by their publicity. The dressings would be presented privately to the Committee, the first considerations being practicability, suitability and originality. It was hoped thereby to create a demand for the coiffures published. This was as much as he could say for the moment without divulging secrets, but other developments were contemplated and would be made public when the time came.

Mr. Cattolico's report with a full endorsement of his action, and a hearty vote of thanks was carried unanimously.

Hairdresser's Weekly Journal 1938

MONTE CARLO RALLY DRIVERS FINISH

BRITISH ARRIVALS

MONTE CARLO, Saturday.

Mr. and Mrs. W. G. Lockhart, in their Talbot, were the first British competitors in the Monte Carlo Rally to arrive here to-day.

"We had lots of fun and a good many minor incidents," Mr. Lockhart said. "Once we hit a boulder, and all our jacking equipment came off."

Mrs. Lockhart was at the wheel all the way from Denmark.

Three women teams were among the early arrivals. Among them was Mrs. A. C. Lace (England) in a Talbot-Darracq, who had started from Stavanger.

The first British car from John o' Groats was the Talbot driven by N. Garrard and S. C. H. Davis. The drivers said the worst part of the drive was the last, from Grenoble, the roads being snow-and-frost-bound.

T. C. Wise and J. F. Clough, driving their Fiat from John o' Groats, lost twenty-three points at Toulouse and two points at Rodez. T. Abel-Smith and E. Smith (Wolseley) lost two points at Rodez.—Reuter.

Sunday Times 1938

26,000,000 GAS MASKS READY FOR USE

9,000,000 IN LONDON

Mr. Geoffrey Lloyd, Parliamentary Under-Secretary for the Home Department, at Birmingham last night, said:—

"The stock of completed civilian gas respirators is 26,000,000. More than 9,000,000 are stored in the London area—others in regional depots. Production is being maintained at about 650,000 respirators a week.

There is little doubt that this rate of production is much greater than that of any other country.

"To ensure that this great stock does not deteriorate but remains fully effective, it is necessary that the respirators should be stored in special depots under careful conditions.

"For these reasons it is obviously impossible for the respirators to be distributed at the present time to the public.

"It is contemplated that each local authority will provide storage for the number required by the population in its area. It is essential that plans for storage and distribution should aim at very quick distribution to the population in emergency."

LONDON'S FIRST SHELTER

The first air-raid shelters to be built for a London local authority will be opened at the Caxton Hall, S.W., by the Mayor of Westminster (Councillor H. S. E. Vanderpant) on Thursday. The shelters consist of a steel-lined gallery and can withstand tremendous pressure. They have air-locks to keep out gas, and luminous paint affords emergency lighting.

Sunday Times 1938

OXFORD PRESIDENT FINED

DEFECTIVE BRAKES

Fifteen Bob Per Crack

MR Patrick Anderson, ex-President of the Oxford Union and a leading figure in the Conservative Association was fined fifteen shillings and costs for an offence against the Road Traffic Act on the Sixth of January.

Mr. Anderson parked his car at the side of the road and was approached by a policeman to enquire about the efficiency of his handbrake.

Mr. Anderson replied to the Police Officer's question with a jocular remark that the car would be all right if the policeman fetched a brick and scotched the wheel.

Varsity Weekly 1938

SIR,—We do not all applaud Mr. Chamberlain. He has released us temporarily from a fear we could have faced courageously, and given us instead the burden of a guilt too heavy to bear.

Even if only a small section of your readers reacts like this, will you not record it as a fact that some people in England today are most bitterly ashamed.

We are, etc.,

SYLVIA TOWNSEND WARNER.
VALENTINE ACKLAND.

Frome Vauchurch,
Maiden Newton, Dorset

Time and Tide 1938

112 Anthony Eden Goes To U.S.A.

Most talked-of English politician at the close of 1938 is Anthony Eden. Will he break away from the Conservatives? Will he lead a united opposition to Chamberlain's foreign policy? Will he be the next Prime Minister? Eden provides no answers in his speeches in England; goes in December, with wife and son, to United States to speak.

Picture Post 1938

Neville Chamberlain arrives back from Munich bearing the Anglo-German Agreement.

Refugee Musicians

" Out of the total of 600,000 or more persons who are suffering from racial, religious or political persecution in certain countries of Europe, no fewer than 12,000 are musicians of various types and grades. The Executive Committee of the Incorporated Society of Musicians and the Musicians' Union have come to the conclusion that it is a primary duty of their Societies as representatives of the musical profession in Great Britain, to undertake some responsibility for the welfare of their unfortunate colleagues.

" For some time the Incorporated Society of Musicians and the Musicians' Union have been in close touch with the Home Office with regard to applications for permits to reside and work in Great Britain. The number of refugees already admitted and allowed to work here is comparatively small, but it has already become evident that there will be few opportunities, if any, for refugee musicians to establish themselves permanently in Great Britain."

Thus begins a short manifesto from the Refugee Musicians' Aid Committee—a strong committee led by Sir Hugh Allen, Sir Thomas Beecham and Sir Percy Buck, with Miss Dorothy Wadham as Hon. Secretary and Sir Robert Mayer as Hon. Treasurer. On the committee too are others to whom we of the gramophone world owe special support—such as Norman Allin, John Goss, Lionel Tertis and Frederick Woodhouse ; and we would suggest that any of our readers who have even the slightest interest in the problem and ability to help with hospitality or cash or organisation should at least write for the manifesto to the Hon. Secretary (Room 209), Bloomsbury House, Bloomsbury Street, London, W.C.1.

Gramophone **1939**

The German-Austrian *anschluss* has led one to wonder whether Hitler may not have his eye on this little mountain paradise. I mentioned this to Dr. Hoop. " Oh, no, no. That is impossible," he assured me. Shortly before my visit to Liechtenstein, the Diet had passed a unanimous resolution in favour of the country's independence. The bond of fidelity to the Prince was renewed, and the Government agreed to adhere firmly to all existing treaties.

Mentioning the possibility of Hitler's entering Liechtenstein to a number of the country's inhabitants, they all stoutly denied such a possibility. Whether they were sure that such an event could not take place, or whether they did not wish to face such a possibility, I could not determine.

Seven policemen attend to the law and order of the country, with 14 " special constables " to aid them should a major crisis take place ! If Hitler or any other dictator should decide to march an army into Liechtenstein, it would meet with no resistance, for the little pocket state has not a single soldier, and Dr. Hoop assured me that Switzerland would not come to his country's aid.

Tourist **1939**

WAR DECLARED

HITLER IGNORES FINAL WARNING

At 11.15 on Sunday morning the Prime Minister made the ominous announcement that as from 11 a.m. Britain was in a state of War with Germany.

The Prime Minister stated that the British Ambassador in Berlin at 9.30 on Saturday night delivered to Germany the final warning that unless the German troops were withdrawn from Poland, His Majesty's Government would fulfil their obligations.

If a satisfactory reply was not received by 11 a.m. on Sunday, Britain would be in a State of War with Germany from that hour.

In a moving speech, the Prime Minister stated that Germany had failed to reply and in consequence Britain was in a State of War with Germany.

Prime Minister's Speech

Mr Chamberlain, in a tense atmosphere, in the course of his moving address said :—

It is a sad day for all of us. To none is it sadder than to me. Everthing I had worked for, everything I had hoped for, everything I believed in during my public life has crashed into ruins.

There is only one thing left for me. That is to devote what strength and power I have to forward to victory the cause for which we have to sacrifice so much.

I cannot tell what part I may be allowed to play myself. I trust I may live to see the day when Hitlerism has been distroyed —(loud and prolonged cheers)—and when a restored and liberated Europe has been re-established. (Cheers.)

Caithness Courier **1939**

Mussolini is probably wondering why he wasted money and lives on the purloining of Abyssinia. It is a treat to know that Hitler has no ambitions about Lapland, and after reading Olive Murray Chapman's *"Across Lapland"* one can only rejoice that there is at least one spot left where the people have no worries of wars or rumours of wars.

" Twelve Against the Gods," by William Bolitho, is just brilliant. I have only space to mention the names of Alexander the Great, Casanova, Christopher Columbus, Mahomet, Lola Montez, Cagliostro (and Seraphina), Charles XII of Sweden, Napoleon I, Lucius Sergius Cataline, Napoleon III, Isadora Duncan, and Woodrow Wilson.

Civil Service Whip **1939**

Books

" Thank you, Allen Lane ! "

Such will be the sentiments of many, including, I should say, the men now serving in the Armed Forces, for there are thousands who will find solace in a book, especially one so convenient in size as a Pelican or Penguin, not forgetting that it is cheap enough to be passed on.

* * *

Civil Service Whip **1939**

Sigmund Freud (May 6, 1856—Sept. 23, 1939)

A broadcast tribute by EDWARD GLOVER

The Listener
1939

THERE are few men of whom it can be said with certainty that their names will live as long as the memory of man endures. Some indeed may acquire lasting fame in their own branch of human endeavour, but sooner or later their memory passes from the mind of that more capricious judge, the man in the street. The genius and the achievements of Freud, who was the founder of psycho-analysis, will not only set his name alongside those of Copernicus, Newton and Darwin, but have made of it a household word to be found in simple dictionaries of the language. For his discoveries were not, as is so often the case, divorced from everyday affairs. They were concerned with the very mind of Everyman, with his happiness and, more important, with his miseries. Following those profound intuitions which are the hallmark of genius, and supporting them with endless patience, Freud succeeded in charting a new continent, a continent of the mind which goes by the name of the unconscious.

CIVIL SERVANTS RECALLED FROM LEAVE

Just prior to the outbreak of war many Civil Servants, including not a few of our members, who were on leave were recalled to duty, while in some instances members who would have been proceeding on leave had to cancel their holidays.

Thus accommodation and board which were not enjoyed had been or had to be paid for, or deposits sacrificed.

The Treasury have now issued instructions to Departments indicating that such losses incurred by officers in receipt of a salary of not more than £400 per annum may be refunded, though it is understood that other cases will be treated on their merits.

Civil Service Whip 1939

The (Silly) Season

★ SUMMER, or "the season," as we optimistically call it, is here. Summer, which to many of us merely means putting our heavy coats in moth balls, using the "rails" a bit more in the hopes of getting a "freight," and working our last couple of hours in daylight.

Some of us dream of future summers when we may enjoy that inestimable boon which (so they say) the employers *might* bestow on us—"Holidays with Pay." We dream of a holiday without the inevitable financial burden overshadowing it, when we will be able to lie in a deck-chair on the sands without thinking of the ten quid we borrowed out of the "club."

Yes, summer has an individual meaning to each of us, but to Esperantists summer-time is Congress-time. In various parts of this parched desert of a world, whose inhabitants are gasping for a breath of peace, for a respite from the eternal clamour of armaments and the shrieking propaganda of maniacs, little green oases spring up. Havens of mental relief, where workers of all nations can discuss problems away from the stultifying influence of nationalism; where the cry is not "Britain for the British" or "One Reich, One Fuehrer," but "The World for the Workers." Where one is "stripped," not of clothes, but of distrust and petty suspicions.

Esperantists make great sacrifices to be able to attend these congresses, some actually cycling across continents to get there, but their reward is the comradeship which permeates these "glimpses" of a future system.

This year the two most important congresses are the S.A.T. Congress at Copenhagen and the I.E.L. Congress at Berne.

Cab Trade News 1939

A Wash-Out.

Behind the inauguration of the B.B.C. foreign language broadcasts lies a little story. According to a report in the *Manchester Guardian*, the B.B.C. advertised for linguists, but made a stipulation that the applicants must be British subjects. The result was a complete wash-out, and so the stipulation about citizenship was dropped. The second advert. brought shoals of letters. There were 2,000 applicants, a great number of these being refugees! Apparently there is some truth in the saying that Englishmen only know two languages—English and Obscene.

Cab Trade News
1939

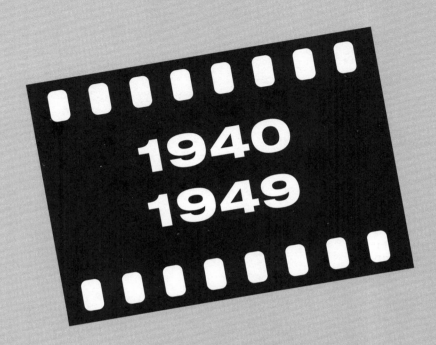

1940
1949

NAZI LOSSES NOW 694

British figures of the losses on both sides in fighting over Britain and the British coast since mass raids began on Thursday, Aug. 8. are given below; the figures in italics showing the number of British pilots who landed safely:

	German	British
Aug. 8	61	18
		(3 Safe)
Aug. 9	1	0
Aug. 10	1	1
Aug. 11	65	26
		(2 Safe)
Monday	62	13
		(1 Safe)
Tuesday	78	13
		(10 Safe)
Wednesday	31	7
		(2 Safe)
Thursday	180	34
		(17 Safe)
Friday	75	22
		(11 Safe)
Saturday	0	0
Yesterday	140	16
		(8 Safe)
Total	694	150

The total number of R.A.F. pilots safe was 57.

Daily Telegraph 1940

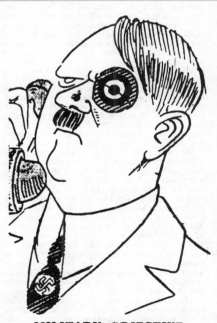

MILITARY OBJECTIVE.
A lovely black-eye from the R.A.F. as Strube saw it. Now see Strube's "Munich Beer Cellar" on Page Four

Daily Express 1940

DUNKIRK OPERATIONS STILL PROCEEDING

ALLIED REARGUARD FIGHT INCESSANTLY

Many thousands of men from the British Expeditionary Force in Flanders, evacuated in the face of great odds by the Royal Navy from Dunkirk, landed in England yesterday and were passing through London on their way to home stations last night.

Numbers of their French comrades from the Allied army, which has fought one of the most stirring actions in military history, have also been landed in Britain.

Weary, unshaven and bearing evidence of the heavy fighting in which they have taken part, the troops were yet in high spirits.

SHIPS OF ALL SIZES USED

Ships and small craft of all classes were used in the evacuation at Dunkirk. Describing the operations, an Admiralty communiqué stated:

"The wounded and a large number of other elements have already been safely withdrawn. These operations are being conducted ceaselessly by day and night, with coolness and determination in the face of fierce opposition particularly from the air.'

Daily Telegraph 1940

THE DUKE OF WINDSOR

GOVERNOR OF THE BAHAMA ISLANDS

The Colonial Office announces that his Majesty the King has been pleased to appoint his Royal Highness the Duke of Windsor, K.G., to be Governor and Commander-in-Chief of the Bahama Islands.

It was announced on Monday that Sir Charles Dundas, Governor of the Bahamas, had been appointed Governor, and Commander-in-Chief of the Uganda Protectorate.

The Times 1940

MR. CHURCHILL AND INVASION

READY, UNDISMAYED, TO MEET IT

"WE SEEK NO TERMS & ASK NO MERCY"

LONDON IN RUINS BETTER THAN ENSLAVEMENT

Mr. Churchill, in a broadcast to British, Empire and American listeners last night, reaffirmed his confidence in the determination and ability of this country to resist invasion and, when the time comes, to lift the dark curse of Hitler from our age. He declared:

"Be the ordeal sharp or long, or both, we shall seek no terms, we shall tolerate no parley. We may show mercy, but we shall ask none."

Never before had Britain had an army comparable in quality, equipment or numbers with to-day's. London itself, fought street by street, could easily devour an entire hostile army, and we would rather see London laid in ruins and ashes than that it should be abjectly enslaved.

Looking to the future, Mr. Churchill declared that we must prepare not only for 1941, but for 1942, "when the war will, I trust, take a different form from the defensive in which it has hitherto been bound."

The Prime Minister said that in a week the Royal Air Force and Fighter Command had shot down more than five to one of the German aircraft which tried to attack convoys in the Channel.

Daily Telegraph 1940

THE LATE MR. NEVILLE CHAMBERLAIN

A TRIBUTE BY MAJOR DESPENCER-ROBERTSON: M.P. FOR SALISBURY DIVISION

It is a sad irony of fate that Mr. Neville Chamberlain should have died before he could see the victorious end of the war that he had striven so hard to avert.

He was completely selfless; he only desired what would conduce to the public welfare; personal ambition had no place in his composition; intrigue and prevarication were abhorrent in his soul. These qualities perhaps were the cause of some defects in his nature. He did not suffer fools gladly, and he had a certain lack of imagination which led him to minimise the effect of some of his utterances and which seemed to show a lack of sympathy which he was, in fact, far from feeling. Indeed there grew up a legend that he was a hard, relentless machine, with none of the milk of human kindness in his make-up. Those who were privileged to see him in his home life know how false was this idea. He was a delightful host, courteous to the humblest guest, ready to talk on any subject (but happiest if it could be birds or fishing); and his devotion to his wife, his inseparable companion, makes us grieve for what she has to endure to-day.

Mr. Chamberlain's patience under the attacks he suffered after Munich was remarkable, though he must have been very sad and sore at heart; and there can be little doubt that the disappointments of the last two years contributed to his breakdown in health which has ended so sadly. Yet even as late as May in this year he gave one final proof of his nobility of character. When he was hounded out of the Premiership he cheerfully and willingly agreed to serve under his successor, and lost no opportunity of urging his followers to give their loyalty and their united support to Mr. Churchill.

He suffered persecution, injustice, disillusionment; but he bore everything with perfect resignation, secure in the knowledge, which was its own reward, that all he had done had been with one end, and one end only in view—the preservation of peace, and the salvation of this country. Posterity will judge him, and his reputation may be safely left to that verdict. To-day we of this generation mourn the passing of a great patriot and a great Englishman.

JAMES DESPENCER-ROBERTSON.

Salisbury and Winchester Journal 1940

The Navy is here!

When the rescuers of the Altmark's prisoners shouted those words, they were not trying to coin a slogan. They were echoing the very thought which has brought comfort to countless thousands of seafarers through the centuries. " The Navy is here ! "

You would no more think of a Britain without command of the seas, than of an England without its inns and beer. And how much comfort and strength have *they* brought to us during these long months of war.

In the pub we have found a common meeting place. Brightness in the black-out. Warmth in the cold. Cheerfulness in the midst of worry.

And we can drink beer there. Mild or bitter, ale or stout, this true drink of Englishmen has done well for England. Its barley malt and hops are wholesome fare.

But there is another reason why we drink beer. We like it !

York Star 1940

CITY NEWS Liquidating the Rich

OSCAR R. HOBSON, City Editor

THE Budget as we know has raised the standard rate of income tax to 10s. in the £ and it has raised the total direct taxation on the highest slices of income to 19s. 6d. in the £.

Despite the obvious purport of these figures, I doubt whether many people have really grasped one fundamental moral of the Budget—that it represents the coup de grace to the rich man in this country. In the rather sinister terminology of Bolshevik Russia, the rich man is being "liquidated" as surely as was the wealthy kulac of that country ten years ago.

Let me give a few examples. One is that cited by the Chancellor in his Budget speech—namely, that to retain a spendable income of £5,000 a year a man must now have a gross income of no less than £66,000 a year. Another I have already I think quoted in these columns. The multi-millionaire with £150,000 a year even two years ago had £47,000 left over to spend: now he will have only £7,000. Six-sevenths of his pre-war net income has gone. The £100,000-a-year man who had £33,000 pre-war will now have less than £6,000; and the £50,000-a-year man will have only £4,600.

News Chronicle 1941

Arrest of a Man Named Schneider

ALLEGED OFFENCE UNDER THE ALIENS ORDER

At Stratford-on-Avon Borough police-court on Wednesday, Henry Schneider (29), described as a grocer, residing at 49, Shipston-road, Stratford-on-Avon, was charged with giving false information on the form prescribed by the Secretary of State under the Aliens Order, to wit, that his name was Henry Taylor.

Supt. Simmons said the charge was brought under article 7 of the Order, by which it was the duty of every person in a boarding-house or hotel to give certain particulars as to his correct name and nationality. On December 4th prisoner arrived at 49, Shipston-road, and filled up the form in the name of Henry Taylor. Information came to the police, and Schneider was arrested on Tuesday night. The Superintendent asked for a remand in custody for a week, as he had to make certain inquiries. Prisoner said he was of Russian parentage, and his parents were naturalised before he was born. The form became operative on the outbreak of war, and the penalty for giving false information was set out on the form.

Schneider pleaded ignorance, and said he thought he was signing a rationing form. He had no friends, except a brother-in-law in London.

Henry Schneider (29), described as a grocer, and staying at 49, Shipston-road, Stratford-on-Avon, made a second appearance at Stratford-on-Avon Borough police-court on Wednesday, charged with giving false information on a form prescribed by the Secretary of State.

Supt. Simmons said that the charge was brought under article seven of the Aliens Order of 1920, as amended by a later order, by which it was the duty of every person in a boarding-house or hotel to give certain particulars as to his name and nationality. On December 5th prisoner went to Shipston-road and filled in a form in the name of Henry Taylor. Information reached the police, who found that his real name was Henry Schneider, and that he was actually a British subject, although his father was Russian. Prisoner said he thought it was a ration form, but there were clear directions on the paper, and also the penalty for giving false information. The landlady mislaid the original form, and the man filled up another the same day, again giving the name of Taylor.

Detective-Constable Morgan said he interviewed prisoner on January 9th. He admitted that his correct name was Schneider, and he produced his identity card. He said he had used the name of Taylor recently, and that he thought the card had something to do with rationing. He added that he had not changed his name by deed poll, and that his parents were either Russian or Polish.

Schneider said it was a silly act on his part. He was born in England after his parents were naturalised.

The Mayor (Mr. T. N. Waldron) said the Bench felt that defendant did not intend to do any harm, but he had caused a great deal of trouble to the police.

Schneider was fined £1.

Stratford upon Avon Herald 1940

MR. CHURCHILL BECOMES PRIME MINISTER

MR. CHAMBERLAIN TO LEAD THE HOUSE OF COMMONS

BY OUR POLITICAL CORRESPONDENT

Mr. Chamberlain saw the King at Buckingham Palace yesterday evening and tendered his resignation. He advised the King to send for Mr. Winston Churchill.

Mr. Churchill was immediately summoned to the Palace and entrusted with the formation of a new Government.

This is to be on an all-party basis. While every Minister has placed his office at the disposal of the new Prime Minister, all are at his request carrying on at present in their posts pending the formation of a new Administration.

Daily Telegraph 1940

George Street, Plymouth, in 1941.

Fighting fires caused by bombing.

BUCKINGHAM PALACE BOMBED

BUCKINGHAM PALACE was bombed for the third time yesterday when the Germans made two mass air-raids over the south-east and London areas.

It was in the first raid that the Palace was attacked, the Queen's private apartments being damaged by a bomb which did not explode.

The bomb crashed through the tapestry room which is used by the Queen as a drawing-room on the first floor. It tore a hole in the ceiling.

Another bomb which fell on one of the lawns also failed to explode.

A number of small incendiaries fell at the same time in the Palace grounds and some of them started small fires on the grass.

These were quickly got under control by the Palace A.R.P. staff and police.

The King and Queen were not in residence at the time and only a skeleton staff of servants and others was in the Palace. They were all in the basement shelters and there were no casualties.

Terrific air battles took place and up to 11 p.m. 175 enemy aircraft had been shot down. Thirty of our fighters were lost, but 10 of the pilots are known to be safe.

Dealing with the first raid an Air Ministry and Ministry of Home Security communiqué stated:—

"This morning a large number of enemy aircraft crossed the coast near Dover in two waves. They were promptly met by strong formations of our fighters and an air battle ensued.

"In the course of this two small enemy formations succeeded in penetrating to the London area.

"Bombs were dropped and, amongst other enemy objectives, Buckingham Palace was again hit.

"The Queen's private apartments were damaged by a bomb which did not explode.

"Elsewhere in the London area houses were hit, some fires broke out, and damage was done to gas and water mains.

"From preliminary reports it is clear that the number of casualties was small.

"At least 50 enemy aircraft were shot down in this raid."

Western Mail
1940

You *can't* have a instead of the siren

ASKED for in Parliament yesterday, by Sir William Davison (Cons., South Kensington) : "A more musical and martial note, in the nature of a post-horn or bugle call, for air-raid sirens."

ANSWER by Mr. Mabane, Parliamentary Secretary to the Ministry of Home Security :—

"Experiments were undertaken recently to discover whether alternative noises would be practicable or effective. The results revealed that better noises are not within the limits of practical possibility."

REJOINDER by Sir William: "I have received many letters from women who say that the sirens are more depressing than the bombs. What the country wants is a trumpet call, a challenge, and not the wailing of the banshees."

JOKE squeezed in by Mr. Shinwell (Soc., Seaham): "Can you utilise the services of the Secretary of State for Scotland ?"—i.e., Mr. Ernest Brown, who is famed for having the loudest voice in the House.

RETORT to Sir William by Lady Astor: "Women are showing more courage than men, and I beg Sir William not to listen to a few nervous letters from a few nervous women."

RETURN to the original question by Mr. Gallacher (Com., West Fife): "Can the adoption of some other kind of warning be considered ?"

FINAL ANSWER by Mr. Winston Churchill : "A suggestion has been made which I did consider—namely, the display of a red flag on particular occasions when it was thought that unpleasant things were going to happen."

Laughter all round.

Daily Express **1940**

The Spectator **1941**

VIRGINIA WOOLF

BY ROSE MACAULAY

She has died at the height of her powers ; her last book, finished but not yet published, is thought by some who have read it to be her best. What she might have written later is uncertain, for she did not write to pattern ; all she wrote had both for her and us, the interest of a lovely exploration. The gap she leaves is unfillable, her loss (and now when so much else is on the way to be lost) intolerable, like the extinguishing of a light.

NAZI BOMBERS WRECK HOUSE OF COMMONS

THE RIDDLE OF 19 "MISTERS"

The Financial Secretary to the War Office can't trace that famous list of Home Guard appointments — the one showing that only nineteen out of 319 officers are plain "Misters."

That was his reply, given in a Parliamentary answer yesterday, to Mr. Alfred Edwards (Lab., Middlesbrough, E.). But, added the secretary:

"Those lists which I have examined show that less than 10 per cent. are peers, baronets, knights or brigadier-generals."

[The list referred to by Mr. Edwards was given in a War Office Order Paper issued on April 14.]

Daily Mirror **1941**

"Frauds On Widows" Habit

In intervals of imprisonment for false pretences, Walter Brackley, of Wain-a-long-road, Salisbury, has made a habit of defrauding women.

"Most of his victims are widows," said the police yesterday when at Poole. Brackley was sentenced to six months' hard labour.

He was alleged to have obtained £87 from Mrs. Alice Bainbridge, of Poole, saying he had served in the Great War with her late husband.

Actually, said the prosecution, Brackley knew Captain Bainbridge only by meeting him in an hotel.

Daily Herald **1941**

CORN PLASTERS TAXED

Purchase Tax must now be paid on corn plasters, but not on first aid dressings.

Exemption for first aid dressings covers: Surgical strapping, wound and first aid dressings, plaster of paris bandages, vaccination plasters or pads.

Pearls, real or imitation, are also to be taxed.

Daily Herald **1941**

DAMAGE TO THE HOUSE OF LORDS

THE ABBEY & BRITISH MUSEUM ALSO HIT

It was revealed last night that several of London's most famous buildings were damaged on Saturday night, when German 'planes unloaded their bombs indiscriminately in the heaviest attack since the " reprisal raid " of April 16, which was the worst the capital has experienced.

Among places hit were:

HOUSE OF COMMONS.—St. Stephen's Hall, the Chamber where M.P.s meet, reduced to a heap of rubble and may never be used again. Big Ben and its famous clock scarred, but still going. Roof of Members' Lobby destroyed.

HOUSE OF LORDS.—Chamber damaged. The Resident Superintendent, Capt. E. L. H. Elliott, was killed.

WESTMINSTER HALL.—Historic roof, dating back to 12th century, damaged.

WESTMINSTER ABBEY.—Roof of the Lantern, the square tower on the centre of the building, has fallen in. The Deanery has been destroyed, but the main fabric of the Abbey is undamaged.

BRITISH MUSEUM.—Fire damage to back of building.

The attack in the brilliant moonlight cost the Germans at least 33 'planes and about 160 trained personnel, the highest penalty they have paid in night raids on this country. Our night fighters destroyed 29, and four others were shot down by A.A. fire.

The German High Command communiqué said that hundreds of high explosives and more than 100,000 incendiaries were dropped in the raid, which was described as a reprisal for the " methodical bombing of the residential quarters of German towns, including Berlin."

London had two Alerts last night, the second being sounded shortly before midnight. An Air Ministry and Ministry of Home Security communiqué this morning announced the destruction of three enemy raiders by our fighters when attempts were made to cross the Dorset and East Kent coasts shortly after dusk.

Daily Telegraph **1941**

HESS LANDS

"Rudolf Hess, the Deputy Fuehrer of Germany and Party Leader of the National Socialist Party, has landed in Scotland in the following circumstances:

" On the night of Saturday, May 10, a Messerschmitt 110 was reported by our patrols to have crossed the coast of Scotland and to be flying in the direction of Glasgow.

" Since a Messerschmitt 110 would not have the fuel to return to Germany, this report was at first disbelieved.

" However, later on a Messerschmitt 110 crashed near Glasgow with its guns unloaded.

" Shortly afterwards a German officer who had baled out was found with his parachute in the neighbourhood, suffering from a broken ankle.

" He was taken to hospital in Glasgow, where he at first gave his name as Horn, but later on declared that he was Rudolf Hess.

" He brought with him various photographs of himself at different ages, apparently in order to establish his identity.

" These photographs were deemed to be photographs of Hess by several people who knew him personally.

" Accordingly, an officer of the Foreign Office, who was closely acquainted with Hess before the war, has been sent by aeroplane to see him in hospital."

Daily Herald 1941

HAD POLISHED TOE NAILS

HESS was immaculately groomed. Before his identity had been proved beyond doubt it was obvious that he was no ordinary prisoner.

Even his toe-nails were beautifully polished.

Mrs. McLean, wife of David McLean, the Renfrewshire ploughman who found Hess, said : —

" We knew when he came into the cottage and spoke to us that he was a man of some standing and accustomed to command.

" When he smiled he showed he had several gold teeth. On one wrist he had a gold watch, on the other a gold compass. His clothing showing below his flying kit was of good quality and his boots were lovely.

Daily Herald 1941

Daily Herald 1941

FINN END OF THE WEDGE

Russia is expressing uneasiness at the arrival in Finland of large forces of German troops.

MENACE OF ROMMEL'S ATTACK

May Compel Our Withdrawal From Benghazi

HEAVILY REINFORCED ENEMY STILL DRIVING EAST

[From CHRISTOPHER BUCKLEY, Our Special Correspondent]

CAIRO, Monday.—The big battle of tanks in Western Cyrenaica, south and south-east of Benghazi, is now in its fourth day. So far it has gone against us.

It will be useful to face this fact and try to deduce the reasons for this German success. Axis forces, believed to be largely German, have advanced some 150 miles in the three days, and there is no evidence that their advance has yet been checked.

They have pushed from Agheila to points north and north-east of Msus, 70 miles south-east of Benghazi. Their position beyond Msus implies that Benghazi is threatened, the enemy having closely followed the strategy which brought them such speedy and spectacular successes last April.

In the course of an advance at this speed we must expect that a certain amount of material has been left behind by our forces. We were, it now appears, not ready for an attack against the Agheila position for the very reason that the heavy armoured vehicles which had stood us in good stead in our advance across Cyrenaica were undergoing a much-needed overhaul.

A TACTICAL SURPRISE

The enemy, greatly reinforced, achieved a tactical surprise, catching our light forces with strong armoured columns of his own.

To take a naval parallel, it was as if a cruiser squadron had borne down in battle on a number of armed merchantmen. Our advanced forces therefore drew back on our main armoured strength, and the battle now going on is a test of strength between these two mechanised forces.

General Rommel has once again shown himself a commander of daring or impetuosity—from whichever angle one chooses to regard it. He is going out for a victory which might help him to recover much or all of Cyrenaica.

On the other hand, he has voluntarily abandoned the decidedly strong position at Agheila, on which we might have broken our teeth if he had chosen to wait for us there. It looks as if he is risking all to win all this time.

There are many questions which readers in Britain will justifiably want to ask, but at the present stage, when a "maul" is going on and tanks are hunting one another over an immense area, it is clearly neither practicable nor advisable to make statements about the course of the battle.

For that reason no official information is forthcoming regarding either our strength or that of the enemy.

The Scotsman 1942

Enough Scrap for 12,500 Tanks

More than 200,000 tons of metal has been recovered from railings and gates all over England, Scotland and Wales—equivalent in weight to some 12,500 Valentine tanks or enough metal to provide steel for 13 35,000 ton battleships.

This vast tonnage given in the latest figures issued by the Ministry of Works last night is about half the original total estimated as likely to be obtained from the nation's railings. Now it seems that the original estimate will be exceeded. Of the total London has contributed just under half.

Provincial totals are rising, the rate of collecting now being between 8,000 and 9,000 tons a week. Highest provincial tonnages are:—

Gloucester, Wiltshire, Somerset, Devon and Cornwall region, 12,692.

Northumberland, Durham and North Riding region, 11,423.

Bucks, Oxford, Berks, Hants and part of Dorset region, 11,057.

Scotland, 9,225.

Cheshire, Lancashire, Westmorland and Cumberland region, 9,115.

Wales, with 1,959 tons, is the lowest.

Yorkshire Post 1942

JAPAN DECLARES WAR ON U.S. & BRITAIN

TOKYO ACTION FOLLOWS BOMBING ATTACKS

SURPRISE RAIDS ON HAWAII AND MANILA

MR. CHURCHILL TO MAKE STATEMENT IN COMMONS TO-DAY

Japan has declared war on the United States and Britain. This was announced late last night in a message from Washington which stated: "The Japanese Government has announced that Japan enters a state of war with the United States and Britain as from 6 a.m. to-morrow (Monday) morning."

This announcement followed surprise bombing attacks on Manila and Honolulu by Japanese planes yesterday.

Late last night the following statement was issued from 10, Downing Street:—

"The Lord Chancellor, after consultation with the Government, has summoned the House of Lords to meet at 3 p.m. to-morrow, and the Speaker, after consultation with the Government, has summoned the House of Commons to meet at the same time. A statement will be made in both Houses."

Mr. Churchill, at the special emergency meeting of Parliament, will make a full statement on the swift developments which followed Japan's attacks on American bases and her declaration of war on Britain and the United States.

News that Japan had attacked U.S. bases at Manila and Honolulu was announced by President Roosevelt at the White House. The United States War Department has ordered the mobilisation of military personnel throughout the country.

Financial Times 1941

Recorder Rebukes Bar For Blitz Gossip

Mr. Hemmerde

MR. E. G. HEMMERDE, K.C., Recorder of Liverpool, rebuked members of the Bar yesterday—for gossiping.

"The amount of foolish gossip after seven or eight days' Blitz on Liverpool was remarkable," he said, at Liverpool Quarter Sessions.

"One member of the Bar told me he himself had seen the Town Hall a mass of rubble. That was completely false.

"At the Temple, in London, another member told me the town had been for some time under martial law and things were desperate.

"That was nothing but a lie.

"I should like to be able to deal with people who circulate rumours, some false and others which they do not know to be true.

"It is time people who are taking no part in the war kept their mouths closed, and that people of this profession should not disgrace the law and the northern circuit.

"The people of this town have behaved admirably under the most terrible conditions."

Mr. Hemmerde's praise for the people of Liverpool was borne out by the size of the calendar—the smallest for 32 years. There was only one new case.

Daily Herald 1941

THE LAST MESSAGES

The last message received in London from our troops in Singapore was one from General Percival to General Wavell. Dispatched from Singapore some time on Sunday afternoon, it stated that, owing to heavy losses and shortage in water, petrol, food, and ammunition, it was impossible to carry on the defence of the island any longer.

On Saturday a telegram was received from Sir Shenton Thomas, Governor of the Straits Settlements, about conditions in Singapore, saying that there were a million people concentrated within a radius of three miles, and that water supplies were very badly damaged and unlikely to last for more than 24 hours. The last telegram received from the Governor, probably sent about the time of the surrender, said that the civil population was quiet but bewildered, that the passive defence and fire services were carrying on, and that the telephone girls were still at their posts.

The Scotsman 1942

THE ESCAPE OF GERMAN WARSHIPS

Many questions are being asked by the public following the news of the action in the Channel between British air and sea forces and the German warships Scharnhorst, Gneisenau, and Prince Eugen, with their escorting surface and air craft.

First there is the inevitable and exceedingly unfavourable comparison between what Japanese torpedoes, launched by aircraft working from bases hundreds of miles distant, did to the Prince of Wales and the Repulse and what British torpedoes, launched by aircraft based a few miles away, did to the German ships.

Next there is the insistent question about the long-drawn-out bombing of Brest and about whether our bombs are satisfactory and our method of using them the best possible.

Finally, there is the question of whether our air reconnaissance discovered the movement of the large German formation of vessels as soon as possible.

Observer 1942

Collaboration in War and Peace

LONDON, Thursday Night

Britain and Russia have signed a 20-year agreement confirming their alliance in war and peace, and have reached full understanding on the creation of a second front in Europe this year. Russia has also reached agreement with Washington on the question of a second front.

THE Treaty, which was signed at the Foreign Office on May 26, provides for joint action in the war against Germany, for mutual assistance against any repetition of violence by Germany or associated States after the war, and for post-war collaboration along the lines laid down in the Atlantic Charter.

Both countries have given an undertaking that no separate peace will be made with Germany without mutual consent.

Neither Britain nor Russia is to seek territorial gains, and the two Governments will work together to organise security and economic prosperity in Europe. In doing so they will take into account the interests of others of the United Nations.

Yorkshire Post 1942

Determined Fighting in the Biggest Raid Yet

180 NAZI 'PLANES DOWN OR HIT

95 Allied Machines Missing

Nine hours after their dawn landing at Dieppe, where they destroyed a radiolocation station, a six-gun battery, an ammunition dump and a flak battery, the first Allied daylight Commando expedition was safely re-embarked. Fighting has been very fierce, and casualties are likely to have been heavy on both sides.

SPECIAL new landing craft were used to enable Allied tanks to make their first appearance on the Continent since Dunkirk in the biggest raid yet carried out by combined operations.

Great air battles, the fiercest since the Battle of Britain, were fought out above the scene of the land fighting. Every Operational Command was in action.

Late last night it was known that the Luftwaffe had lost 82 'planes for certain—and that may not be the final figure—with over 100 probably destroyed or damaged. We lost 95 'planes, but 21 fighter pilots are known to be safe, and others may have been rescued.

Yorkshire Post 1942

START A SAVINGS GROUP ANYWHERE

Help in the fight by forming a Savings Group in your street, factory or office. Get in touch with the Hon. Secretary of your local Savings Committee, he will give you full particulars. The Post Office has his name and address.

Bareheaded Women — Archbishops' Statement

QUESTIONS are frequently asked in these days regarding the ancient custom that women should not enter a church with their heads uncovered. The scriptural authority for this rule is to be found in St. Paul's writings, but this required that women should be veiled—a custom long since discontinued.

After consultation with the Bishops, the Archbishops of Canterbury and York have issued a statement on the question in the course of which they say, " We wish it to be known that no woman or girl should hesitate to enter a church uncovered, nor should any objection to their doing so be raised."

Church of England Newspaper 1942

Ringing World 1942

Leicester.

DEATH OF MR. JOB SAWYER.

We regret to announce the death of Mr. Job Sawyer, who passed away at his home in the village of East Hagbourne on Friday, August 28th.

Mr. Sawyer, who was 70 years of age, had been a ringer for half a century and had taken part in many peals of Grandsire and Stedman Triples. He was keen and active in the tower and on handbells, and up to the last took a great interest in ringing matters and in 'The Ringing World.' He will be remembered for his cheerful spirit and devotion to duty as a churchman and Sunday service ringer. The funeral was at East Hagbourne on Monday.

EIGHTH ARMY STRIKES

Bitter Battle Rages On El Alamein Front

NAVAL ATTACK AT SAME TIME

Britain's Eighth Army and Rommel's Afrika Korps are again locked in a bitter struggle in Egypt.

The latest news of General Montgomery's new attack, launched on Friday night at El Alamein after day-and-night air preparation, is that fierce fighting is continuing.

The German news agency claimed last night that the Axis system of defences was reached only at a few points and that as a result of powerful counter-attacks British shock troops suffered losses.

While General Montgomery was launching his land attack naval forces attacked enemy coastal positions near Mersa Matruh. They were attacked by enemy aircraft, but all returned safely.

Observer 1942

A GRAVE VOTE

THE Labour Party has officially voted against the Government attitude on the Beveridge Report, despite the exhortations of its prominent leader, Mr. Herbert Morrison.

Mr. Morrison's principal argument was that the Government had made up its mind on the Report quicker than anyone had expected. He omitted to say that its conclusion was that the Report had to be drastically whittled down.

It was a grave decision that the Labour Party made, for we are in the midst of a war which will determine the whole future of the British people and we have still to make our major military contribution to the winning of that war.

It can only be won by the preservation of the unity of the British people. It is that unity which the reactionary forces, who have influenced the Government's attitude, are seeking to destroy.

Mr. Morrison, who reminded the Labour Party that "there is a war on" should have addressed his remarks to the reactionary forces. The Beveridge issue is a war issue. If the reactionaries succeed in paring the Report down to an unrecognisable skeleton of its former self, they will strike a deadly blow at war morale.

Daily Worker 1943

U-BOATS MEET DECISIVE DEFEAT: 5 MORE SUNK, MANY OTHERS DAMAGED

FOR THE SECOND TIME WITHIN SIX DAYS NEWS CAME LAST NIGHT OF A MAGNIFICENT NEW VICTORY IN THE BATTLE OF THE ATLANTIC. IN A TWO-DAYS' DRAMATIC FIGHT AGAINST 20 U-BOATS WHICH HAD CONCENTRATED TO ATTACK TWO VALUABLE CONVOYS, AT LEAST FIVE OF THE ENEMY WERE SUNK AND THREE CRIPPLED.

The U-boats never got a chance to launch the major attack which they had planned. Admiral Sir Max Horton, Commander-in-Chief Western Approaches, described their defeat as "decisive."

Such was the success of our sailors and airmen that 99 per cent. of the escorted ships sailed safely into harbour.

Not one of our warships was so much as scratched. The total Allied casualties were two aircraft of Coastal Command shot down by the U-boats' guns and three damaged.

The People 1943

The story of the brilliantly successful action comes quickly after an Admiralty announcement that in a previous convoy battle six U-boats were sunk and nine others attacked.

These successes provide new meaning to the Anglo-U.S. official statement on Friday that for the past four months more U-boats have been sunk than ships lost.

Some of the first enemy prisoners to be taken during the battle of El Alamein.

Capturing a tank at the battle of El Alamein.

Primate's Call To Nation

'SEX MORALITY AND HONESTY COLLAPSING'

A CALL to men to resist the present "really alarming collapse of honesty and sex morality" was made yesterday by Dr. Temple, Archbishop of Canterbury.

"It used to be said that an Englishman's word is his bond," said the Primate. "We took it as a clear sign of the corruption of the Italian people when goods could not safely be left in public places such as railway trains.

'But what we despised in our neighbours is now to be observed among ourselves.

"There is a danger that we may win the war and be unfit to use the victory."

The Archbishop was addressing a meeting for men only, held at Central Hall, Westminster, by the Church of England Men's Society.

'After the war," he said, "we shall all be extremely tired, and weariness is a selfish condition So we must expect, unless we successfully guard against it, a great access of selfishness, in the individual family, class and nation.

"Along with this there will be a mood of relaxation in reaction from the restraints and discipline of war time."

When they surveyed the moral situation of the country today, they found two apparently contradictory features.

In respect of endurance, mutual helpfulness and constancy which, during the "blitz," reached heroic proportions, the morale of the country was magnificent.

Against that was a really alarming collapse in respect of honesty and sex morality.

"I am sure," the Primate went on, 'that it is one of our primary duties to be talking constantly about the evil of the prevailing dishonesty and untruthfulness.

"Every lie, every bit of cheating, tends to undermine the principles of respect for one another's personality and mutual trust and confidence, and is treachery to our cause

"PASSING AMUSEMENT"

"It is just the same with sex relationships. To use that function as an opportunity of passing amusement always involves treating another person as a plaything or a toy. That is destructive of the freedom we are fighting to maintain.

"There is nothing nasty about sex. There is no reason why it should not be spoken of in a natural and matter-of-fact way; but it must be treated with respect and even with reverence because it is the means by which men and women are enabled to act on behalf of God in the creation of his children.

"Sexual sin is not the only sort of sin, nor the worst kind of sin; the supreme sin and the fountainhead of all the others is pride, not lust.

The People
1943

Camera 'Ace' Dies In Crash

Cairo, Saturday.

MR. F. W. BAYLISS, Paramount war photographer, has been killed in an air crash in the Western Desert.

He had been three years in the Middle East and had covered every campaign beginning with Abyssinia and ending with Tunis.

In an early bombing raid he was forced to bale out on one occasion, and took pictures as he parachuted to earth.

The People 1943

Manchester Guardian 1943

CLIMBER'S FALL IN SNOWDONIA

Manchester Man Injured

John Cooke, of 3, Holt Terrace, Longsight, Manchester, was admitted to the Caernarvonshire and Anglesey Infirmary, Bangor, on Christmas night suffering from injuries received while walking in Snowdonia.

With other members of a party who were spending the holiday at a hostel near Ogwen lake, Cooke was descending the Tryfan mountain at the top end of the Nant Ffrancon pass when he lost his footing and fell some distance. Luckily the rope which the party were using checked his fall. His friends attended as best they could to injuries which he had received to his head and legs and carried him over the rocky path in the dark to the main road where an ambulance, summoned in the meantime by a member of the party who had gone on ahead after the accident, was waiting to take him to Bangor.

Last night Cooke was stated to be fairly comfortable.

So Sally Was Court-Martialled

SALLY, the dog mascot of H.M.S. Polruan was attracted by a saucer on the deck of H.M.S. Rothesay. So she changed ships.

Their work done, the two minesweepers were turning for home when Rothesay flashed a signal to the Polruan: "We have a deserter from your ship on board. Please collect."

A motor-boat was lowered, and an armed escort under A.B. W. Pye, of Dunkinfield, Cheshire, crossed to the Rothesay and placed Sally under "close arrest."

At a subsequent "court-martial" the "prisoner" had fourteen days' leave stopped, "as she had nothing to say in her defence."

But as Sally has never been ashore since she joined the ship, she didn't care.

The People 1943

Daily Worker 1943

KATYN MURDERS: SOVIET INQUIRY

A SPECIAL Soviet committee has been investigating the circumstances of the shooting of the Polish prisoner-of-war officers in the Katyn forest, near Smolensk. The committee is completing its work and in the near future will publish a statement on its findings.

This was disclosed yesterday by Moscow radio, which said that in connection with the liberation of the Smolensk region and on the decision of the Extraordinary State Commission for the Investigation of the Crimes of the German Invaders the special committee was formed.

Among the members of the special committee are Academician Alexei Tolstoy, famous Soviet novelist, N. N. Burdenko, chief surgeon of the Red Army, and the Metropolitan Nikolai.

The Soviet people are expressing great satisfaction that the committee will soon report its findings, says a cable from John Gibbons, Daily Worker Special Correspondent in Moscow.

"Those who fell head over heels into the trap laid for them by the Nazis will be made to look very foolish," was the comment of people reading Pravda at a newspaper stand in the Nikitsky Boulevard, Moscow, he reports.

INVASION BATTLE

FALL OF BAYEUX "GOOD NEWS"

Airborne Link-Up

OFFICIAL news and correspondents' reports from France yesterday indicated that one of the fiercest and bloodiest battles of the war was in full swing in the towns and villages of Normandy and on the green fields and roads flanking the coast between Havre and Cherbourg.

Our airborne forces, according to yesterday's communique from Supreme Allied H.Q., have made contact with Allied seaborne troops and have been engaged in desperate fights with the German defenders.

A reporter who dropped with the paratroops says, in the course of a dramatic story full of the atmosphere of conflict: "I believe that the things they (the paratroopers) have done are almost solely and completely responsible for the great success our invasion has had so far in this sector."

The fall of Bayeux, tapestry town, five miles inland on the road to Caen, is described as Allied H.Q., as "very good news" and an event "which may open up the advance from that particular point."

There has been fierce armoured fighting in this region of the Normandy battle area but progress continues despite determined enemy resistance.

Building Up Supplies

And while our men on shore airborne and seaborne, fight grimly to exploit the position and perform countless deeds of high courage, the vast and complicated work of building up our bridgehead forces and maintaining supplies under tremendous air and naval protection goes on almost without intermission.

Unloading on the beaches was stopped at times on Wednesday by bad weather but with better conditions and by superhuman efforts of Allied crews the time leeway has been made up.

Great Air Superiority

In the air, too, our forces have maintained their colossal superiority despite increasing reaction by the Germans. The Luftwaffe, in fact, came out and went down heavily.

During the 24 hours ended at midnight 102 enemy planes were accounted for, including 20 destroyed on the ground.

Geared for Victory

The Germans at any rate have been through a unique experience because they have felt the full weight of a United Nations' war machine geared for victory.

One of the units in this machine was described officially yesterday — a vessel fitted entirely with rockets which puts an amazing weight of explosives on the beaches and has a very high moral effect. It was developed as a result of experience gained at Dieppe.

Warships' Support

Support fire from Allied warships continued throughout Wednesday. Our air forces have given invaluable support to the ground troops on all sectors of the front.

Hampshire Telegraph and Post 1944

Our War Babies

These blood oranges haven't 'arf got a kick in 'em, Alfie.'

More Lease-Lend Millions Wanted

WASHINGTON, May 6 President Roosevelt to-day submitted to Congress a request for an appropriation of an additional £862,642,500 to carry out the Lease-Lend programme during the year ending June 30, 1945.

This appropriation would be to provide industrial products necessary for the production of planes, tanks, guns, and other war supplies in Allied countries.

Mr. Donald W. Davis, Vice-Chairman of the United States War Production Board, said at Boston that the American output of war supplies in the coming year would amount to £17,500,000,000.—Reuter.

Daily Mail 1944

D-Day Landings, 1944: Soldiers descend on Sword Beach, Normandy.

Flying Bomb Counters

Attacks On Sites And New AA Measures

A MIGHTY force of bombers and fighters was seen flying across the Channel towards the Boulogne area last night.

German flying bomb stores as well as their pilotless aircraft installations on the French coast were among their targets.

It is confidently believed that the night's assaults may mark a new heavy offensive against the German pilotless plane.

Allied Air Command are confident of pin-pointing these and other "secret" weapon target areas and striking an effective blow against the flying bomb.

Since this latest frightfulness weapon was first used against this country R.A.F. and U.S. heavy bombers by night and day have been diverted back to the Pas de Calais area.

They have laid a blanket of some 1,500 tons of high-explosives on the launching areas and replacement dumps.

The Germans began the construction of scores of concrete and rail take-off tracks for this type of aircraft in the area across the Strait closest to this country a year ago.

Sunday Dispatch 1944

The Fatal Shooting Incident at Kingsclere

General Eisenhower's Regret

REPORT TO THE DISTRICT COUNCIL

General Eisenhower's sorrow and regret has been expressed to the inhabitants of Kingsclere through the Rural District Council on Tuesday in regard to the recent shooting incident at Kingsclere, when there was a fusillade of shots at the Crown Inn and the landlady, Mrs. Napper, and two coloured American soldiers were killed.

The matter arose in a report from the Clerk (Mr. F. A. H. Keates), who stated that on October 5th, a regrettable and unfortunate incident occurred at Kingsclere when, apparently following a dispute between the American Military Police and coloured troops, a shooting incident took place outside the Crown Hotel, resulting in the death of the licensee's wife and two coloured American soldiers. Following this incident, he had on Saturday morning, the 7th October, received a telephone communication from Col. Lumsden, a local resident, suggesting that a petition should be submitted to the appropriate authorities and that the Council should give this petition their official support. He had informed Colonel Lumsden he would report the matter to the General Purposes Committee for instructions.

Mr. Keates reported that the same afternoon he received a visit from the Second-in-Command to General Eisenhower and other United States officers in the United Kingdom, who stated that General Eisenhower had requested them to convey to the local authority and to the general inhabitants of Kingsclere his personal sorrow and regret and also of the whole United States Army Command that this most unfortunate and regrettable affair, resulting in the death of a local resident, should have occurred and have been caused by United States troops. He sincerely hoped that the effect of this occurrence would not tend to excite public opinion and to detract from the friendly good-feeling and spirit of co-operation which existed between our two English-speaking nations, which was so necessary and essential to the world now and in years to come. They also gave General Eisenhower's assurance that the fullest possible investigation would be made into the matter and appropriate action taken.

Arising from the report, it was resolved to recommend that the Council communicate with the United States authorities.

The report and recommendations were unanimously adopted upon the proposition of Lady Portal, the chairman of the committee.

Newbury Weekly News 1944

France Revolting as Allies Advance

Tank Battles near Caen: New Gains Along Whole Front

More Armour Ashore: 5,000 Prisoners Taken

Insurrection and sabotage are increasing throughout France as the Allies advance, it was learned at S.H.A.E.F. last night. Every village offers help information, and medical assistance to our troops, and those still beyond our reach are rising against the Germans.

Reports received by French circles in London last night said that plans destined to facilitate the Allied operations have been put into effect over the whole of the Vosges district. The French Forces of the Interior have engaged German forces of over 2,000 men and have taken 300 prisoners.

In the Nord Department, the Saint Quentin, Merville and Bac-Saint-Maur canals have been cut. In the Aisne Department 50 railway engines, two turntables, and a work shop at Amberieu have been destroyed.

Fighting is going on at Bourg and Macon. Transformers have been attacked in the Luneville district in the east, reducing the production of electricity by two-thirds.

Guerrillas Out in Brittany

In the Nord Department and in the Saone-Loire Department the F.F.I. and the local population are said to have declared a state of insurrection against the German army. In Brittany guerrilla bands have attacked German troops, killing about 20 of them and capturing supplies.

Heavy fighting between French patriots and the Germans is going on at Grenoble, in south-east France, according to reports reaching the Swiss Press.

Martial law has been proclaimed. A large force of patriots surrounded the town on Thursday night. They were led by the Chasseurs Alpins—the "blue devils"—crack mountain troops. Grenoble has long been a centre of patriot resistance.

Observer 1944

Daily Herald 1944

It's Field Marshal Monty Now

By Major E. W. SHEPPARD

GENERAL SIR BERNARD MONTGOMERY has been promoted Field-Marshal, supernumerary to establishment, as from to-day.

The promotion does not, of course, mean that he vacates his command of the 21st Army Group.

Nor does "supernumerary to establishment" mean that the promotion is not substantive or does not take effect at once.

The establishment of field-marshals allowed for in the British Army List is eight, and there is already that number of field-marshals in the Army. Indeed, there are more. Lord Wavell, for instance, is a supernumerary field-marshal.

Rare Honour

Montgomery is one of the few generals who have been made Field Marshal without having been Chief of the Imperial General Staff, the highest Army appointment.

He relinquished command of his victorious Eighth Army in Italy to become C.-in-C. of the British group of armies for the liberation of Europe.

"Monty," to the Army and the British public—and the "Calculating Machine" to the Germans—he has captured the imagination of soldiers and public as no other general in modern times.

He is 56, and was promoted Major-General in 1938 and full General in 1942.

(Eisenhower's Praise—Page 3)

Britain Able to Bear the Cost of Beveridge

By E. F. Schumacher

"THE Tory Reform Committee does not believe that measures of Social Reform which it has championed are beyond the taxable or economic capacity of the nation to bear, or beyond the willingness of the majority of individuals to provide by personal effort and sacrifice."

This is the main conclusion reached in Bulletin No. 5 of the Tory Reform Committee, after a statistical survey of the present and future income of the nation. Due allowance is made for the increased cost of interest and management of the National Debt, for war pensions, the maintenance of substantial fighting forces, increased votes for health and education, and for the adoption of the Beveridge Report in full.

The second main conclusion is that the limits of what this country will be able to afford "have for the time being been nearly approached" by the measures of social reform already proposed, and that "the time has come to concentrate upon increasing the national income in the cause of Social Progress by every means, and in particular by increased industrial efficiency."

Observer 1944

Melody Maker
1945

GLENN MILLER IS MISSING

'Plane Vanishes on Journey to Paris

DANCE BAND FANS ALL OVER THE WORLD, AND THE HUNDREDS OF THOUSANDS OF ALLIED TROOPS WHO HAVE BEEN CHEERED AND ENTERTAINED BY HIS MUSIC, WILL LEARN WITH THE VERY DEEPEST CONCERN THE GRAVE NEWS THAT MAJOR GLENN MILLER, CELEBRATED LEADER OF THE AMERICAN BAND OF THE ALLIED EXPEDITIONARY FORCES, HAS BEEN OFFICIALLY REPORTED MISSING.

His last broadcast in person in this country was on December 12, and he left England by air on December 15 to fly to Paris and join the rest of his band, who had already arrived there safely.

SINCE THEN THERE HAS BEEN COMPLETE SILENCE. NO NEWS HAS COME FROM HIM OR THE PLANE IN WHICH HE WAS TRAVELLING; IN FACT, HE AND THE MACHINE SEEM COMPLETELY TO HAVE VANISHED, AND ON CHRISTMAS EVE SHAEF ISSUED A SHORT STATEMENT — WHICH WAS BROADCAST BY THE B.B.C. IN ITS NEWS BULLETINS—OFFICIALLY ANNOUNCING HIM TO BE MISSING.

Right up to the moment of closing this issue for press on Wednesday morning (December 27), the MELODY MAKER has been in constant touch with the authorities, hoping that good tidings would come through. We regret to report, however, that no news has been forthcoming of his whereabouts or — we hate to have to write the words, but the stark facts must be faced— of his fate.

One gleam of hope is the conjecture that his plane may have been forced down in enemy lines, and that he is now a prisoner of war, since it is understood that his flight was in connection with the arranging of troop concerts on the Continent, and therefore there is no reason necessarily to suppose that the plane took the direct cross-Channel route to Paris.

OSWIECIM REVELATIONS

Worst Death Camp Captured

Oswiecim (Auschwitz), most infamous of all the Nazi death camps, has been captured by the Red Army, as reported in THE JEWISH CHRONICLE last week, and first investigations reveal that the horrors perpetrated there put even those of Maidanek in the shade.

Several thousands of completely exhausted prisoners in the last stages of emaciation were rescued by the Russians.

When the Maidanek atrocities were exposed to the world, the Germans began to try and hide what was taking place at Oswiecim.

They destroyed an electrical machine which was able to kill several hundred victims at once, the bodies then being dropped on to a conveyor belt which carried them to the electric furnace, where the bodies were burned and reduced to powder.

A mobile plant for slaughtering children was removed by the Nazis, and the gas chambers were reconstructed to make them appear to be garages. Mass graves in the camp were levelled.

According to the survivors, the death factory was a great industry with many departments. There were offices where the deportees were sorted according to their age and capacity to perform slave labour before being slaughtered. Other offices were set aside for the aged, for children, and for invalids doomed to immediate execution.

The powdered remains of the victims were used as fertiliser for the fields surrounding the camp which was several square miles in extent.

Between 1941 and 1943, five to eight sealed trains filled with deportees used to arrive at the camp daily. They drew up at a special siding built in the camp. It is estimated that over 1,500,000 victims were done to death in Oswiecim, and hundreds of thousands of them were Jews.

Jewish Chronicle 1945

PADRES REPORT ON DEATH CAMP

What Jewish Chaplains Saw

The Rev. I. Levy, Senior Jewish Chaplain to the B.L.A., in a letter to THE JEWISH CHRONICLE, writes: The world has heard of the notorious death camp of Bergen Belsen, recently liberated by our Forces. The press and radio have made references to it and to the " sights " which many come to see. What thought has been given to the 25,000 odd Jewish inmates, I wonder?

I have just returned from a four-day stay there. My colleague, the Rev. L. H. Hardman, has been there since the second day of its liberation and has done yeoman service in helping the Military Government to bring some order into this disastrous chaos. I was with him for a short period to lend a hand. We need help and more help. Are there any Jewish groups of relief workers ready to join us? We need hundreds of them.

I feel that I owe it to the Jewish Community at home to give them some idea of the scenes in this horrible camp, but I cannot describe the indescribable. There are no words to convey the tragedy and misery of those tens of thousands of hapless victims.

Jewish Chronicle 1945

Greater London Plan :

PROFESSOR ABERCROMBIE and the team of which he has been the brilliant leader and inspiration have completed their gigantic task of designing the remodelling of the metropolitan area to fit the needs of the future. The result of their work is to be seen in the Outline Plan for Greater London. Mr. F. J. Osborn has described this as a " town planning classic," and the description need not be regarded as extravagant. The proposals now brought forward continue and expand those contained in the first Outline—that for the area governed by the London County Council. The latest Plan deals with an area of 2,599 square miles extending outwards from the London County Council boundary for roughly 30 miles from the centre of London and which in 1938 had a population of 6¼ millions. The area includes the whole of the counties of Middlesex, Hertfordshire and Surrey and parts of Kent, Essex, Bedfordshire, Buckinghamshire, and Berkshire.

Local Government Journal 1945

Primate: distress

The Archbishop of Canterbury (Dr. Fisher) said last night :—
" I do not think that anyone can feel anything but distress at the scenes which followed the shooting of Mussolini in Milan."

Daily Express 1945

THE GUNS HAVE DIED AT LAST

THE world is at peace, and the guns at last have died away in silence. It is victory over Japan day.

"The last of our enemies is laid low" were almost the first words used by Mr. Attlee in his dramatic midnight announcement to a tense and expectant people that Japan had surrendered unconditionally. He read the terms of the Japanese reply to the Allied demands, and announced that to-day and Thursday would be public holidays.

LET ALL RELAX

After expressing gratitude to the fighting Forces, Mr. Attlee said:

"Here, at home, you have a short-earned rest from the unceasing exertions you have all borne without flinching or complaint through so many dark years. I have no doubt that throughout industry generally the Government lead in the matter of Victory holidays will be followed, and that Wednesday and Thursday everywhere will be treated as days of holidays.

"There are some who must necessarily remain at work on these days to maintain essential services, and I am sure they can be relied upon to carry on. When we return to work on Friday morning we must turn again with energy to the great tasks which challenge us. But for the moment let all who can relax and enjoy themselves in the knowledge of work well done.

"Peace has once again come to the world. Let us thank God for this great deliverance and His mercies. Long live the King."

Exeter Express and Echo 1945

MR. CHURCHILL APPEALS FOR "SPECIAL RELATIONSHIP"

SUREST BASIS OF EFFECTIVE UNO

SOVIET "IRON CURTAIN" IN EUROPE

Speaking at Fulton, Missouri, yesterday, Mr. Churchill said that the " sure prevention of war " and the rise of a world organization demanded a special relationship between the British Commonwealth and Empire and the United States.

Such a relationship implied a common study of potential dangers, a similarity of weapons and instruction, an interchange of officers and cadets, and a joint use of naval and air bases throughout the world. So far from being inconsistent with the overriding loyalty to a world organization, this was probably the only means by which the organization would achieve full stature.

Mr. Churchill said also that Uno must immediately begin to be equipped with an international armed force. It would be wrong, however, to entrust the secret knowledge or experience of the atomic bomb to a world organization still in its infancy.

Since the end of the war a shadow had fallen on the scene; nobody knew what Russia and its Communist international organization intended to do in the immediate future " or what are the limits, if any, to their expansive and proselytizing tendencies." There was, however, in Britain a resolve to persevere through differences and rebuffs in establishing friendship. Difficulties and dangers would not be relieved by a policy of appeasement; what was needed was a settlement.

The Times
1946

John L. Baird — Television Pioneer

By B. CLAPP

Electronic Engineering
1946

As a result of this positive evidence of the possibilities of television, a small company was formed known as " Television Limited " and opened new offices and laboratories in Upper St. Martins Lane, and it was here I first saw John Logie Baird early in 1926 where he was carrying on his experiments without any technical assistance whatever. Even at this stage he was fully confident of solving the main problems and perfecting the science.

A few months later, towards the end of 1926, I became his first technical assistant and was connected with him very intimately for many years.

Even during the most exciting moments in our experiments he was a most considerate man, and although time meant nothing to him—night being the same as day, Sundays the same as weekdays—he was always most thoughtful for his staff and insisted that while working long hours they had adequate food and drink. As a Scot he dispelled the idea that as a race they are mean—he was most generous.

ROYAL ROMANCE HINT

Princess Elizabeth and Greek Prince

An Associated Press despatch from Athens states that the Greek monarchist newspaper, "Hellenicon Aema," yesterday hinted at an intimate relationship between the royal houses of Britain and Greece, and Greek royal family circles in Athens said last night that the reference might be to the engagement of Princess Elizabeth and Prince Philip of Greece.

The newspaper said :—" During his stay in London Regent Damaskinos may attain a happy solution which will connect intimately the British and Greek royal houses."

Prince Philip, who is 24, is a son of the late Prince Andrew and Princess Alice (née Mountbatten). He is now serving as A.D.C. to his uncle, Admiral Lord Louis Mountbatten, Supreme Allied Commander, South-East Asia. He was on active service as a sub-lieutenant with the British Mediterranean Fleet from 1939 to 1941, and was mentioned in despatches.

Inquiry at Buckingham Palace last night produced the reply that nothing was known there of the Greek rumours.

Glasgow Herald 1945

MR. H. G. WELLS

NOVELIST AND THINKER

Mr. H. G. Wells died at his London home on Tuesday at the age of 79.

Through half a century of material and intellectual change that has shaken all foundations H. G. Wells created, argued, admonished, planned, and prophesied to a single purpose. Wherever there were visions of a new world in the making, wherever there were schemes for a more rational ordering of human affairs, there also was H. G. Wells. Whatever the shortcomings as artist or thinker of this irrepressible, non-stop genius, there can be no question of the unity of his versatile labours. Novelist, fantasist, analyst of society, amateur of science, popularizer of ideas, his profuse and astonishing literary career exhibits the constant and guiding passion of a single-minded personality. Wells did not believe in the inevitability of progress—far from it. He did believe, above all else, in the possibility of planning and shaping the progress of mankind, and in the doom and destruction that awaited us in the absence of such purposive control.

In support of that belief came a flow of words, a torrent of ideas, a mounting spate of enthusiasms from year to year that did not a little to form the mental climate of his times and that made the word "Wellsian" almost a household term of criticism. Wells was never anything but successful as a writer and at one time was possibly the most widely read author in the world. Although of necessity his public diminished as the purpose of everything he wrote grew more familiar and more emphatic, he always remained one of the biggest intellectual influences in the English-speaking world. For many years now it had been taken for granted that there would be two or three new volumes a year from him, fiction or sociology or science or what not, and pronouncements upon every leading topic of debate; and it is all the harder to realize the loss of that restless and lively intelligence, that vivid and youthful personality, the short, confident figure with his squeaky voice, twinkling gaiety, and alert, penetrating expression known to a host of people simply as "H. G."

Times Educational Supplement 1946

HEALTH

THE Government was on velvet during the National Health Service debate. Here is a Bill which aims at bringing the best medical care within reach of all persons, rich or poor. Few will quarrel with that purpose, which was in fact accepted by the Coalition and carried some way towards legislation. Moreover, the Bill follows broadly the pattern set by the Coalition White Paper; Mr. Bevan has refused to go as far as many of his own party supporters would wish in applying strict Socialist doctrine to medical affairs. True, the hospitals are to be nationalised, but there is general agreement that our hospital system needs fairly drastic reorganisation of some kind, and Mr. Bevan seems to be genuinely anxious to run the hospitals on a loose rein. The terms of service for doctors, not yet announced, are expected to be generous; there is no doubt that in many ways the scheme will offer the young doctor more attractive prospects, and certainly fewer anxieties, than he has now. And equally no doubt that it will give great numbers of people access to a wider and more efficient range of medical services than they have enjoyed hitherto.

A measure which promises so much is no easy target for criticism. One might have expected that it would be opposed only by selfish reactionaries. Yet the fact remains that it is mistrusted—for various and not always convincing or consistent reasons, but still mistrusted—by a fairly high proportion of doctors, and not merely by a few ancient diehards.

Observer 1946

CHURCHILL STATUE ON WHITE CLIFFS

From Our Own Representative

HYTHE, KENT, Saturday.

Fourteen mayors of the Cinque Ports and their associate towns in Kent and Sussex met here today to consider the proposal to erect a 120-foot statue of Mr. Churchill on the cliffs at Dover. It was stated that Mr. Charles H. Davis, of Cape Cod, Massachusetts, wants to raise all the money needed, £25,000, in America, and that offers of money have been received from many parts of the British Empire. The mayors are to hold another meeting.

Sunday Times 1946

BBC Closing for 5 Hours Each Day

BEGINNING today the B.B.C. will be entirely off the air from 9 a.m. to midday and from 1.30 to 3.30 p.m.

The B.B.C. will thus save 32,000 power units a day, or 40 per cent of the power it normally consumes.

In the morning and afternoon transmitting hours, up to 6 p.m. the Home and Light programmes will be

'Waiting Days'

Any "waiting days" served on or after February 10 will rank for payment of unemployment benefit where the claimant is unemployed for 12 days or more.

Under new regulations issued by the Minister of National Insurance, payment for the three days, February 10 to 13 inclusive, will be made on Friday, February 28. The Ministry of Labour may arrange to pay earlier.

Latest unemployed total is 1,918,400.

Daily Worker 1947

ELEVEN PLUS IS TOO EARLY

WE are forced to the conclusion that eleven plus is too early an age for the child to be subjected to the mature educational disciplines; he is not ready to embark upon a genuine secondary phase. In Scotland this seems to be recognised, and the transfer age is fixed at twelve. In another, quite distinct educational system that flourishes in England—that which involves the transition from a preparatory school to a public school—the transfer age is much later at thirteen or even fourteen.

There is another point. The choice of eleven plus makes the *complete* secondary course very long—covering seven or eight years in its grammar school form. One school of thought believes that this is too long, and that the differences between boys of eleven and eighteen are so great, that to try to organise this wide age-range in one school under one headmaster is unwise. This is probably an exaggeration, especially when we remember that in this particular case the junior boys will most likely have mental ages a year or so in advance of their chronological ages. Many who have taught in successful grammar schools would probably not admit the existence of a problem at all.

Schoolmaster 1948

Princess Elizabeth's Wedding

"An Act done with Simple Reverence in the Presence of God"

A WEEK has now passed since the British people and the friends of Britain everywhere gave themselves up to a day's rejoicing in celebration of the marriage of Princess Elizabeth and Lieutenant Philip Mountbatten, R.N. (now the Duke of Edinburgh). But not even the days of austerity can dim the memory of November 20—a day that will live in the hearts and minds of millions of men and women and be reborn again and again on the lips of mothers and grandmothers when coaxed by the children for a story about a Prince and a Princess.

To me, as one who was privileged to be present in Westminster Abbey last Thursday, the day must ever be one of imperishable memories. Not merely because of the historical significance and setting, the colour, the splendour, the pageantry, the music, and the famous and illustrious company; but because the solemn simplicity of the religious service made such a strangely deeper impression than all the material magnificence. Despite all that has been written in the popular Press, the news-reels and colour films, the tumult and the shouting; despite the jewels, the velvets and brocades; despite the banners and the flags, that which took place in London last Thursday was a religious act—something done, and done with simple reverence, in the presence of God.

British Weekly
1947

MR. T. S. ELIOT.
Awarded the Nobel Prize for literature. He has long been in the forefront of English letters as a poet, dramatist, essayist and critic. An American by birth, he became a British subject in 1927. He was awarded the O.M. in the New Year Honours.

Illustrated London News
1948

Sir John Cockcroft, director of the Harwell Atomic Energy Research Establishment, told a London audience that the medieval alchemists' vain search for the "philosopher's stone" had now been solved. By means of the atomic pile we could produce many hundreds of pounds of new elements which had not existed on the earth before . . .

Prediction **1949**

Barbirolli and the Hallé

After many rumours, it was good to hear Barbirolli had elected to remain with the Hallé Orchestra. It was announced in Manchester that Barbirolli was influenced to stay with the orchestra instead of going to the B.B.C. by changes which include an increase of minimum pay rates to players, decision to send the orchestra abroad at least once a year and enlargement of the orchestra to pre-war strength of one hundred players.

Pianomaker **1949**

GROUNDNUTS SCHEME IS 'WRITTEN OFF' AS IMPOSSIBLE

Daily Mirror
1951

By BILL GREIG

THE great East African groundnuts scheme, designed to supply Britain with oil and fats, has failed. A White Paper issued by the Government yesterday admitted that the "original aims of the scheme have proved incapable of fulfilment."

What is left of the scheme is being taken out of the control of the Ministry of Food and handed over to the Colonial Office to run as an experiment in development on a much smaller scale.

About £36,500,000, spent over the past four years, is being written off. All this, however, is not dead loss. There are many assets on the ground and much land has been cleared.

FIRST public tribute to Bernard Shaw since his death has come from St. Pancras, the borough in which he lived at the beginning of the century.

From 1897 to 1903 he served on the Vestry and the Borough Council, with the programme "Push up the rates and pull down the death rate."

On his 90th birthday he became the first freeman of the borough.

Stage and public

Famous actors and actresses joined in the tribute organised by St. Pancras public libraries and held in the Town Hall on Wednesday night.

Admission to the assembly hall was by ticket only. Tickets were available at the public libraries and the hall which holds 1,000, was full. A library spokesman told the Express and News: "We wanted the general people of St. Pancras to join in and we think we succeeded."

The council received a message of good wishes from Miss Blanche Patch, who was unable to be present. Miss Patch was Mr. Shaw's secretary.

At the end of the evening the audience stood in silence before dispersing.

Hampstead and Highgate Express
1950

By Daily Graphic Reporters

A COUNTRY-WIDE search for the 1,100-year-old Scone Stone stolen from Westminster Abbey was extended last night to railways, lorries, seaports and airports.

Urgent messages from Scotland Yard asked rail and road transport employees and Customs men to examine unusually heavy packages.

J F S initials clue

Details of the theft of the 3 cwt. stone, taken from beneath the gilded Coronation Chair, had been flashed already to Paris and New York.

The initials J. F. S., newly carved on the chair, may be a clue to the thieves, who are believed to be fanatically patriotic Scots. One suggestion last night was that J. F. S. represented Justice For Scotland.

If caught, the thieves can be charged with sacrilege, for which up to 14 years' jail can be imposed.

So many Scots have sworn to aid in restoring to their country the Stone of Destiny, as it is described in official records, that the list of possible suspects is the longest for any crime in history.

Daily Graphic
1950

REX HARRISON and his wife, LILLI PALMER, look forward to repeating their perfect holiday in the autumn

Woman
1950

14 YEARS FOR GIVING SECRETS TO RUSSIA

SOVIET WAS SAVED 5 YEARS IN COMPLETING ATOM BOMB

DAILY TELEGRAPH REPORTER

The maximum penalty of 14 years' imprisonment was passed by the Lord Chief Justice, Lord Goddard, at the Old Bailey yesterday on KLAUS EMIL JULIUS FUCHS, 38, chief of the theoretical physics branch of the Government's secret atomic research establishment at Harwell, Berks. [Full Report—P7.]

He had admitted giving to Russian agents information about atomic research which in the words of the charge was calculated to be directly or indirectly useful to an enemy and prejudicial to the safety or interests of the State.

Dr. Fuchs had for years been passing details of British and American atomic developments to Soviet agents in both this country and the United States. He was one of six men in Britain, the atomic mission sent to America, who knew one of the most vital secrets of the atomic bomb—how to explode it.

DR. K. E. J. FUCHS, who was yesterday sentenced to 14 years' imprisonment for four offences under the Official Secrets Act. Another picture—P7.

Daily Telegraph 1950

ON his 70th birthday Ernest Bevin has shown the grace and the strength to give up the great office of Secretary of State for Foreign Affairs. He has put his country before himself.

The 'Daily Mirror' in the past has not failed to criticise him for faults, as we see them, of prejudice, of obstinacy and of arrogance. They are the faults of a big man.

For let no one forget it. Ernest Bevin is one of the great Englishmen of the 20th Century. Time alone can judge his handling of foreign policy, but his place in history is already secure. He is one of the great leaders in the upsurge of the people that began in his generation. He gave his strength and his health in that struggle.

Daily Mirror 1951

The Voice that Reads the News

Radio Times 1951

THE recent announcement by the BBC that the reading of news bulletins in the Home Service and Light Programmes would be confined to a limited number of readers seems to have caused widespread interest and, indeed, judging by comments and letters, some misunderstanding.

Let it be said in the first place that there is nothing new or original in this arrangement. In 1940 a small body of announcers took over these duties in the Home Service and Forces programmes. The only difference was that at that time and until 1946 their names were given with each bulletin and then only for security reasons; for, in fact, the purpose of defeating any attempt by enemy radio stations working on BBC wavelengths from across the Channel to broadcast false news in English. The voices with the names became familiar in every household. The number was then eight. The number today is eight. Why and how were these eight selected?

STUART HIBBERD
Veteran of the team. Military service in Gallipoli, Mesopotamia, India, 1914-21. Retired from Army in 1922. Joined BBC in 1924

ALAN SKEMPTON
Left school August 1939. Joined R.A.F. 1941. Flying instructor; later trained as night fighter pilot. Joined BBC January 1949

ROBERT DOUGALL
Joined BBC 1934. Became 'Radio Newsreel' reporter 1940, released to join Navy and served eighteen months in North Russia

COLIN DORAN
Educated at Eton (King's Scholar 1931). Fought in Kohima, campaign as Infantry Officer. Joined BBC in 1947

AMERY—MACMILLAN

Left: The marriage took place at St. Margaret's, Westminster, of Mr. Julian Amery, son of Mr. and Mrs. L. S. Amery, and Miss Catherine Macmillan, daughter of Mr. Harold Macmillan, M.P., and Lady Dorothy Macmillan

Queen 1950

MONKEY-NUT SUITS WILL SOON BE ON THE MARKET

Daily Mirror 1951

By RONALD BEDFORD

THOUSANDS of British men and women next winter will be wearing suits made of a mixture of monkey-nut fibre and wool.

Because of wool shortages and high prices, the new fibre will be vitally important to Britain

Called Ardil, it has been developed after years of research by scientists of Imperial Chemical Industries. It is made from what is left after margarine-makers have extracted the oil from monkey nuts.

At a new £2,000,000 plant, specially built for the purpose, near Dumfries, 500 men and women are now beginning to produce the fibre.

Target output for this year is 3,500 tons—enough, when mixed with wool on a fifty-fifty basis, to make 3,500,000 suits. Next year's target is 10,000 tons.

For the past eight months I have been wearing one of the few monkey-nut suits specially made for test purposes. So has Board of Trade President Harold Wilson.

Mine is brown, with a fawn and red pin-stripe. It wears as well as an expensive all-wool suit, though it is slightly heavier. And it is as warm as any all-wool suit I have had.

It does not shine so easily at the seat and the elbows, and stands up to dry-cleaning as well as a normal suit.

The only fault I can find with the suit after a rigorous test in all weathers, and after wearing it continuously, is this: It gets baggy at the knees more easily than an all-wool suit.

STONE OF DESTINY

Dr DON VISITS ST ANDREWS THIS WEEK-END

St Andrews students were among the most interested people in Scotland to learn of the appearance of the Stone of Destiny at Arbroath Abbey, as two of the chief protagonists in the matter visit the city within a few days of each other.

Dr J. M'Cormick, chairman of the National Covenant Committee, addressed the St Andrews University Scottish Nationalist Society on Wednesday, when there was great jubilation among the students at the gesture that had been made at Arbroath. On the other side, the Dean of Westminster, Dr A. C. Don, arrives in St Andrews this week-end to deliver a sermon at the University Chapel on Sunday.

Dr M'Cormick, in the course of an interview prior to his meeting, said: "The removal of the Stone of Destiny from Westminster and its return to public light in the Abbey of Arbroath has been symbolic of the determination of the new generation of Scots to insist on their national rights.

"Some deplore their methods, but no one can be blamed for their purpose.

."They have now made it clear that they sought neither personal glory nor private advantage, but thought only of compelling attention to a historic wrong and to a present need.

"I have no doubt that, in their choice of Arbroath Abbey, they had in mind the words of the ancient Declaration of Independence.

"It seems that the authorities have now, with indecent haste, removed the stone to police custody in Forfar. Surely that is not a way to venerate the most ancient symbol of Scottish nationhood.

"Surely, even for one day, the Stone might have been allowed to lie in public view on the consecrated soil of Arbroath.

"Whatever the outcome of this latest development, I feel sure the whole people of Scotland will unite in demanding that the Stone be finally and publicly returned to Scotland.

St Andrew's Citizen 1951

Illustrated London News 1951

AFTER THE SERVICE COMMEMORATING THE GLORIOUS STAND OF THE GLOUCESTERS AT THE IMJIN RIVER ACTION MEN OF THE GLOUCESTERSHIRE REGIMENT MARCHING FROM GLOUCESTER CATHEDRAL ON JUNE 17. On June 17 about 1800 people attended in Gloucester Cathedral a service of intercession and commemoration for the men of the 1st Battalion, The Gloucestershire Regiment, who took part in the heroic action in Korea in April. Men from the regimental depôt, Territorials, National Servicemen, British Legion, and Old Comrades' Association were present at the parade and service. The Duke of Gloucester was represented by Maj.-General C. E. A. Firth.

Party Backing for Bevan in Constituency

From J. C. Griffith Jones
TREDEGAR, Mon.,
April, 28

MR. ANEURIN BEVAN returned to his home town this evening to explain his resignation from the Government to his chief supporters.

After a private conference of the Divisional Labour Party (Ebbw Vale Division), asked for by Mr. Bevan and attended by 340 delegates, the following statement was issued :

"Mr. Bevan explained why he had found it necessary to resign. He expressed his profound belief in the ultimate triumph of the Labour movement. The delegates unanimously approved of Mr. Bevan's action and assured him of their wholehearted support."

'Socialist Instinct'

I understand that some delegates intended to criticise Mr. Bevan's "threat to the unity of the party," but his eloquence, his appeal to the "true Socialist instinct of our people," and his call for "no repetition of 1931," with the almost fanatical support of the majority of the delegates, carried the meeting.

Outside, the hall, on the bus and in the town square, in the cafés and public-houses, opinion was strongly pro-Bevan. At his home in Queen's-square, where his sister now lives, there was a sheaf of telegrams and letters congratulating him on his stand.

The real test of Labour opinion in the constituency will be the public meeting at Ebbw Vale to-morrow. The 1,400 seats could be filled three times over.

Observer 1951

DISPUTED ISLANDS IN THE CHANNEL

RULING SOUGHT FROM THE HAGUE COURT

FROM OUR DIPLOMATIC CORRESPONDENT

The British Government have requested the International Court at The Hague to settle a dispute between Britain and France that has existed, if not from time immemorial, at least for 300 years.

The question at issue is the sovereignty of the Ecrehos and the Minquiers. These groups of tiny islands, situated between Jersey and the French coast, have been the scene of a succession of lively brawls, it seems, between French and British fishermen throughout the centuries. The Ecrehos are two islands some 300 yards long, on one of which there are a few occasionally inhabited fishermen's huts. The Minquiers are a group of rocks barely visible at high water.

The dispute concerned both fishery rights and territorial sovereignty. After discussions at the Foreign Office in July, 1950, an agreement was reached on the fishery rights. This has since been ratified by the British and French parliaments. By a separate agreement on sovereignty Britain and France agreed last December that the case should be submitted by Britain to the International Court, and, this agreement having now also been ratified, the British Government have applied to the Court for a ruling. It remains for both sides to submit "memorials" to the Court, which may well be an intricate and detailed process, but it is hoped that the story will before long have a happy ending at last.

The Times 1951

"DAILY MIRROR" REPORTER

THE note, the theme, the very heart of Britain's Festival was sounded by the pealing bells and brazen trumpets, echoed by the cheering crowds and passed on by the waving flags—"Rejoice. Be glad," they sang. The Festival had begun.

The mood of Britain's happy day was set by the King and Queen as they drove to St. Paul's for the opening ceremony.

They smiled. And it was as though a floodgate was unlocked.

Through the crowds went that smile. It raced along the Royal road. It flashed ahead of the prancing horses. It was at Ludgate Circus before the cavalry outriders drew near. A Festival smile that went on wings.

And the cheering! And the waving! And the flags, the songs, the joyfulness! In the streets they sang and laughed and the drummers thumped with vigour.

And the colours! The scarlet and gold of Beefeaters, the crimson and buff of Pikemen, the brilliant gold and black and silver of the trumpeters of the Household Cavalry.

The jingling harness and clattering hooves took up the song. The Windsor greys, the scarlet coach swept up to the broad steps of great St. Paul's. The service was simple, yet splendid. It was a family gathering—with the Royal Family never more a family than now, sitting and kneeling at the front of the great nave.

'A Joyful Season'

"We will show what we have done in working out our own salvation. We will be joyful for a season," said the Archbishop of Canterbury.

Three thousand people from every walk of life and every corner of the land—civic leaders, ordinary folk, foreign dignitaries—joined in this dedication. The young Duke of Kent, singing lustily, did his best to catch the eye of cousin William of Gloucester, a seat or so away. His mother reprimanded him with a sidelong glance that left nothing unsaid.

Outside, on the steps, the King proclaimed the Festival begun. "This is no time for despondency," he said. "For I see in this Festival a symbol of Britain's abiding courage and vitality."

Back towards the Palace went his coach. The bells were pealing still. The fanfares echoed yet. Little children, placed carefully in the front by London policemen so that they could see all, waved their flags. Women waved their handkerchiefs and men their morning papers.

Happiest Crowd

"The happiest and yet the most orderly crowd I've ever known," said a cheery bobby.

Some people had been sharing Trafalgar-square with Nelson and the pigeons since six o'clock in the morning. They meant to have a kerb-side view. For many had come thousands of miles, from many parts of the world, to see the start of Britain's Festival. They did not mind the wait. Not when they could smile. Not when they could sing and cheer. Not when the bands played and the King came by.

And so the Festival was started. A fine, happy start. "Rejoice, Be glad," was the keynote. A note sounded by the King.

FESTIVE WAS THE DAY—THE KING SET THE MOOD

Observer 1951

London search for 'Rubber Bones' Webb

A FLYING SQUAD team was standing-by at Scotland Yard last night to move to any district where Harold "Rubber Bones" Webb (30), who escaped from Dartmoor on Sunday might be reported.

Webb, who escaped by crawling through a heating duct, got his nickname from his reputation of being able to slip out of handcuffs—and through narrow openings.

He was sentenced to eight years' penal servitude and 20 strokes of the birch at the Old Bailey in 1946 for robbery with violence.

News Chronicle 1951

BRITAIN'S A-WEAPON

Daily Mail
1952

6,000-ft CLOUD MILE WIDE

'It Rose in Ragged Shape— Unlike Usual Mushroom'

Onslow, North-West Australia, Friday.

BRITAIN'S first atomic weapon has been successfully exploded in a secret test in the Monte Bellos islands off the north-west Australian coast, it was officially announced today.

The explosion is the climax of two years' secret planning in these desolate islands—known locally as the Devil Islands.

According to a correspondent at Rough Range North-West Australia, the weapon was exploded at 8 a.m. local time today (1 a.m. B.S.T.).

The cloud from the blast had a ragged shape, wide at the base, unlike the familiar mushroom smoke of the American explosions.

A stringent security blackout covering an area some 200 miles across, centring on Flag Island in the Monte Bellos group, indicated the test was near. Ships and planes had been forbidden to visit the islands for some weeks.

One minute after the detonation the cloud had reached 6,000ft. Three minutes after the explosion the cloud was a mile wide at its centre, and the shape at the top was that of a ragged letter "Z."—Reuter.

GREAT FOG

Firemen run in front of their engines

By Daily Graphic Reporters

THE great fog which has paralysed London has entered its fourth day.

Weather men last night offered no early hope of a let-up.

They saw no sign of the wind or temperature rise which would shift the Thames valley fog belt caused by cold air on the ground and a warmer layer above.

And smoke from Londoners' weekend fires, well built up against the frost, added to the density of the black-out.

Transport by road, river and air was paralysed again yesterday over a radius of 20 miles.

Daily Graphic 1952

10-EGG HEN IS DEAD

JENNIFER, the wonder hen, died yesterday — 24 hours after her marathon ten-eggs-in-an-hour feat.

Said her owner farmer Charlie Rogers, at Bodymoor Heath Farm, Warwickshire last night: "I have asked a Birmingham taxidermist to set

Jenny up in a glass case with those ten eggs.

We will keep her on the sideboard near the spot where she laid them."

Said Margaret, Mr. Rogers' 18-year-old daughter: "Jenny spent last night in her cardboard box and I tried to make her eat. But the laying effort had been too much for her."

Daily Express 1952

EDEN THREE MINUTES OVER

By ARTHUR BRITTENDEN
News Chronicle Reporter.

MR. ANTHONY EDEN, in his television appearance for the Conservatives last night, overran his time by 3min. 5sec.

The B.B.C. had allotted him 15 minutes, beginning at 8 p.m., when the T.V. service opened. But Mr. Eden took just over 18 minutes.

On Monday night Lord Samuel, making the first election speech ever on British television, was faded out after 15 minutes. His talk for the Liberals was uncompleted.

In a statement after Mr. Eden's appearance the B.B.C. said last night: "We asked the speakers of all parties to keep their programme to 15 minutes. Mr. Eden was rehearsed for that period. But we realised it is very difficult to insist that this time is kept to. Television conditions are entirely different from those in a sound studio where a person is reading from a script. On TV it is impossible for us to be ruthless.

"Lord Samuel was not faded out because of time. It was entirely due to a misunderstanding between him and the producer in the control gallery, over a signal passed between them."

★

News Chronicle 1951

Tiddly? Perhaps— Harding

Gilbert Harding

MR. GILBERT HARDING admitted last night he might have "over-fortified" himself against asthma and fog before appearing in TV's "What's My Line?" show.

Scores of viewers telephoned the B.B.C. after the show to say they thought Mr. Gilbert Harding was ill.

A spokesman for the corporation said: "We noticed a difference in Mr. Harding's manner and intend to make full inquiries to-morrow."

Daily Graphic
1952

The Government Scraps Identity Cards

Saving Of 1,500 In Staff And £500,000 In Cost

Don't Tear Them Up Yet

Mr. H. Crookshank, Health Minister, announced amid cheers in the Commons this afternoon, that the Government had decided that it was no longer necessary to require the public to possess and produce an identity card.

Mr. Crookshank said it would also be no longer necessary to notify change of address for National Registration purposes, though the numbers would continue to be used in connection with the National Health Service.

The Minister said he was circulating other details of the decision and people should await these before disposing of their cards.

Answering Mr. Shinwell (Lab. Eastington), Mr. Crookshank said the result of this action was estimated to save in staff about 1,500 people and in cost about £500,000 (Government cheers).

"PUBLIC SERVICE"

There was no Government reply when Mr. Clement Davies (L. Montgomery), asked if the Minister would consider refunding Mr. Willcock (he brought a test case—see below) who did a very con-

Another souvenir of the Second World War.

siderable public service in calling attention to these cards and to the fact that they were unnecessary and degrading, and also whether he would recommend to the Foreign Secretary to follow his good example and try to get rid of passports as well.

When Mr. Barber asked if this action could have been taken a long time ago with the consequent saving mentioned. Mr. Crookshank replied: "Certainly, the suggestion was pressed upon the previous Government."

When Mr. H. A. Marquand (Lab, Middlesbrough East), former Minister of Health, rose, the Speaker said he understood from the Minister's answer there was to be a fuller statement circulated in the official report, and perhaps it would be in the interests of other members who had questions on the order paper—

At this stage, Mr. Shinwell,

rising on a point of order, said, apart entirely from the merits of the question, was there any reason for the Minister of Health to make an attack on the late Government—(there were Conservative cries of "Yes" during the ensuing uproar)—without affording Mr. Marquand an opportunity of asking a question on these allegations.

"May I ask," Mr. Shinwell continued, "what relationship was there between the merits of the question and the insinuation which the right hon. gentleman made?"

The Speaker said he thought it was in the interests of members as a whole that they should pass on.

HOW THEY STARTED

Identity cards first came into operation at the beginning of the war when the Government's National Registration Bill, called for registration of all persons in the United Kingdom, except members of the armed forces. That was nearly 12½ years ago.

The maintenance of a National Register it was said, was to support and facilitate National Service arrangements, to provide manpower and population statistics, and for other services, like preserving contact between families split up by evacuation.

When the war ended, identity cards remained. It was maintained that they were invaluable as a check on National Service registration, security and rationing and also administration of the Health Service, family allowances and post-war credits.

In July last year, when the Lords passed a resolution in favour of ending the cards. Lord Shepherd, the Labour Chief Whip, said that the National Register had enabled the forces to call up 10,000 men who disobeyed the call-up proclamation in the previous two or three years.

FRAUDS CHECK

To help in checking on frauds the Post Office Savings Bank insisted on the production of a person's card before a withdrawal could be made.

Lost ration books could be replaced only if the losers took their identity cards to the food office.

It was estimated that about 300,000 identity cards were lost each year.

The courts heard several protests against the cards. Most notable was the case of Mr. Clarence Harry Willcock, of Hadley Wood, Barnet, who appealed last year against his conviction for failing to produce his, when, as a motorist, he was asked by the police to do so.

The conviction was upheld in the King's Bench, but the Lord Chief Justice criticised the police practice of demanding a card whenever they stopped a motorist, whatever his offence might be.

Soon after, the Metropolitan Police were given instructions to demand identity cards only when absolutely necessary.

Liverpool Echo 1952

DEBORAH KERR, co-starring in M.G.M.'s "QUO VADIS," Colour by Technicolor

DEBORAH KERR...Lustre-Creme presents one of the 12 women voted as having the world's loveliest hair. Famous Hollywood stars use Lustre-Creme to care for their glamorous hair.

The Most Beautiful Hair in the World

is kept at its loveliest . . . with
Lustre-Creme Shampoo

Yes, when lovely Hollywood stars tell you they use Lustre-Creme, it is high praise for this unique shampoo, because beautiful hair is vital to their glamour-careers.

In a recent issue of the magazine "Modern Screen," a committee of famed Hollywood hair stylists named Deborah Kerr as one of 12 women with the most beautiful hair in the world.

You, too, will notice a glorious difference in your hair after a Lustre-Creme Shampoo. Under the spell of its rich, lanolin-blessed lather, your hair shines, behaves, is eager to curl. Hair dulled by soap abuse, dusty with dandruff, now is fragrantly clean.

Hair robbed of its sheen now glows with new highlights. Lathers lavishly in hardest water, needs no special after-rinse.

NO OTHER cream shampoo in all the world is as popular as Lustre-Creme. For hair that behaves like the angels and shines like the stars . . . ask for Lustre-Creme Shampoo.

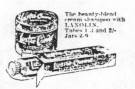

The beauty-blend cream shampoo with LANOLIN. Tubes 1/3 and 2/- Jars 2/9

Famous Hollywood Stars use Lustre-Creme Shampoo for Glamorous Hair

Daily Express 1952

JUST FANCY THAT—A SHIP WITH A WINDOW
UNDER-SEA BOFFINS WATCH BUBBLES

Express Staff Reporter

NAVAL scientists have been photographing the surge of water round a moving ship's propellers—the first men ever to see just what happens under water when a ship gets under way.

The Admiralty revealed yesterday that observations were made through thick panes of glass set into the hull of the frigate Helmsdale.

Scientists crouched in tiny compartment behind the windows, studying the effect of the whirling water on struts and propellers.

They watched, particularly, the sort of bubbles created by the ship, for these revealed much about the resistance of a propeller against water.

To cut down that resistance without losing thrust is one of the problems the scientists are

out to solve. They first of all studied model propellers rotating in tunnels. But this, though instructive, did not go far enough.

Hence the windows in the Helmsdale, one of eight ships used by naval boffins.

High-speed cameras photographed the view from the windows. Sometimes it was so clear that fish could be seen swimming under the hull.

Each time the Helmsdale returned to Portland Harbour she had to have her windows cleaned. A diver went down and wiped off the salt and slime.

THE THREE

STAND ALONE

Heavily veiled, the three mourning Queens stand together as the coffin of the King is borne from its gun-carriage to the catafalque in Westminster Hall. . . . They joined the procession behind the coffin and as they turned to do so the Queen Mother stood back for the new Queen to precede her.

Daily Herald 1952

BENTLEY DIES

Daily Herald 1953

FIXED to the gate of Wandsworth Jail late last night was this notice: THE SENTENCE OF THE LAW PASSED ON DEREK WILLIAM BENTLEY, FOUND GUILTY OF MURDER, WILL BE CARRIED INTO EXECUTION AT 9 A.M.

So today, 19-year-old Bentley will be hanged for his share with 16-year-old Christopher Craig in the murder of Police constable Sidney Miles.

The final " No reprieve " came after a day and night of last-ditch efforts. It was written by the Home Secretary, Sir David Maxwell Fyfe, in his own hand in reply to a deputation of six Labour M Ps, headed by Mr. Aneurin Bevan, who presented a petition signed in the Commons by 200 M Ps last night.

This move followed a dramatic but unavailing bid by more than 50 M Ps, led by Mr. Sydney Silverman (Lab., Nelson and Colne), to get the matter debated in the House. Said Mr. Speaker Morrison: A motion can be put down when the sentence has been executed.

THE QUEEN'S FIRST STATE OPENING OF PARLIAMENT

COLOURFUL LORDS CEREMONY

BY OUR OWN REPRESENTATIVE

WESTMINSTER, Tuesday.

The Queen literally " ascended the throne " to-day when for the first time she performed the State opening of Parliament. Both Lords and Commons were deeply moved by the grace and self-possession with which she underwent this taxing ceremony.

A fair, girlish figure in those august surroundings, she recaptured to an unusual degree the ancient spirit of Parliament; the Sovereign calling together her great men and commoners to parley and take counsel together about—in the words of the writ of summons—" the difficulties of the said affairs and dangers impending."

The Lords is a matchless chamber for such a ceremony, and long before 11 a.m. it was crowded with an assembly seen nowhere else in the world.

Peers in scarlet and ermine robes filled the cross benches on the floor of the House and overflowed, all party divisions forgotten for the occasion on benches on both sides.

The rows of peeresses on both sides of the House in gowns of every hue and many wearing glittering tiaras, seemed almost subdued by comparison.

Ambassadors of every race in an assortment of exotic uniforms, head-dresses, formal evening dress and decorations, filled the Diplomatic box on the right of the Throne. In front was the Bench of prelates, led by the two Archbishops, of Canterbury and York.

GALLERY FILLED

Mrs. Churchill Watches

On the symbolical bench in front of the throne, nearly a score of judges in full robes of scarlet, black and gold formed a solid phalanx. Every seat in the public galleries was filled, Mrs. Churchill and Mrs. Attlee being easily recognisable among the spectators.

The Times 1952

The funeral cortège of King George VI passes through Horse Guard's Parade

West Indian immigrants arriving in Britain.

Ginnie, the cat, brings home diamonds

GINNIE, four years old and ginger, is a cat in a million—a cat that brings home diamonds. Yes—*diamonds.*

That is why every time Ginnie goes for a stroll now she is closely followed by one of her owners, the Mansell family, of Westerham-road, Keston, Kent.

Ginnie was noticed to be limping after she jumped through the dining room window at the Mansell home the other day. Eight-year-old Ivor called his mother. "Perhaps she has a stone in her foot," said Mrs. Winifred Mansell. She lifted the cat's left forepaw and saw what looked like a small piece of glass. She took it out. Then she saw another piece and removed that, too.

After a closer look, she called her husband, Mr. Ivor Mansell, a building contractor. "These bits of glass," she said. "Do you think they could be diamonds?"

Mr. Mansell laughed—but his wife polished the bits and took them to a jeweller. They *were* diamonds and very finely cut. Unofficially they are worth £30 each.

Daily Herald 1953

Duke of Windsor just too late

QUEEN MARY died in a peaceful sleep at twenty minutes past ten last night.

The announcement was made at 11.11 by the Prime Minister in the House of Commons. A bulletin on the gate of Marlborough House at 11.15 told the silent waiting crowd:

"While sleeping peacefully, Queen Mary died at 20 minutes past ten o'clock."

Then as a thousand people pressed forward to read the notice, the personal Standard of Queen Mary was seen to be slowly hauled down from the staff on Marlborough House, where it had flown all day.

Men bared their heads. Women, many of whom had been waiting eight hours, were weeping as they queued to pass by the last bulletin.

The Princess Royal was the only member of the family at the death-bed. But at 10.28 the Duke of Windsor, making his third call of the day, drove up to Marlborough House. He did not know that his mother had died eight minutes before. An hour later the Duke drove away through the silent crowd. His head was bowed.

Daily Herald 1953

Lancashire Evening Post 1953

KATHLEEN FERRIER DIES AT 41

KATHLEEN FERRIER, world-famous contralto, died in a London hospital, to-day. She was 41.

Miss Ferrier was at the height of her powers and, by her death, the country loses one of the finest singers of our time.

A contralto with the rare ability to convey a sense of exaltation to her audience, she was considered by many critics to be without rival in the world.

Miss Ferrier was born at Higher Walton, but came to Blackburn as a child with her father, the late Mr. William Ferrier, headmaster, for many years of St. Paul's School, Blackburn.

For most of her childhood music and singing were no more than a spare-time activity. She learnt the piano, practised the violin and sang with the local choral society.

TELEPHONE OPERATOR

But when she left Blackburn High School for Girls at the age of 14, she went not to study at the Royal Academy of Music or some foreign conservatoire but to work in Blackburn Post Office.

For the next nine years the singer, who was to be acclaimed from Vienna to San Fransisco, worked as a telephone operator.

During her off-duty hours she began to reveal unusual talent as a pianist and, in 1931, won a grand pianoforte award in a national competition for entrants under 16 years of age.

Subsequently she won many distinctions at music festivals all over the North and obtained the joint degrees of L.R.A.M. and A.R.C.M. at the first attempt.

Even so, it was not until 1937, after going in for a competition at a local musical festival for a wager, that singing became her chief interest.

Sir Malcolm Sargent heard her in Manchester and strongly advised her to go to London to study.

SANG IN ABBEY

Wartime tours with C.E.M.A. in factory, barracks and canteen were the prelude to her first London engagement in 1943 when she sang the "Messiah" in Westminster Abbey.

Three years later she made her operatic debut at Glyndebourne in Benjamin Britten's "The Rape of Lucretia."

For Miss Ferrier the post-war years meant endless touring all over Europe and America. She sang at La Scala in Milan and the Carnegie Hall in New York. She appeared every year at the Edinburgh Festival.

A wreath will go from Lambeth

by ALAN DICK

MARY PORTER
30 stone of rollicking good nature.

A GREENGROCER'S van from Lower Marsh Market, down Lambeth Way, goes to Marlborough House tomorrow with a wreath to Queen Mary from the street traders of the market.

They have never forgotten Queen Mary's visit to their market in the spring of 1939, and the way she melted to their Cockney warmth.

They wrote to her regularly and every birthday they sent her flowers and a birthday wish. And every time Queen Mary wrote back.

Tomorrow the street traders of Lower Marsh Market send their last flowers to Marlborough House.

The wreath is being made up by Mary Porter, the market flower-girl, 30 stone of rollicking good nature whom the boys call "Mother Jolly." She has three boys of her own, and a girl into the bargain.

Mary was born in Covent Garden, where they called her mother Queen of the Punnets, after her dainty baskets of mustard and cress.

Daily Herald 1953

Why was I born?

FOR half a century I have been stuck on this earth and I still do not know what I am, where I am or why I am on earth at all.

Must I give up hope, or is there a light somewhere?—Kerree Collins, Petersham-road, Petersham, Surrey

? *Can any reader answer this question? Address your letters to Viewpoint.*

Daily Mirror 1953

The Duke of Edinburgh pays homage to the Queen during her coronation in Westminster Abbey, on 2 June 1953

Barber's bill came to £8 17s. 6d.

THE barber cutting Bob Howarth's hair told him his scalp was in a poor condition.

"Do something about it," said Bob, and the barber did. Came the bill. For haircut, scalp treatment and two bottles of lotion—£8 17s. 6d.

Bob—his full name is Robert Francis Howarth—is a student from Kenya and lives at Palace Gate, Kensington.

He paid up, but when he told his friends they went back with him to the barber's shop—the Adelphi salon in Villiers Street, W.C.2, run by Mr. Ronald George Evenett.

Telling his story to the L.C.C. Public Control Committee yesterday, Bob said: "I asked the person who attended me to give a detailed list of the charges for the treatment I had received.

"They added up, as far as I remember, to £2 14s. I was told the balance was the price of two bottles of lotion.

"Then Mr. Evenett ordered out my friends, saying that they were trespassing, and I was asked to go into a small room to discuss the matter.

"I asked them to take the bottles of lotion back but they said they could not as the money they had received for them had been banked."

The committee was hearing an application to revoke Mr. Evenett's licence for manicures, head massage, vapour baths and high-frequency treatment.

After Bob's evidence, Mr. Evenett walked out.

A chemist said he analysed three bottles of hair tonic.

Each was worth less than 1s.

Nineteen-year-old Anthony Clifford Cook, 9s.-a-day aircraftman, said he had a bottle of hair tonic.

"I poured the contents on the ground, put a match to it, and it went up in flames." he said.

The committee decided to revoke Mr. Evenett's licence. An official said he can still carry on business as a hairdresser.

News Chronicle
1953

Fine news for the Queen on her Coronation Morn—

EVEREST IS CONQUERED

THE Queen will be told this morning that Everest was conquered on May 29 by the British expedition.

The report came from India and was broadcast throughout America. The climbers to reach the 29,002-ft. summit were E. P. Hillary and a sherpa, Tensing Brutia.

This is the climax of 11 attempts, eight of them British.

The 13-man Everest team is led by 47-year-old Colonel John Hunt, CBE, DSO. He is a rifleman.

Daily Herald
1953

400-an-hour in queue for tour of city

LONG queues formed last night for Coronation tours of Cardiff by bus and the corporation transport department were hard pressed to cope with the demand for the 20-mile sightseeing trips to view the city's decorations.

The itinerary covered the city centre. Cathays Park area, Splott, Grangetown, the Docks area, Cowbridge-road, Whitchurch-road, Llandaff, Gabalfa and other districts. The tour occupied one-and-a-half hours.

All drivers were given a list of 17 points of interest at which to make brief stops for the benefit of sight-seers. Loaded doubledeck buses were leaving the Greyfriars-road starting point last night every few minutes at a rate of nearly 400 passengers an hour.

Department problem

"Our problem to-night is shortage of buses," a busy corporation transport official told the *Western Mail*. "A number of our vehicles are already out on private hire for other Coronation trips in the city.

"Sight-seers are well pleased with the tour and they have expressed appreciation of the brief stops made in streets where the decorations are outstanding."

The tour was mapped out some days ago by officials of the transport department. The 1s. 6d tours will continue every day this week from 2.30 p.m. onwards.

Western Mail 1953

Pettit found dead—with a confession in his pocket

DAILY MIRROR REPORTER

WILLIAM PETTIT, 27, whom the police wished to see in connection with the murder last month of Mrs. Rene Brown, was found yesterday in a bombed London building—dead.

It was in the very heart of the city where thousands passed daily on their way to and from work.

And in Pettit's pocket was found a last confession. It read: "Forgive me for what I have done. I could have gone on living with Mr. and Mrs. Brown, but I cannot live without her. I loved her, I loved her, I loved her"—the signature, Bill, was in Pettit's handwriting.

Among other papers found in Pettit's pocket was a letter he had received from Mrs. Brown.

Dr. Keith Simpson, the pathologist, established that Pettit, who was suffering from an advanced state of tuberculosis, died about four and a half weeks ago.

His body was in a sleeping position "as if he had simply lain down to die," police said.

Daily Mirror 1953

14 Days' Agony

SIR,—There are many farmers who, whilst they agree that the rabbit population must be kept under control, are so appalled by the suffering caused by myxomatosis that they refuse to take any part in spreading this terrible disease.

It is not the duty of the RSPCA to defend the Ministry of Agriculture, whom Mr. Barwise accuses of "sitting on the fence" (Letters, July 16 issue), but it is true that the Ministry, to its credit, did try to limit the spread of this plague.

Mr. Barwise implies that the housewife would like to see more rabbits dying of myxomatosis, but I have yet to meet the woman who would advocate the spreading of a disease which leaves its victims blind and deaf and agonised over a period of 14 days. I would remind Mr. Barwise that this is a Christian country and that the injunction to "be merciful that ye may obtain mercy" still carries weight with the majority.

ARTHUR W. Moss,
Chief Secretary, RSPCA.

105 *Jermyn Street,*
London S.W.1.

Farmer's Weekly 1954

EXECUTION OF CHRISTIE

Children in crowd read notice

TWO hundred people outside Pentonville today watched the posting of the notice announcing the execution of John Reginald Halliday Christie, the strangler, of No. 10, Rillington Place, Notting Hill, London. W.

It was a gossiping, laughing and joking crowd. Women with shopping baskets and children on holiday were among those who rushed forward to read the execution and death certificate notices.

About half a dozen police remained between the crowd and the door.

After five minutes the police moved the crowds away from the door.

A verdict of "Death by judicial execution" was recorded at the inquest on Christie in Pentonville Prison.

Oxford Mail 1953

NURSERY WORLD

Vol. 47. No. 1442   THURSDAY   JULY 30th · 1953   EIGHTPENCE

THE young musician on our cover this week is Andrew Lloyd Webber, photographed at 4½ years of age. He is the son of Dr. W. S. Lloyd Webber, musician and composer, who is professor of theory at the Royal College of Music.

The Editor

Husband returns home to find—

DANCING WIFE MURDERED IN ARMCHAIR

Police theory of killing by jealous woman

By Daily Mail Reporter

MRS. PENELOPE MOGANO, aged 43, was found murdered in the dining-room of her home in Holland-road, Coventry, last night. She was lying in an armchair with her head battered in.

The discovery was made by her husband, Mr. Carlo Mogano, when he came home from work. His son, Adrian, 14, home from school, had been waiting an hour trying to get in.

Police found a blood-stained carving-knife and were also looking for a blunt weapon.

Mr. and Mrs. Mogano were keen old-time dancers, and regularly visited an old-time dancing club near their home.

Pantry ablaze

And detectives are working on the theory that the killer is a maniac who hates old-time dancing, possibly a woman with a fanatical hatred not only for dancing but for anyone who is any good at it.

Daily Mail 1954

He put the milk in your chocolate

THE man who put the milk in your chocolate died yesterday at the age of 76—George Cadbury of the famous chocolate firm.

He was on holiday in Switzerland 50 years ago and a cowherd to whom he was talking suggested that plain chocolate—which was the only chocolate known in this country — would be better with milk in.

Back home he tried it, liked it —and sold it with great success.

George Cadbury was the man, too, who suggested the advertisement which shows two hands pouring a glass-and-a-half of milk into a bar of chocolate.

Mr. Cadbury, who died at his Birmingham home, was a former managing director of Cadbury Bros. He retired in 1943.

His idea was on the hoardings, in the newspapers, on cinema screens.

Daily Herald 1954

Pipe down, please

This summer there have been too many vagrant bagpipers playing in Fort William, Invernesshire, streets—some "filthy and often half drunk." So the town council yesterday decreed that all must be licensed first by the burgh surveyor.

News Chronicle 1953

THE PILTDOWN MAN: A RECONSTRUCTION BY A. FORESTIER FROM "THE ILLUSTRATED LONDON NEWS" OF DECEMBER 28, 1912, SUPERVISED BY DR. (LATER SIR) A. SMITH WOODWARD.

IT was revealed on November 21 that as a result of investigations carried out in the Department of Geology at the British Museum (Natural History) and in the Department of Anatomy, Oxford, it had been established that, although the fragments of the cranium of Piltdown Man were genuine remains of primitive man, the mandible and canine tooth on which the ape-like appearance of Piltdown Man was based are deliberate fakes, and are those of a modern ape. The Museum Report states: "The faking of the mandible and canine is so extraordinarily skilful, and the perpetration of the hoax appears to have been so entirely unscrupulous and inexplicable, as to find no parallel in the history of palæontological discovery." The fluorine test, the nitrogen test and chemical analysis have all played their part in exposing the fraud.

Illustrated London News 1953

MP's attempt to renounce title fails

Wedgwood Benn Bill rejected by Peers

SIR WINSTON CHURCHILL wrote this month to Mr. Anthony Wedgwood Benn, Socialist MP for South-East Bristol, who wants to renounce his father's title so that he can remain in the House of Commons: "I am personally strongly in favour of sons having the right to renounce irrevocably the peerages they inherit from their fathers. . . ."

Nevertheless, after hearing this expression of opinion, read in the House of Lords last night by Lord Stansgate, Mr. Wedgwood Benn's father, the Peers refused by a 28 majority to give a Second Reading to the Wedgwood Benn (Renunciation) Bill.

Lord Stansgate told the House that in 1941, when the announcement that he was to be raised to the peerage appeared, his son, Anthony, now 30, was very angry, and "abused" him.

'Infringement of rights'

Viscount Samuel, the Liberal leader, who supported the Bill, said the present situation was an infringement of the rights of the individual. "A king may abdicate but a peer may not," he declared.

Lady Stansgate and Mr. Anthony Wedgwood Benn and his younger brother sat in the Special Visitors' Box as the debate proceeded.

Conservative and Socialist Peers also spoke in favour of the Bill, but the Lord Chancellor, Viscount Kilmuir, advising its rejection, said that while sympathising with the position of any young man who had given service in the House of Commons, the remedy must be general in character, and not, as in this case, of particular application.

Serious constitutional issue

A great and serious constitutional issue was involved. The acceptance of the principle that the heir to a peerage could renounce his eventual rights would effect a great constitutional change.

The Second Reading of this Private Member's Bill was moved by Lord Stansgate, who, speaking of his son, Anthony, said the death of his elder brother "heaped on the unwilling shoulders of this young man honours which were going to debar him all the ambitions of his life."

After the Lord Chancellor's advice to the House to reject the Bill, Lord Stansgate, greeeted with loud cheers, rose again, saying: "There is an injustice and because it is a right claim, a fair claim, and supported by powerful opinion both here and in the other House, I propose to carry the banner into the Lobby." He then pressed the Bill to a division.

Yorkshire Post 1955

GUILTY CHIMNEYS

"Smog" is the enemy. Here is the way battle must be joined, by each and every one of us. (*In Black and White. 16 mm. or 35 mm. Running time: 20 minutes.*) *Suitable for general showing, schools, institutions, factories, etc. On loan free to approved borrowers. Apply to your Gas Showrooms or send coupon below.*

Townswoman 1955

Harlem's 'Royal Family'

Billie Holiday arrives at London Airport. On left is her pianist, Carl Drinkard. On right, Taps Miller, who flew in on the same 'plane.

Melody Maker **1954**

'Good-bye' words were obscene—Russian wife did not know

THE Russian-born wife of an English colonel bid her guests good-bye after a bridge party " by using a term of the grossest possible obscenity," said Mr. Justice Collingwood in the Divorce Court yesterday.

But the judge said that the only possible conclusion was that the words, prompted by the husband, had been repeated by the wife with no knowledge of their implication.

He awarded a decree nisi on the ground of cruelty to 44-year-old Mrs. Marina Wilkinson, of Abercorn-place, St. John's Wood, N.W., and dismissed a cross-petition alleging cruelty by 60-year-old Colonel William Alexander Camac Wilkinson, D.S.O., M.C., O.M., of Storrington, Sussex.

Daily Mail **1954**

You May Like to Know . . .

that Mobile Trailers are touring Britain with an "Atoms for Peace" Exhibition. Staying approximately one week in each place, it will be in Nottingham from September 27th, Birmingham from October 7th, Cardiff from October 20th, Bristol from November 1st, and Southampton from November 11th. The Exhibition is presented by the United States Information Service in co-operation with the United Kingdom Atomic Energy Authority and is housed in five 21-ton trailers which are expandable into exhibition units. Its purpose is to explain graphically and simply the endless possibilities for improving the standard of life and tackling the problems of health through international co-operation and the pooling of atomic materials for constructive purposes.

that a Great Autumn Exhibition of Flower Arrangements will take place at the Royal Horticultural Society Hall on October 7th and 8th in aid of the Hospital Annexe of the Country Home of the Gardeners' Royal Benevolent Institution. Townswomen who are interested either in making or seeing unusual flower arrangements can get further information from Julia Clements, 132 Sloane Street, London, S.W.1, on application (enclosing a stamped addressed envelope).

that a Dairy Cookery Week, organised by the National Milk Publicity Council, will be held from October 24th–29th. Special cookery demonstrations, using milk and milk products, will be arranged by Gas and Electricity Boards in many parts of the country.

that the English Electric Company provide specialist speakers, within a 50-mile radius of London, in a variety of subjects, ranging from " X-Ray in Modern Medicine " and " The Development of Television," to " Kitchen Planning " and " From Soup to Nuts with a Mixer." They are also able to arrange special demonstrations in all domestic subjects at their model kitchen in London for groups up to fifty at one time. Further particulars from Patricia Hardie, Assistant Press Relations Officer, The English Electric Company Ltd., Marconi House, Strand, London, W.C.2.

WAS THIS MADE BY A SNOWMAN?
Footprint found at 14,000 ft

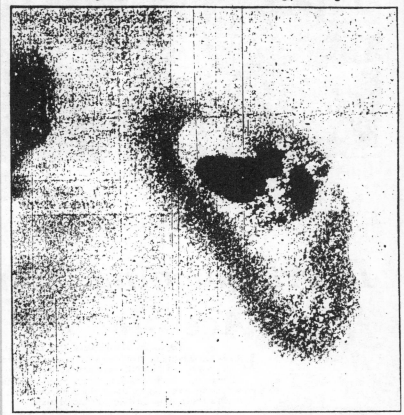

THIS is one of the footprints found by Mr. Charles Stonor, of the *Daily Mail* Himalaya Expedition, during the reconnaissance of the slopes below Everest which he reported last week.

In a patch of melting snow at 14,000ft. he came across a maze of such tracks each the size and shape of a human foot. Expressing his belief that these were genuine Abominable Snowman (or Yeti) tracks, Mr. Stonor said their average length was ten inches with a maximum breadth of five inches and the breadth across the heel three inches. He estimated that they had probably been enlarged by melting, perhaps by a third of their size.

By no possible chance could any Sherpa have been wandering about in these bleak heights in winter, and in any case the prints were too sharply outlined for the shapelessness of the invariable Sherpa boot.

Daily Mail **1954**

Townswoman **1955**

● Bannister, first man to beat the four-minute mile, breaks the tape. . . . There was electricity along that side-line. . . . He was fighting for breath, his head rolling with fatigue—but his stride was superb.

BANNISTER DOES IT
English victory beats world

Express Staff Reporter

THE dream of world athletes through the years was achieved yesterday by an Englishman — 25-year-old Roger Bannister, who became the first man on earth to run a mile in under four minutes.

His feat at Oxford last evening—against a 20-mile-an-hour cross-wind—was equal in dramatic achievement to the crashing of the sound barrier in the air.

Bannister's time, officially recorded, was 3MINS. 59.4SECS. —beating the record of Sweden's Gundar Haegg by 2secs.

Daily Express 1954

Heart-warming Scenes as Crowds Acclaim Sir Winston

By J. D. MARGACH, Our Political Correspondent

LATE last night, in response to repeated calls from the crowds in Downing Street, Sir Winston Churchill, appeared at a window of No. 10.

Eleven times the beaming figure raised his hand in the famous V-sign. The crowds sang "For he's a Jolly Good Fellow" . . . and thus, memorably, ended Sir Winston's last day as Britain's Prime Minister.

Sir Winston went to Buckingham Palace at 4.30 yesterday afternoon. Half-an-hour later came the official close of his historic Premiership, with this statement:

It is announced from Buckingham Palace that the Right Hon. Sir Winston Churchill had an audience of the Queen this evening and tendered his resignation as Prime Minister and First Lord of the Treasury, wh'ch her Majesty was graciously pleased to accept.

Thus the famous Churchill era ended.

Aberdeen Press and Journal 1955

RUTH ELLIS

A LAST-MINUTE plea to save Ruth Ellis from the gallows on Wednesday was made yesterday to Major Gwilym Lloyd-George, the Home Secretary.

He is spending an anxious weekend pondering, away from Whitehall officials' assistance, this plea and other petitions— 10,000 more signatures asking for a reprieve were delivered last evening.

The new appeal, sent to the Home Office by Ruth Ellis's solicitor, Mr. John Bickford, accompanied dramatic new information concerning her life.

It was this: She was a sick woman at the time she shot her lover, racing motorist David Blakely. She was a self-confessed alcoholic.

And only a few days before the shooting on Easter Sunday she was a mother-to-be. But a miscarriage intervened.

Ruth Ellis's insane drinking was a by-word in the Little Club, the fashionable bar on the fringes of Mayfair of which she was manageress. She was known often to drink a bottle of gin in two hours.

Mr. Vernon Charles, specialist head of a Hastings alcoholics' clinic, has sworn a statement concerning her alcoholic disease. It throws new light on her state of mind at the time of the killing.

Reynolds News 1955

Fabian News 1956

GAITSKELL REPLACES ATTLEE

FABIANS will wish to be associated in the expressions of respect and goodwill that C. R. Attlee has received on his retirement as leader of the Parliamentary Labour Party.

Mr. Attlee, who was then living in Stepney, joined the Society in 1907 and has an unbroken record of membership. In March 1920 his ' Metropolitan Borough Councils' was published as Tract 191 and throughout his later career he was willing to help the Society at all times. Less than six months ago he wrote the preface for Margaret Cole's pamphlet on the Webbs.

Fabians will also welcome **Hugh Gaitskell** as his successor.

Mr. Gaitskell joined the Society by way of the New Fabian Research Bureau to whose publications he had been a frequent contributor. He served on the Executive Committee in 1939-40 and again in 1952-53. In the last four years he has spoken at many Fabian functions and has written for the Society.

Broadstairs and St Peter's Mail 1955

KILLER GRABBED A TYPIST

Girl's dramatic story at Manston inquest

A MARGATE girl, 21-year-old Margaret Shirley Hull, employed as a typist-secretary at Manston air base, told a dramatic story of her encounter with a killer when she gave evidence at the inquest on the R.A.F. Corporal who was shot dead on August 24th.

Eye-witness evidence of the shooting was also given by a Ramsgate man, Mr. William Charles Emptage, of 16 Wilfred-road, who is employed at the base as a finance clerk.

At the inquest held in Ramsgate Courthouse on Friday, 26th August, the Coroner for East Kent (Mr. W. R. Mowll) and a jury heard how 22-year-old R.A.F. Police, Corporal Raymond Peter Grayer, of Clyde-road, Brighton, stationed at Manston, died almost instantly from three bullets —one in the middle of the back — when he was mown down by the rifle of the coloured American Airman Napoleon Green, who also shot and killed two others and wounded nine.

The nine-man jury returned a verdict of murder.

The Times 1955

CLEANER AIR

The EARL of MUNSTER, Minister without Portfolio, replying to a question by Viscount Thurso on the Government's plans for stimulating action on the Clean Air Bill, said it was the intention that the provisions relating to the establishment of smoke-controlled areas should become operative before the end of this year, and that the other provisions of the Act, which mainly affected industry, should come into operation early in 1958.

This accorded with the recommendation of the committee on air pollution and with the statements made in Parliament during the passage of the Bill. The interval was designed to allow time for any improvements or alterations to plant that might be necessary to enable industry to comply with the Act. The main stimulus for such improvements was provided by the requirements of the Act. The Government could not undertake to vary their present monetary policy, but the importance in the national interest, both of fuel economy and of measures to reduce air pollution, was recognized.

He understood that the Board of Trade were conducting an inquiry into the plans of industry for capital expenditure in 1957, but it was too early yet to assess the results of that inquiry.

Townswoman 1955

You May Like to Know

that it is possible to " adopt " one of the 250,000 people uprooted from their homelands who still live in camps in Germany, Austria and Trieste. The organisation known as "Aid to Displaced Persons " arranges a system by which anyone who wishes in a small measure to alleviate human misery is put in touch with an individual D.P. to whom she writes and sends perhaps an occasional parcel. Arrangements are made for the translation of letters. Since most of the D.P.s are too old or too sick to qualify for emigration, letters are of very great significance, since the recipients regard them as an indication that someone still cares for them as individuals. Further particulars may be obtained from Mrs. J. B. Duff, Hillwood Cottage, College Road, Woking, Surrey.

LOCH NESS MONSTER SEEN AGAIN

Good View from Above Dores

Inverness Courier 1955

On Wednesday evening, shortly after 9 o'clock, Mr A. M. Mackenzie, Inveran Farm, Invershin, and Mr J. Calder, Markinch, Fife, along with another eight people, witnessed an appearance of the Loch Ness Monster. Mr Mackenzie told a "Courier" reporter that on Wednesday evening, he and Mr Calder were motoring down from Torness to Dores, when they were stopped by an excited group of people, several hundred yards from the Loch side, and on the hill above Dores. The people were six holiday-makers from Fochabers, and Mr J. Brown and a friend, both from Inverness. Mr Mackenzie said that they were watching an object which was moving at about 25 m.p.h. along the surface of the loch, throwing up a large wash.

The object, which appeared to be about 25 feet to 30 feet in length, with a big head and one hump, was moving about in the middle of the loch.

Mr Mackenzie said that had it not been for its size, it might well have been a seal, because several times it dived below the surface of the water, each time re-appearing several yards along the loch. After watching from the hillside for about 15 minutes, Mr Mackenzie decided to go down to the side of the loch to get a better view, but when he and his friend arrived at the water's edge, the Monster had disappeaerd. appeared.

GAG ON RADIO TALKS IS TO STAY

By HUGH PILCHER

IN a free vote last night MPs approved by a 145 majority the rule which gags TV and radio from discussing political topics for 14 days before they are debated in Parliament.

But they agreed to an inquiry into the working of the gag and whether it should be reduced to one week.

Politics were pushed aside in the Commons for the debate. Instead MPs split into two new "parties."

On one side were stars of radio and TV (with their admirers). On the other, stars of Parliament (with their supporters).

Both declared passionately that free speech and democracy were in mortal danger—but for opposite reasons.

● The "Broadcasting Party" DENOUNCED the 14-day gag.

● The other side, led by a strangely assorted pair, Mr. Attlee and Dr. Charles Hill, the Postmaster-General, INSISTED that the rule must stay if the dignity and authority of Parliament were to be upheld.

Daily Herald 1955

DISGUSTED WITH SHOW BUSINESS—'I MAY QUIT'

By LAURENCE WILKINSON

AFTER twenty days of the Hughie Green case the jury took just 20 minutes yesterday to decide that his charges of bribery at the B.B.C. were baseless.

Then Hughie Green met his rival, Carroll Levis, outside the court. Green said a few words to Levis, who put his arm round his shoulder. Hughie Green then hurried away.

Said Levis : "Hughie Green said something very fine and wonderful ; it was the gesture of a sportsman and a gentleman."

Levis wiped his eyes with a handkerchief. His wife, Mrs. Mina Levis, who also had been a defendant, leaned her head against a wall and wept.

"This was her birthday ; she could have had no finer present than clearing her name of bribery and conspiracy," said her husband.

Judgment had been entered, with costs, estimated at £35,000, for Mr. Carroll Levis and seven other defendants. Mr. Green had alleged a conspiracy to keep his show "Opportunity Knocks" off the air in favour of the Carroll Levis "Discoveries" programme.

Daily Herald 1956

Daily Mail 1955

OH, WHAT A RUSH FOR THE B & K DINNER AT No. 10

A WHIRLWIND drive whisked Mr. Bulganin and Mr. Kruschev from cheering crowds at Claridge's to cheering crowds at Downing - street last night — IN THREE AND A HALF MINUTES.

Pedestrians leaped to safety as the 11-car convoy, flanked by 20 motor-cycle policemen, tore along at over 50 mph, tyres screeching at every corner.

The Russian leaders were whisked past the cheering crowds in Downing Street, and were inside No. 10 within seconds of their car pulling up.

They stayed for two and three-quarter hours at the dinner party given by Sir Anthony Eden. . . .

A party which Mr. Hugh Gaitskell described as "very gay and informal with no official talks."

Mr. Bulganin sat next to Earl Attlee, Mr. Kruschev next to Sir Winston Churchill, with Sir Anthony in the middle of the four.

First of the guests—who included Mr. Morrison and the TUC chairman Mr. Wilfred Beard—to leave was Sir Winston, who had been telling anecdotes of pre-Communist Russia.

Sir Alexander Korda dies suddenly

Dorset Daily Echo and Weymouth Dispatch 1956

SIR ALEXANDER KORDA, chairman of London Film Productions and one of the leading figures of the British film industry, died today. He was 62.

His death occurred suddenly at his home in Kensington Palace Gardens. He had appeared to be in normal health yesterday, although in the last six months he had felt tired.

Clean Air in Our Time
—Part for All to Play

By STANLEY CAYTON
Chief Public Health Inspector and Cleansing Superintendent, West Bromwich

THE Clean Air Act, 1956, is the achievement of a long and arduous campaign by many individuals, organisations and committees, spread over many years. The high cost of smoke to the community in terms of washing and cleaning, damage to buildings, structures, metals, textiles and paintwork, the shutting out of sunlight from our towns and the injury to the health of human beings has at last commanded the serious attention of Parliament. But the introduction of an Act of Parliament does not mean that the battle is over. It is not an end; it is only a beginning.

The greatest menace to the new Act is not its weakness in which the lawyers may revel, but the apathy of the public, of some local authorities and even of some officers. Only when the value of clean air has been successfully demonstrated throughout the length and breadth of the country will the cause receive adequate support. As the Beaver Committee on Air Pollution said: "Real improvement can be secured only by a continuous programme urgently and insistently carried out over a number of years," calling for a "combined effort by many different interests" and "continuous propaganda and education." In this great endeavour there is a part for everyone to play.

*Birmingham Post
1956*

Britain's Latest A-Explosion

View on 'Backyard Shelter Protection'

Britain's latest atomic weapon was exploded at Maralinga, South Australia, yesterday, leaving a mile-wide red scar across the vast desert.

The blast left a litter of iron sheets scattering the ground like confetti. Concentric rows of buildings suffered heavy damage—the nearest vanished and those further away were buckled and twisted out of shape.

Six supermarine Swift jet fighters within a mile of the centre were tossed over and over on the ground, and the high slim steel tower from which the weapon was detonated disappeared without trace.

Maj.-Gen. Ivan Dougherty, one of Australia's Civil Defence chiefs who watched the explosion, said atomic bombs had "definite limitations" as a weapon against civilians. "A backyard shelter with 3ft. of earth or concrete over it would protect a family from the effects of the blast, heat and direct radiation."

*Birmingham Post
1956*

WEEK-END BREAK-IN AT THIRSK CAFE

Rymer's Cafe, in Westgate, Thirsk, was entered over the week-end and about £12 was taken from the cash register.

It is thought that the thief or thieves obtained entry from the rear of the premises, which include a confectionery shop on the ground floor, and a cafe above.

The property is almost immediately opposite Thirsk Police Station.

Thirsk, Bedale and Northallerton Times 1957

Egypt Seizes the Suez Canal

Cairo Offices Sealed Off By Police

President Nasser announced last night that Egypt had framed a law nationalising the Suez Canal; it would become effective on publication in the official gazette. In Cairo last night Egyptian police cordoned off the administrative section of the Suez Canal building. Officials sealed off the main entrance to the offices with red wax.

The State-controlled Cairo Radio made the following announcement later last night: "The take-over of the Suez Canal installations was completed after it had become the nationalised Egyptian company."

Speaking in Alexandria, Nasser said that shareholders would be paid in accordance with the last closing prices at the Paris Bourse. All Suez Canal Co. funds in Egypt were now frozen, he said.

He added: "The Suez Canal is an exploiting company. We shall build the high dam by restoring our rights in the Suez Canal. We shall take the income from the Suez Canal —$100m. a year—and build the high dam."

Workers Retained

He said the Government had approved a law nationalising the company "in the name of the nation." The company would be transferred to the State with all its assets and commitments.

Article Four of the 'law nationalising the canal states: "The body shall keep all officials of the nationalised company, as well as its employees and workers, who shall continue the discharge of their duties. None of these may leave work or stop doing their duties for any reason whatsoever except with permission."

"The Suez Canal Company's annual income is £35m.," Nasser said. "At present Egypt takes a share of just over £1m. In five years we will be able to acquire £178m. after the nationalisation of the Suez Canal Company. We don't have to seek American and British aid for building the dam. We will build it ourselves and with our own money."

A senior official representing British interests in the Suez Canal Co. said in London last night: "The Egyptian Government has no right to take this step, because it is bound by an agreement until the middle of November, 1968. The company's lease has never been contested."

Sir Anthony Calls Midnight Talks

By a Diplomatic Correspondent

An urgent conference was called at Downing Street late last night to deal with the situation created by President Nasser. Sir Anthony Eden had an hour's talk with the three Chiefs of Staff. About midnight the French Ambassador called, accompanied by M. George Picquot, the director-general of the Suez Canal Co.

Mr. Selwyn Lloyd, the Foreign Secretary, Lord Kilmuir and Lord Salisbury arrived later and at 1.30 a.m. the conference was continuing.

Official reaction in London is that Nasser's coup is a reprisal for withdrawal of the offer to help in financing the Egyptian dam project.

Unjustified Action

Nasser has no legal right to expropriate the company whose operating rights are guaranteed. No Egyptian government has yet contested the company's legal status in Egypt—it is not subject to Egyptian law.

Nasser himself recognised the international status of the company in the Anglo-Egyptian Agreement of 1954. Both Powers pledging themselves to uphold the Convention.

However unconstitutional Nasser's action it does not seem likely that the Suez Canal Zone will be reoccupied by British troops, whose right to return exists only in meeting an imminent threat of war.

PREMIUM BONDS SALES IN MIDLANDS

Estimated at About £100,000

Reports from the main cities and towns of Great Britain indicate that, in general, there was no excessive demand for National Savings Premium Bonds when 20,000 Post Offices and 13,000 bank branches opened for business yesterday—the first day of the bonds offer. Sales figures were not available last night.

Post Office officials pointed out that as bonds bought this month will go into the first draw at the end of next May there was no need to buy early.

Some Merseyside dockers, when they drew their pay last night, stated that they were buying bonds on the way home—and were cutting down their pools investment.

For many buyers, no doubt, the great attraction was the chance of winning £1,000 by purchasing a £1 bond. The bond must be held for six months and there are smaller and more numerous prizes ranging down to £25.

*Birmingham Post
1956*

*Birmingham Post
1956*

BRITISH FORCES MASS TO REOCCUPY SUEZ

Dawn Action in Canal Defence

TROOP PLANES LEAVING CYPRUS

Swift Moves After Egypt Rejects Ultimatum

Mrs. Golda Meir, the Israeli Foreign Minister, to whom Gen. Burns, Chief of Staff of the United Nations Truce Organisation, delivered a protest yesterday. He asked for a cease-fire.

Birmingham Post
1956

Mr. Ben-Gurion, the Israeli Prime Minister.

EARLY to-day British and French forces in the Mediterranean were moving into key positions, awaiting an order to occupy bases in the Suez Canal area. This was the consequence of the rejection by Col. Nasser of an ultimatum from Britain and France to Israel and Egypt to stop fighting and withdraw their forces at least 10 miles from the canal.

The ultimatum expired at 4.30 a.m. to-day. Before dawn R.A.F. transport planes began taking off from Nicosia for a southerly destination. They left at regular intervals from an R.A.F. base packed with planes. French transport aircraft took off from Tymbou, near Nicosia.

The ultimatum, Sir Anthony Eden told the House of Commons, was decided upon " to separate the belligerents," to safeguard British nationals and secure free transit through the canal. The forces would be withdrawn as soon as present hostilities ceased. [Sir Anthony's statement to the Commons —Page 7.]

Cairo Radio, announcing rejection of the ultimatum, said that Col. Nasser summoned the British Ambassador to give him the news. He said that the ultimatum constituted " an attack on the rights and dignity of Egypt and a flagrant violation of the United Nations Charter." Nasser also reported his decision to the Soviet and American Governments.

Early to-day Israel accepted the Anglo-French ultimatum to stop fighting with Egypt and withdraw her forces " on condition that Egypt also agreed."

Katie said : Tell no one I'm dying

KATIE JOHNSON, stage and screen actress—she was the gentle old lady in the Alec Guinness Comedy " The Lady-killers" — has died at Elham, near Folkestone. She was 78.

Katie Johnson

Miss Johnson widow of Mr. Frank G. Bayly, the actor, went to Elham, where her son lives, about five weeks ago, and stayed in furnished rooms with a woman companion.

She asked that nobody should be told about her dying, and few people in the village even knew she was there. She died on Saturday and the funeral took place at Elham yesterday.

The vicar, the Rev. Isaac Williams, said: " She came here to die, and she didn't want anybody to know that she was here. I think I was the only person in the village apart from her relatives who knew who she really was."

For her part in " The Lady-killers " she was voted the best British actress of 1955.

News Chronicle 1957

Retford, Worksop, Isle of Axholme and Gainsborough News 1957

Travel Talk To Gringley W.I.

A much-travelled young Gringley man, Dr. R. Asher, B.A., Ph.D., gave an illustrated talk on his visits to India, Ceylon and Singapore, at Gringley W.I.'s monthly meeting.

He told vivid stories of the Orient, its people and its customs.

Mrs. Thomson, president, was in the chair.

The thanks of the Institute were accorded to the speaker by Mrs. S. Firth.

Mrs. Walpole, of Laneham, catered for the W.I. party held last month. The tables presented a most attractive appearance with new W.I. crockery. The president gave a birthday cake and members enjoyed whist and a beetle drive. An entertainment was given by Mrs. K. Ball and helpers.

Chichester and Southdown Observer 1957

HOW THE BODY WAS FOUND

WHEN 40-year-old Mr. John Randall, of Snow Goose, Cutmill, Bosham, set out on an innocent fishing trip with brothers Ted and Bill Gilby on Sunday, he revived a 14-month-old international mystery.

Floating 250 yards off Pilsey Island they found a headless body in a close-fitting rubber suit and flippers.

Soon the world was asking: " Is this the body of ex-Naval frogman Commander Crabb?"

At the time of the discovery Mr. Randall had a hunch it was Commander Crabb. So he acted accordingly.

TIED ALONGSIDE

" We tied the body alongside the dinghy," he said. " Then Ted and Bill rowed it carefully ashore. We didn't pick it up.

" We put an anchor-rope on it and took it to the edge of the beach, still floating, putting the anchor on the beach. As the tide receded the body dried out, and by the time the R.A.F. and police came by launch and helicopter it was high and dry on the beach."

Mr. Randall said that he left a message for the R.A.F. at Thorney and then went off in his six-ton trawler, Red Goose, to try his hand for the prime fish off the Pilsey sands.

When he got home at nine o'clock that evening he was besieged by Press and television men.

Mr. Randall has a retail fur business in Portsmouth near the Sallyport Hotel, where Commander Crabb stayed the day before he disappeared.

" I saw him in the hotel on several occasions," he said.

Telling the story of the dramatic find, Mr. Randall explained that they went out to get a few lobsters and then some sole and skate, intending to experiment with his new invisible net.

" We stopped the engine to start fishing," he continued, " and then somebody said: ' What's that?'

" At first we thought it was a buoy or log of wood, and then, when we saw the rubber, we thought it was a tractor tyre. I got on the engine casing and said: ' It is a tractor tyre and you can see the two treads.'

" Then Ted Gilby said: ' It's a body.' I thought it might have been an empty suit, but we felt it was firm and heavy."

BRITAIN NEVER SO WELL OFF—Premier

Warning that Inflation Could Throw Away All Gains

'CLEAR DUTY' ON PENSIONS

By JAMES MARGACH, Political Correspondent of The Sunday Times

BRITAIN'S economic prospects are good and the country has never known such prosperity in its history, declared the Prime Minister in a buoyant, optimistic speech at Bedford last night on the state of the nation. "Let's be frank about it—most of our people have never had it so good," he said. There is no sudden crisis, he emphasised.

Sunday Times 1957

But while expressing healthy confidence that inflation would be conquered by rising activity, high investment and high savings, he warned his audience that the only answer to what he called the "64,000 dollar question" was increased production.

Wages had risen far beyond prices, by 40 per cent. against 20 per cent. over the past six years. "The great mass of the country has, for the time being at any rate, been able to contract out of the effects of inflation."

He then delivered this straight - from - the - shoulder warning: "They will not be able to contract out forever if inflation prices us out of world markets, for if that happens we will be back in the old nightmare of unemployment. What folly to risk throwing way all that we have gained!"

HUGE ARMADA AT SPITHEAD

Portsmouth Will Be Host To 10,000

ACTIVITIES reminiscent of wartime fleet manoeuvres were evident in Portsmouth Harbour and at Spithead today as warships from many countries arrived to complete the big assembly of NATO forces at the end of the autumn exercises.

Throughout the week-end warships of the United Kingdom, from Canada, the United States, France, Belgium, and Federal Germany have been berthing, to give Dockyard pilots their busiest time since the Coronation Review in 1953.

Because of the various stations they were holding when the exercise ended, the ships arrived at Portsmouth at unexpected times, completely altering the pre-arranged plans for berthing, writes our Naval Correspondent.

But the biggest units — those of the United States Fleet — arrived today according to plan, and by 11 a.m. Spithead was crowded with warships.

Present were the giant American carrier Saratoga, the American cruiser Northampton (both wearing admiral's flags), the British carrier Ark Royal (going to Southampton tomorrow), the Royal Navy's guided-missile ship Girdle Ness (whose ship's company is seriously hit by the influenza epidemic), and the cruiser Sheffield.

Saratoga's sister ship Forrestal is expected at Spithead later in the day, and will proceed to Southampton. The British aircraft-carrier Albion is due shortly after 4 p.m., and will enter harbour before evening.

Completing the assembly in Portsmouth Dockyard is the British aircraft-carrier Victorious, which was moved on Saturday into tidal waters for the first time in seven years. She is nearing the end of her big reconstruction.

Portsmouth Evening News 1957

SAUCERS MAY HAVE BEEN WAR BALLOONS

A NEW theory on flying saucers came to-day from Mr. Alec Niblic, who described to Belfast Rotary Club some of his experiences as a "back-room boy" in the Royal Navy during the last war.

"Barrage balloons sent up during the war could have stayed up for quite a while and they could have been taken for flying saucers by people who claimed to have seen strange objects in the sky a couple of years ago," he said.

Belfast Telegraph 1958

The Wolfenden Report

PORTSMOUTH has a particular interest in the controversy which is bound to follow publication of the Sir John Wolfenden committee recommendations. Where a port has also a large Service population, it is bound to become tainted by the immoral behaviour of both men and women, and the fact that Portsmouth is no exception is shown by the conviction figures. In the list dealing only with males, the City is third, being exceeded by London and Birmingham. Taking total populations into account, it indicates a disturbing number of offenders. On the other hand, it also shows a high degree of police vigilance in securing such a large number of convictions.

There are no statistics which could show the number of male offenders in each town, and the percentage brought to the courts, but it would be reasonable to expect that, if such figures were available, Portsmouth would appear in a favourable light. Behaviour is nothing like so blatant as in London, and it is usually found in two or three notorious areas. This makes it less of an affront to public decency, and easier for the police to exercise supervision. The only occasion when most decent - minded citizens are ever able to notice vice at its worst is during a big influx of visiting naval personnel. It is apparent, when this occurs, that London must be left looking a little less iniquitous.

Though there is little likelihood of an early Cabinet decision on the Wolfenden report, the next session of Parliament is expected to include a big Commons debate, and a major clash is probable over the proposal that immoral behaviour between consenting males over the age of 21 should no longer be a criminal offence. The report puts forward the thesis that it is not the function of criminal law to try to regulate private morals, and that there is an important distinction between crime and sin. This part of the debate will be of special interest to those dealing with Portsmouth vice, because many of the cases here fall into this category, though they would still lead to prosecutions if the offences were in public places. There will be many with doubts about the wisdom of allowing this recommendation to become law, and even those in favour might regard 21 as too young an age to be outside the control of the police. It will certainly be necessary to have special safeguards in the Services, as a protection for those of inferior rank, whatever the age.

Portsmouth Evening News 1957

False Beards and Moustaches

MR. GERALD NABARRO (Con., Kidderminster), who has a bigger moustache than any other MP, asked the Chancellor of the Exchequer in the House of Commons last week whether he was aware that false beards and moustaches were liable to 30 per cent. purchase tax, whereas if each hair was separately shaped and threaded to a backing designed to be gummed to the face, they were tax free.

MP Gerald Nabarro

He also wanted to know how much tax had been collected on false beards and moustaches in the last few years.

This is part of a campaign which Mr. Nabarro has kept up for months. The week before he wanted to know why tweezers under 4½ in. long and nail nippers 3½ in. were taxed at 90 per cent., but the same articles in larger sizes were tax free.

Hairdresser's Journal 1958

THIRD-TIME ESCAPE ROUTE

PRISONERS CLIMBED THIS WALL

CAR WAS WAITING HERE

NEWS CHRONICLE REPORTER

ALFRED HINDS is free again. He made his third getaway yesterday, from Chelmsford jail, Essex. The escape, like the other two, had been carefully planned with outside help.

This was obvious to police last night from the evidence of Mrs. Margaret Whigham. She saw it all from Trinity Road School, which adjoins the jail. Mrs. Whigham's husband is the school caretaker.

"I saw two men silhouetted against the sky on the prison wall," she said. "Then they jumped down into a clump of weeds and ran across the school playground to a light green Morris Minor

News Chronicle 1958

"There was a man in the driving seat, and the car shot off.

"*I couldn't get the car's number, but I saw the two men start to take off their prison clothes as soon as they got in*"

Punch 1959

Hoffnung

Gerard Hoffnung, who died last week at the tragically early age of thirty-four, first appeared in *Punch* in 1952 with a drawing about a lovesick trombonist. From then on he contributed often, usually on musical subjects, though not infrequently with elephants, which had the same fascination for him as his beloved tuba. He was a fully-integrated humorist, who found fun in everything and was the greatest fun himself, though he could be passionately serious about the burning questions of the day. His style was highly personal; it had no obvious antecedents and leaves no descendents. Hoffnung was Hoffnung, unique and irreplaceable.

Barnet Press 1959

THE NORTHERN LINE

SIR.—At approximately 6 p.m. on Monday, I, with many other would-be Barnet travellers, waited at Tottenham Court Road for a Barnet train We waited and waited. The following sequence of trains arrived :

(1) Edgware. (2) Edgware. (3) Edgware. (4) Barnet. (5) Mill Hill. (6) Edgware. (7) Barnet. (8) Colindale. (9) Edgware. (10) Mill Hill. (11) .dgware.

The Barnet trains were so overcrowded that it was impossible for most passengers to board them Were it not for the fact that in the utter confusion the train labelled for Mill Hill eventually found itself at Barnet, many of us would have been waiting still It was touch and go, however, for while one Finchley porter was announcing that the train would go to Barnet, a second was exhorting passengers to 'All change.' as its destination was Mill Hill.

Is it any wonder that exasperated Barnet travellers are forced to indulge in sit-down strikes " Heaven knows London Transport are providing more than sufficient provocation.

Surely the time has arrived for the train service from the West End to Barnet to be the subject of a top-level inquiry Two Barnet trains out of 11 is not by any stretch of the imagination a fair or intelligent allocation of rolling stock. No doubt London Transport will say that conditions on Monday were exceptional. Unfortunately the exception is too often the rule on the West End section of the Northern Line Again and again two Edgware trains are followed by a Mill Hill or Colindale with yet another Edgware before a Barnet train arrives in front of the packed platform

I hope Barnet Council and interested local organisations will press London Transport for an immediate and independent investigation of services allocated to Barnet travellers. I stress " independent " because the sit-down strikes are a clear indication that the situation is becoming far too serious for yet another bucket of London Transport whitewash

JAMES REEDY.
24. Coppice Walk.
Totteridge. N 20.

The last Presentations

At Buckingham Palace last week three historic functions were held. In future years debutantes will only be presented to the Queen if they are invited to one of the Garden Parties. On this page are some of the girls who attended the last of the Presentation Parties

Miss Dominic Riley-Smith
Daughter of Mr. and Mrs. Douglas Riley-Smith, of Loxwood, Sussex, she was chosen recently by couturier Pierre Chardin to model his designs at the Berkeley Debutante Dress show to be held in April to aid the N.S.P.C.C.

Miss Teresa Hayter
Only daughter of Sir William Hayter, the diplomat, and Lady Hayter. Miss Hayter was born in China, and has travelled extensively. She will go to Oxford in October to Lady Margaret Hall, and will study modern Russian

Tatler 1958

TOMMY STEELE KNOCKED OUT

Mobbed on stage by teen-agers

STEWARDS FIGHT TO SAVE STAR FROM GIRLS

Shirt ripped and hair torn out

Tommy Steele was almost torn apart by young fans in amazing scenes at Dundee Caird Hall last night.

He was mobbed and collapsed, unconscious. The scene happened at 10.45 p.m.

With two choruses to go in "Mabeline," a song written by Tommy himself, he let out an enthusiastic "Oh yeah," and fans, mostly girls, who had been flooding down on to the stage from the capacity audience, took that as a signal for the end.

Three hundred girls, mostly teenagers, and a few youths caught the strong body of stewards off guard and mobbed the stage.

They poured down the aisles, over the footlights, and down from the organ gallery.

A centre entrance to the stage had been brought back into use for the first time for several years as an additional security measure.

Fans jumped, in some cases 10 feet, from the organ gallery into the passage, and cut off Tommy's escape.

Tommy was submerged in a sea of screaming girls. He stood bemused for a moment, and appeared to attempt to reason with them.

But it was no use! Manager Larry Parnes took control and fought his way to Tommy's side. He pushed aside the fans and tried to force his way through the doorway.

Tommy's right arm had been twisted up his back, his shirt ripped from his back, and hair was pulled from his head by his admirers.

In agony

The battle for Tommy between the mob and the stewards lasted several minutes. His manager at one stage struck out at the fans as Tommy pleaded, "Let me go," and screamed in agony.

He was pulled almost unconscious to the door leading backstage and collapsed in the passage.

As he fell to the floor, the crowd was held back, and

stewards and a "Courier" reporter carried him unconscious, his guitar still hanging from his neck, to the dressing-room.

He was laid on the floor. His manager rushed for a cup of water for him while the guitar was tenderly removed and Tommy was made comfortable.

Mr Charles M. Macdonald, city factor, in charge of backstage security, cleared the dressing-room of all but Tommy's team.

Doctor called

A doctor and an ambulance were sent for but the doctor was not required. The ambulance men treated Tommy, who had by this time regained consciousness, for an injured shoulder.

Meanwhile, as soon as Tommy had been carried from the battleground, all the doors leading to the hall itself had been locked and chocks knocked in at the bottom to stop them being forced open.

Another "Courier" reporter out front watched as the crowd began to fight with stewards.

For several minutes the struggle continued, and one girl fainted and had to be carried outside the hall.

Hall in darkness

The battle on stage ended when someone momentarily plunged the hall into darkness. After this the audience, with a few exceptions, began to file out of the hall.

Several small bands hung about chanting "We want Tommy," but they were dispersed.

One steward said, "I have never experienced anything like that. I thought he was going to be killed."

After the hall had been cleared

Dundee Courier and Advertiser
1958

The semi-conscious Tommy Steele is carried to his car by two policemen.

Two girls in the audience express their rapture with a "hand jive."

COCO THE CLOWN HURT IN ROAD CRASH

The leading clown of the Bertram Mills Circus, Coco (Nicolai Polaikov), suffered a suspected spinal injury and a broken nose and other facial injuries in a road accident at the weekend between Perth and Dundee.

The Times **1959**

MARGOT FONTEYN IN NEW YORK

Refusal to Talk of Events in Panama

Dame Margot Fonteyn, who was released from detention in Panama early yesterday, arrived in New York by air last night and refused to answer questions on a reported anti-Government plot in Panama or the present whereabouts of her husband, Dr Roberto Arias. She said she hoped to spend a day or two in New York before leaving for London.

Dame Margot spent two nights in prison in Panama City on suspicion of being involved in the alleged plot.

The British Ambassador in Panama, Sir Ian Henderson, and the First Secretary, Mr Robert Farquharson, were kept waiting nearly four hours on Tuesday for a call from the prison to collect Dame Margot and take her to the British Embassy for the night. Then early yesterday Mr Farquharson was suddenly asked to pick up her bags from the hotel where she had been staying and take them to the airport.

Dame Margot was already on the aircraft when Mr Farquharson arrived with her luggage. She insisted that she was leaving Panama at her own request. This is also what British Embassy officials were told by Panamanian officials.

In London, however, the Panamanian Ambassador, Senor Don Carlos Fernando Alfaro, said that he had been officially informed that Dame Margot had been requested to leave Panama after proper investigation of charges laid against her. The charges were not specified.

Glasgow Herald
1959

A HISTORIC OCCASION
THE FIRST OF THE
LIFE PEERESSES

Illustrated London News 1958

With intelligent folk —
it's save *and* smoke

MINORS

20 for 2/8
PLAIN OR CORK TIPPED

Issued by
GODFREY PHILLIPS LTD

TWO BRITISH PROTESTS TO ICELAND

Reckless Shooting by Ship

The Government yesterday protested in the strongest terms to the Icelandic Government about methods which Icelandic coastguard ships are adopting against British trawlers on the high seas near Iceland.

Two Notes were delivered to the Icelandic Government by Mr Summerhayes, the British Chargé d'Affaires in Reykjavik.

The first Note said that during the night of April 30 the trawler Arctic Viking was intercepted by the Icelandic coastguard ship Thor. In attempting to arrest the British ship, the Thor fired a number of live shells, the nearest of which was stated by the skipper of the Arctic Viking to have fallen extremely close to his ship and tried to board the trawler.

"The Government protest emphatically at this reckless shooting by the Icelandic coastguard ship directed towards an unarmed British trawler, and note with concern the tendency for Icelandic coastguard vessels to employ increasingly violent and provocative methods in attempts to interfere with the legitimate activities of British trawlers on the high seas."

In the second Note the Government draw attention "to a further instance of the dangers and unseamanlike methods employed recently by the Icelandic coastguard service on the high seas."

"The Icelandic coastguard ship Maria Julia repeatedly executed dangerous manoeuvres in attempts to obstruct British trawlers while on the high seas." The tactics were provocative and went beyond any measures necessary for obtaining identification of the ships concerned.

On one occasion the Maria Julia's manoeuvres nearly caused a collision with the British naval ship H.M.S. Contest, which was said in Iceland to be responsible for the danger. This was contrary to the facts.

"The Government express their serious concern at such incidents, which constitute a danger to the safety of both Icelandic and British crews and ships, and strongly urge that the Icelandic coastguard ships be instructed to observe the internationally recognised rules of conduct on the high seas."

Glasgow Herald
1959

AN ARREST IS MADE (LEFT) DURING THE RIOTING BETWEEN COLOURED AND WHITE PEOPLE WHICH TOOK PLACE IN NOTTING HILL, LONDON, ON SEPTEMBER 1.

Illustrated London News
1958

TWO CHARGED UNDER VICE ACT

POLICE REPORT CLEAR WEST END STREETS

Two women were arrested in London at the weekend and charged with soliciting for the purposes of prostitution, "being known prostitutes," under the Street Offences Act, 1959, which came into force a minute after midnight on Saturday. One of the arrests was made at 11 minutes past midnight.

The police reported a "very quiet weekend." Few women who could obviously be taken for prostitutes were to be seen in Piccadilly, Park Lane, Curzon Street and other places in the West End of London where in recent years their presence has become a nuisance both to residents and passers-by.

A spokesman for the West End police said that so far the Act was having the desired effect of driving such women off the streets. He added that it was early to say whether this was only a temporary effect and in any event the weekend was not a good time to judge what was likely to happen, as many of the women on Saturdays and Sundays were not to be found in their usual haunts.

Normally, at West End Central police station some 20 prostitutes are charged on Saturday and Sunday nights.

The Times **1959**

SIR STANLEY SPENCER

A CONTROVERSIAL FIGURE IN ART

DAILY TELEGRAPH REPORTER

SIR STANLEY SPENCER, who has died aged 68, was the centre of controversy in the artistic world for many years. Many of his paintings on religious themes were among the best known of our times.

Born at Cookham, Berks, in 1891, he was the seventh son of a professor of music. He studied at the Slade School of Art. His painting of the "Resurrection," exhibited at the 1950 Royal Academy, began a fierce controversy.

In the same year he made his peace with the Academy after a 15-year quarrel. He had resigned as an A.R.A. in 1935 after two of his pictures had been rejected. But in his later years few questioned the authenticity of his insight. He was knighted last June.

Daily Telegraph **1959**

KILLED INSTANTANEOUSLY ON GUILDFORD BY-PASS
Road Surface 'Treacherous After Rain'

MIKE HAWTHORN, the fearless young Farnham man who diced with death on race circuits to become Britain's first world motor racing champion, was killed when his powerful 3.4 litre dark green Jaguar sports car crashed on the Guildford By-Pass on Thursday on his way to a lunch appointment in London.

Hawthorn gave up racing only seven weeks ago because it was 'too dangerous.' Yet he died on the wide asphalt covered by-pass about 200 yards on the Guildford side of Coombs Service Station. His death was the greatest tragedy that has as yet occurred on the By-Pass.

The news of Hawthorn's death flashed through the town and people were stunned when they heard of the tragedy. Within an hour of the crash, which happened at about 11.45 a.m. calls were coming into the 'Surrey Times' newsroom from people asking if the story was true.

People halted to look at the newsbills proclaiming 'Mike Hawthorn killed in Guildford crash,' and fumbled quickly for the money to buy a paper. Rapidly newspapers containing the barest details were sold out.

On the buses, in cafes, on street corners, everywhere, people were saying unbelievingly, Mike Hawthorn is dead.

This popular, fair-haired, 6ft young sportsman was known and liked by innumerable people locally, as it was only a few years ago that he was an apprentice at Dennis Bros. Ltd.

The inquest will be held at Guildford on Monday afternoon.

Surrey Times and Weekly Press
1959

Meet The Election Candidates
The Parties Have Chosen Their Contestants

Mrs. Margaret Thatcher, Conservative Candidate, seen here with her twins, Mark and Carol, and her husband, Mr. Denis Thatcher.

Ivan Spence, barrister, Liberal Candidate

Eric Deakins, aged 26, Labour Candidate

The Conservative

Mrs. Margaret Thatcher, who is in her early thirties, is a barrister, a qualified research chemist — but now prefers to entitle herself "housewife". The mother of twins, a boy and a girl born in August, 1953, Mrs. Thatcher began her education at a Council school and won her way to Somerville College, Oxford, emerging as a Master of Arts and Bachelor of Science.

Until her marriage to Major Denis Thatcher in 1951, Mrs. Thatcher was a research chemist in the plastics industry. She gave this up and continued to study, and less than a year after the twins arrival, was "called to the Bar" and found herself qualified as a Barrister-at-Law. This profession she practised from Kings Bench Walk, Temple.

From early political affiliations to Conservatism, her work for the cause found outlet while a student at Oxford, and she had the distinction of being elected President of the Oxford University Conservative Association in 1946. Steadily gaining political experience, Mrs. Thatcher worked as an active officer of the University Association, canvassed during the 1945 General Election and spoke at many branches, and going to her home district, the Grantham area, to speak for the candidate there.

Her platform speaking ability which has since brought national recognition continued to gain strength and command over the intervening years, and led to her adoption — twice — in Dartford, Kent, where she reduced a Socialist majority by 8,000 votes.

Mrs. Thatcher's selection from a long list of applicants for the Finchley candidacy, when Sir John Crowder's retirement was announced, caused a surprise in Tory ranks no less than in the rest of the constituency. The Conservative selectors claimed a major triumph when, at an introductory meeting her off-the-cuff speech to the assembled Conservatives — a meeting containing not a few critics — won them over, and they publicly stated their satisfaction at the choice. Since then, Mrs. Thatcher has pursued an intense "meet the people" personal campaign.

Finchley Press 1959

DR. FISHER SPENDS AN HOUR WITH THE POPE

EXCHANGES MARKED BY "HAPPY SPIRIT OF CORDIALITY"

From Our Own Correspondent

ROME, Dec. 2

The Archbishop of Canterbury, Dr. Fisher, spent more than an hour with the Pope today in the Pontiff's private library. Their conversation is stated from both sides to have been marked by a spirit of cordiality. The Archbishop said later that the whole interview was "as friendly, and natural and sympathetic as possible".

The meeting was notably longer than the usual courtesy visits at the Vatican, but as this was the first meeting of an Archbishop of Canterbury and a Pope since the Reformation precedents provide little help.

ARRIVED EARLY

Dr. Fisher arrived at the Arch of Bells, by St. Peter's, about a quarter of an hour earlier than expected; this is said to have been because traffic was light. He was received almost immediately on reaching the Papal apartments.

The Archbishop was able to give his Holiness, according to a Church of England statement later, some of the impressions he had gained from his recent visits to Jerusalem and Istanbul, which were of special interest to his Holiness, in view of the fact that, as Apostolic Delegate at Istanbul for 10 years, he had close personal experience of the religious situation in the east.

His Holiness expressed to the Archbishop, the statement continued, his great desire—as he did on many other occasions—to increase brotherly feelings among all men, and especially among all Christians; and the Archbishop confirmed from his own knowledge and experience how keen and widespread was the desire in many Churches to act for the same purpose.

Death of woman who worked with Charlie Chaplin

Mrs. Lily Maria Craig died at the age of 80 at St. Barnabas Hospital, Thetford, on Tuesday. She was the mother of Mr. H. G. W. Craig, of 7, Saxon Place, Thetford, and had been at St. Barnabas' for three years. Previous to that she was in a London hospital.

Mrs. Craig started her life as a circus artist and became an acrobatic dancer. Her husband and Sid Chaplin were the people who talked Sid's brother, the famous comedian Charlie Chaplin, into a stage career and Mrs. Craig worked with Charlie Chaplin in his first show. She spent all her life in show business and had been a widow for over 30 years. She leaves a stepdaughter and son. The funeral takes place today.

Thetford and Watton Times **1960**

The Times **1960**

BRITISH MAGAZINE TO BE PUBLISHED IN RUSSIA
New cultural agreement signed

MOSCOW, Monday.—Britain will be allowed to publish a Russian-language quarterly magazine in Russia as a result of talks between officials who signed a new cultural agreement to-day. But British newspapers and magazines will not be sold on Moscow bookstalls, and Russia will not stop jamming B.B.C. programmes until they cease offending Soviet views.

The agreement provides for increased exchanges and contacts in science, technology, education, and culture.

A separate agreement on the sale of the magazine—" Angliya"—is expected to be signed in a few days, but the magazine is not expected to appear for six months. The title, in Russian, means the United Kingdom.

Mr Georgi Zhukov, chairman of the Soviet state committee for cultural relations with foreign countries, signed for Russia, and Mr Joseph Godber, Parliamentary Under Secretary for Foreign Affairs, signed for Britain. The new agreement, which extends to the first quarter of 1963, replaces the present one which expires next April 1.

MUSIC FESTIVALS

The agreement, which refers to the importance of easing tourist restrictions and promoting athletic contacts, makes the following specific points:—

Britain's Royal Ballet and National Youth Orchestra will visit the Soviet Union this year and a festival of British music will be staged in Moscow Leningrad's Kirov Ballet and the Ukrainian Folk Dance Ensemble will make British tours lasting a month, and a Soviet music festival will be held in London in the second year of the agreement.

Both Governments will encourage special showings of each other's films, and there may be exchanges of photographic exhibitions. Delegations of the British and Soviet film industries will exchange visits.

The Scotsman **1961**

Grandpa joins in

NOW a 72-year-old grandfather plans to do the John O'Groat's Land's End walk—*on a diet of raw eggs and warm bullock's blood.*

Says ex - hairdresser William Tulley, of Portsmouth: "If Dr. Moore can walk a thousand miles on fruit juice, I can do it on bullock's blood."

Five-foot tall Mr. Tulley is entering the £5,500 Billy Butlin prize walk, which starts on February 27.

He says his eggs-and-blood diet saved his life when he had tuberculosis fifty years ago.

"It's the best thing there is to build you up," he said at his Walden-road home yesterday after a five-mile training walk.

"My only problem is whether I shall be able to get supplies of blood during the walk."

Sunday Graphic **1960**

Lawrence book summons

An application for a summons against Penguin Books Ltd. under the Obscene Publications Act was granted at Bow Street, London, to-day by Mr R. H. Blundell, the Chief Metropolitan Magistrate.

The application was made by Mr C. Leaf, for the Director of Public Prosecutions, in respect of an unexpurgated version of D. H. Lawrence's book "Lady Chatterley's Lover."

Penguin Books Ltd. stated later they would elect for the case to be tried by jury.

Penguin Books announced on Wednesday that they were postponing publication of the book, in view of "anticipated legal action."

Edinburgh Evening Dispatch **1960**

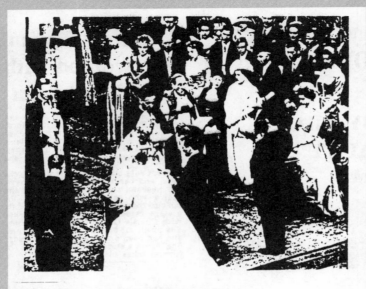

THE CEREMONY

The guest list for the Abbey reached further outside court circles than for any previous royal wedding, and the TV cameras made the audience nation-wide. Also present were the Commonwealth Prime Ministers (in London for their conference). On her way out after the service Princess Margaret paused (*below*) on her husband's arm to drop a pretty curtsy to the Queen

Tatler 1960

BBC broke rule and asked him

BY IAN WOOLDRIDGE

THE B.B.C.'s "This Is Your Life" team planned its biggest surprise for the programme tomorrow week.

They hoped you would switch on and meet ... Danny Blanchflower.

It was 12 weeks ago that 35 - year - old Blanchflower, captain of Tottenham Hotspur, turned from their cameras after being lured to a TV studio.

His action brought a barrage of criticism against the prying eye of *This is Your Life*. But the B.B.C. didn't give up. They went back to Blanchflower last week and *asked* him to appear.

Rule broken

It was the first time in the six-year history of the programme that producer Leslie Jackson had broken his secrecy rule. Nobody has ever been *asked* to appear.

Jackson told me : " It would have been a wonderful scoop if we could have pulled it off. It would have been screened two days after he captained Spurs in the Cup Final.

" But I would ask you to point out that I have never done this kind of thing before. When Stanley Matthews discovered we were doing his life, for example, we cancelled the programme and brought him on months later."

But Blanchflower's life is to remain private.

The Irishman who was yesterday elected · England's Footballer of the Year has turned his back on the B.B.C. for the second time in three months.

Sunday Dispatch 1961

MR. GAITSKELL WINS BY 85 VOTES

◆

DEPUTY LEADERSHIP STILL IN DOUBT

LEFT WING CHALLENGE IN COMMONS

From Our Political Correspondent

The Times 1960

Mr. Gaitskell is Labour leader still. He made it much as expected. When the result of the ballot in the parliamentary party was announced last night it was found that he had beaten Mr. Harold Wilson by 166 votes to 81—a majority of 85 votes. In all, 247 Labour M.P.s out of a possible total of 254 had cast a vote. It is said that at the private meeting in the House of Commons where the figures were made known Mr. Gaitskell's supporters cheered him for a full minute.

The deputy leadership is still in doubt. Mr. George Brown, the most favoured candidate, needed 129 votes to get the necessary clear majority over his two opponents. He polled 118 votes. Mr. Fred Lee was runner-up with 73 votes, and Mr. James Callaghan got 55 votes.

NOBODY can be more delighted about Princess Margaret's engagement than the other Joneses. For now, once and for all, an honourable name will be restored to its former dignity; and will take its place with Bowes-Lyon, Lascelles, Carnegie and the rest. It may seem presumptuous of me to compare plain Jones with the noble houses of Strathmore and Harewood. I am not trying to say, as one of our maids in Ireland once said, that Jones is an uncommon name. But I hope to prove that Jones is a better name than Smith, which has already gained a foothold in the Royal Family.

Tatler 1960

The Forgotten Prisoners

ON BOTH SIDES of the Iron Curtain, thousands of men and women are being held in gaol without trial because their political or religious views differ from those of their Governments. Peter Benenson, a London lawyer, conceived the idea of a world campaign, APPEAL FOR AMNESTY, 1961, to urge Governments to release these people or at least give them a fair trial. The campaign opens to-day, and "The Observer" is glad to offer it a platform.

OPEN your newspaper any day of the week and you will find a report from somewhere in the world of someone being imprisoned, tortured or executed because his opinions or religion are unacceptable to his government. There are several million such people in prison—by no means all of them behind the Iron and Bamboo Curtains—and their numbers are growing. The newspaper reader feels a sickening sense of impotence. Yet if these feelings of disgust all over the world could be united into common action, something effective could be done.

In 1945 the founder members of the United Nations approved the Universal Declaration of Human Rights : —

Article 18.—Everyone has the right to freedom of thought, conscience and religion ; this right includes freedom to change his religion or belief, and freedom either alone or in company with others in public or private, to manifest his religion or belief in teaching, practice, worship and observance.

Article 19.—Everyone has the right to freedom of opinion and expression ; this right includes freedom to hold opinions without interference and to seek, receive and impart information and ideas through any media and regardless of frontiers.

There is at present no sure way of finding out how many countries permit their citizens to enjoy these two fundamental freedoms. What matters is not the rights that exist on paper in the Constitution, but whether they can be exercised and enforced in practice. No government, for instance, is at greater pains to emphasise its constitutional guarantees than the Spanish, but it fails to apply them.

Observer **1961**

SPOKESMAN AT RUSSIAN EMBASSY

A SOUTH NORWOOD woman, Mrs. Margaret O'Connell, who recently served a month's imprisonment for ban the bomb activities, was leading spokesman for the Committee of 100 at the Russian Embassy on Tuesday.

Mrs. O'Connell, a 41 year old teacher, of Warminster Road, spoke to Russian officials for over an hour in an attempt to gain assurance that the 50-megaton bomb Mr. Kruschev referred to on Monday would not be tested.

" I think the first man we spoke to in the Embassy was a public relations officer," Mrs. O'Connell told an " Advertiser " reporter.

" When he understood we were determined to stay, he fetched other officials, and we argued with them for about an hour."

Mrs. O'Connell then left the Embassy to tell those waiting outside what had happened. The rest of the delegation remained until they were forcibly removed by the police.

Croydon Advertiser **1961**

'SECURITY' PROBE AS VASSALL GETS 18 YEARS

Daily Worker Reporter

THE sentencing of Admiralty clerk John Vassall yesterday to 18 years imprisonment for espionage had an immediate sequel in the announcement by the Prime Minister of a committee of inquiry into the case.

Mr. Macmillan hopes to forestall any Labour campaign over the Vassall case comparable to that which led to the setting-up of the Radcliffe Committee.

Chairman of the committee will be Sir Charles Cunningham, Home Office chief; Sir Harold Kent, Treasury solicitor, and Sir Burke Trend, Second Secretary to the Treasury.

It will inquire whether there was any neglect of duty by those responsible for Vassall's employment and will draw attention to " any weakness in existing security arrangements."

When Parliament reassembles Labour spokesmen are likely to criticise the committee's composition as too " official." They would have preferred a judge as chairman.

Plea of guilty

At the Old Bailey 38-year-old William John Christopher Vassall pleaded guilty to four charges under the Official Secrets Act. He had been a minor Civil servant in the Admiralty since 1941.

The Attorney-General, Sir John Hobson, told the court that for the past six years Vassall had been " actively supplying Russian agents with secret information."

He extracted documents from files, photographed them, and returned them the following day.

He was not, said Sir John, " activated by ideological ideas or any political bias."

Moscow pictures

His entanglement had begun when he served in Moscow in the office of the British naval attache. He had been taken out for drinks by Russians and later shown photographs of himself in compromising sexual acts.

For the defence Mr. Jeremy Hutchinson, Q.C., said that Vassall was a homosexual, a " vulnerable, irresolute man who became the victim of ruthless and pitiless parties."

Remarking that Vassall was " no master spy," Mr. Hutchinson added :

" Just so long as this canker of espionage continues to rot the good will between men, so there will be trials such as this."

'Pure greed'

Sentencing Vassall to a total of 18 years the Lord Chief Justice (Lord Parker) told him : " I take the view that one compelling reason for what you did was pure, selfish greed."

Vassall was said to have lived in a flat at Dolphin Square, Westminster, with rent and rates of £500 a year, when his net salary was under £700.

" Almost from the inception," said the Lord Chief Justice, " you were accepting money and accepting money to the extent, it may be, of doubling your salary."

Daily Worker **1962**

She Is 75 To-day

AMONG the most notable converts to the Roman Catholic faith is Dame Edith Sitwell, whose 75th birthday falls to-day (September 7th).

Dame Edith, sister of Sir Osbert Sitwell and of Mr. Sacheverell Sitwell of Weston-by-Weedon, Northants, is not only one of the nation's most distinguished poets, but is generally accounted one of its most bizarre personalities.

At the end of last month, her new book "The Queens and the Hive" was published by Macmillan (price 42s. net) together with "The Outcasts," a new collection of her poems (10s. 6d. net), and a re-issue of "Fanfare for Elizabeth," her book about the great Queen's earlier life (21s. net).

A birthday concert is shortly being held for her at London's Festival Hall, at which Benjamin Britten, Peter Pears, Sir William Walton, Northampton-born Alan Civil and Dame Edith herself will be performing.

Northampton Independent **1962**

24 *Daily Telegraph and Morning Post, Thursday, March 28, 1963*

WOMEN LIBERALS TOLD TO BUY A NEW HAT

"SLOVENLY SOLDIERS DO NOT WIN BATTLES"

DAILY TELEGRAPH REPORTER

INVIGORATED by a series of battle orders for the next General Election, including the tonic advice from their president, Mrs WINIFRED GRUBB, to buy a new hat, women Liberals in conference at Cheltenham yesterday came up with their own ideas for halting the population drift to the South.

In the presidential address, Mrs. Grubb, of Gerrards Cross, Bucks, said: "We must keep an eye on how we look. The slovenly soldier cannot win battles, and while, as Liberals, we do not judge exactly by what we see, let us not feel ashamed at a little personal extravagance in the shape of a new hat.

"Let us grasp the opportunity of appearing to the world in our very best colours. A minor point, you may think it is, but important none the less both actually and metaphorically."

Daily Telegraph 1963

Croydon Advertiser 1961

TEA-BREAK MEN BACK

All the men employed at the Fairfield Halls site were back at work on Monday after a two-week "on-off" strike caused when the employers — Holloway Brothers—refused to allow the men to have free tea-breaks in the canteen.

They will work for a trial fortnight under the new rules—that the men should drink their tea on the job. Next Thursday, union representatives will meet the agent to discuss the situation.

MR. BENN "RENOUNCES" HIS PEERAGE

LETTERS PATENT RETURNED TO LORD CHAMBERLAIN

COMMONS PETITION FOR RULING ON ELIGIBILITY TO REMAIN M.P.

From Our Political Correspondent

Mr. Anthony Wedgwood Benn has withdrawn from his bank the letters patent conferring the dignity of a viscounty on his father and has posted the parchment to Lord Scarbrough, the Lord Chamberlain. This action was symbolic of his renunciation of the succession to the peerage.

The next step will be the bringing into the Commons by a sympathizer within the next few days of a petition for the appointment of a Select Committee to pronounce upon Mr. Benn's eligibility to continue as a commoner without disqualification from a seat in the Commons. He hopes that the outcome might be the drawing up of a simple resolution "which would protect me or anyone else in my position from being plucked away from the Commons."

In his first public statement on his moves to avoid disqualification from sitting as the member for Bristol South-East, Mr. Benn told political correspondents last night that he has had consultations with Mr. Butler, the Leader of the House, Mr. Gaitskell, and (by implication) the Speaker.

The Times 1960

COMMON MARKET: CAN OUR INDUSTRY COMPETE?

STRONG feelings about Britain's projected entry into the Common Market were exchanged at a crowded meeting of South Suburban Co-operative Society members at West Croydon on Saturday.

"Shall Britain enter the Common Market?" was the topic of a three-hour debate.

Mr. Bob Edwards, Co-operative and Labour M.P. for Billston, spoke in support of Britain's entry: "Our living standards will be completely shattered unless we face up to our responsibilities of trading with the countries of the world. If we don't join the Common Market we shall get very poor and become like Portugal or Spain."

The real opponents to Britain joining the Common Market, Mr. Edwards went on, were the "white Commonwealth with Tory Prime Ministers.

"In any case, we should not go into the Common Market dragged behind the coat tails of Macmillan," he said. "We must go forward with a Labour leadership."

Speaking against Britain's entry, Mr. Percy Bell, vice-chairman of the National Committee of the Co-operative Party, told the meeting: "I am not prepared to vote for entry into the Common Market until I know much more about its problems. I am not convinced we should stay out for ever, but if you ask me today to go in then I say 'No, don't.'"

We did not know enough about the Common Market, he said, and there was no guarantee that, if we did enter it, the British market would be able to compete with the other organisations there already.

"Of course, British industry should be made efficient and should be able to compete, but can it at present?" Mr. Bell asked. "I think that too much emphasis has been placed on easy exports to Europe, once we are inside the Common Market."

Answering a question from a member of the audience, Mr. Edwards said that, if Britain joined, the nation would have to have a greater Co-operative movement, both wholesale and retail.

"We would have to modernise the whole of our organisation," he said.

Food prices up?

Mr. Bell told the meeting he though there would be a rise in the cost of food to the consumer if Britain joined.

"But if the average housewife has to pay more for her food, she will have less to spend on other things," he explained. "As a result, we may see a rise in the value of wages."

At one stage, after the debate was open for general discussion, a member of the audience accused Mr. Edwards of evading a question and asked him to reply to it again.

Mr. Edwards replied: "I never evade questions. The answer I gave to the question may not have been to your satisfaction."

He asked for the question to be repeated. It was: Is it true that the Common Market is really a device to propagate capitalism and, if we accept that, is it true that it will delay Socialism ever being brought about?

Mr. Edwards told the questioner: "My reply was that we had a mixed economy in Europe and that the Common Market was not a device to propagate capitalism."

CLERGY INTO RETREAT

The Bishop of Croydon, the Rt. Rev. J. T. Hughes, is taking members of Croydon clergy into retreat on Monday and Tuesday. This period of meditation and prayer will be held at Elphinsward, Haywards Heath, Sussex.

Croydon Advertiser 1961

IT'S FANTASTIC

RUNNING true to form, Orpington's by-election ended with a shattering, bombshell victory for the Liberals which left even them breathless and shaken. Not only demolishing the Conservatives' majority of 14,760 in 1959, but running up a 7,855 majority of their own, was beyond even the wildest dreams of their most optimistic supporters. Declared the victor, Mr. Eric Lubbock: "It is fantastic. I can hardly believe it."

Orpington and Kentish Times 1962

Watched by millions of people throughout the country on both B.B.C. and IT-V. television, the count took place at the Civic Hall and the result declared by the Acting Deputy Returning Officer (Mr. Stephen King) after two hours of mounting excitement. The candidates' names were given in alphabetical order, which put Mr. Lubbock last, and, as his tally of votes was announced, it was greeted with a great roar from his supporters which drowned completely the last few figures and it was some minutes before those in the hall knew the exact result.

Procedure was swept aside and there were none of the normal speeches of thanks. The first to congratulate Mr. Lubbock was the Chairman of Orpington Council (Mr. G. G. Romain), and then Mrs. Lubbock was pushed forward and greeted her husband with a kiss. Then a crowd of supporters chaired him and to resounding cheers and the singing of " For he's a jolly good fellow," he was carried from the hall to be greeted by more cheers and singing from the couple of hundred people waiting outside.

Midday in the City of London, December 1962.

THE LEADING LADY

Junia the Great

Dane uses her theatrical

talents to help

raise money for guide dogs

for the blind

JUNIA is a Great Dane, and she is also an actress. She can give you a look as melting as Audrey Hepburn's. She can, if her director demands it, be as tough as Honor Blackman, with whom she has acted in *The Avengers*. There are times when you suspect that she has as much sense of humour as Margaret Rutherford.

There's no doubt about it, Junia is a scene-stealer. But no actress, or actor for that matter, could possibly resent it, because as you can see from these pictures, she's a heart-stealer too. Junia, like other famous stars, has now reached the stage when a certain proportion of her time is devoted to charity. Her latest project is to offer her services free for a starring part in a film, *Junia and the Trophy*, to help buy guide dogs for the blind. The script has been written by Mrs. Barbara Woodhouse, her owner, in conjunction with Philip Ford, director of the *Lassie* series, who has offered to come from Hollywood to direct it.

Mrs. Woodhouse estimates that, over a period of ten years, the film should raise about £25,000 for guide dogs—and she and Junia are now engaged on raising the £10,000 necessary for financing the production from dog-lovers all over the country. Our first picture shows Junia putting washing in the laundry basket. The next shows her with her devoted friend, Mini Minor, and in the last two you see just two of her many accomplishments; opening a window and drawing the curtains.

Woman's Realm 1964

Yes, he DID tip off Burgess and Maclean

'THIRD MAN' PHILBY—A NEW MI5 SHOCK

By VICTOR KNIGHT and HOWARD JOHNSON

FORMER British diplomat Harold "Kim" Philby was officially named yesterday as the "Third Man" who tipped off his Foreign Office colleagues Guy Burgess and Donald Maclean that the security services were on their trail.

Burgess and Maclean fled to Russia in 1951, and Philby, 51, who turned journalist after being asked to resign from the Foreign Office, is himself believed to be behind the Iron Curtain. He vanished last January from Beirut, capital of the Lebanon.

Harold Philby — "admitted working for Soviet."

Disclosures

These shock disclosures were made to the Commons yesterday by Mr. Edward Heath, Lord Privy Seal. They came as yet another sorry episode in the history of MI5 security failures.

The admission follows years of official denial that Philby had anything to do with the security aspects of the defection of Burgess and Maclean, both of whom are now permanently installed in Moscow.

It is likely to lead to demands for a completely new inquiry into the fantastic events surrounding the disappearance of Guy Burgess and Donald Maclean on the night of May 25 1951.

In particular, MPs want to know why it took TWELVE YEARS for Philby to be revealed as the "Third Man" who warned them to leave the country because the security services were about to take action against them.

They also want to know how Philby, as a Foreign Office employee, knew of security service plans. Did a "Fourth Man" tip off Philby?

Daily Mirror 1963

Tragic death of Michael Holliday

AN inquest is being held today (Friday) on 35-year-old singer Michael Holliday whose tragic death on Tuesday shocked his show business friends.

Derek Johnson writes : The public knew Mike as a relaxed, easygoing entertainer — an impression created by his records and TV shows. But this facade covered a nervous and tense disposition—for Mike was an inveterate worrier.

"I am undoubtedly the most unrelaxed singer in Britain today," he once told me.

MICHAEL HOLLIDAY.

Mike, who sang with the Eric Winstone Orchestra before joining Columbia in 1955, had eight major hit discs, including two No. 1's— "The Story Of My Life" and "Starry Eyed." Other hits included "Nothin' To Do," "Gal With The Yaller Shoes," "Hot Diggity," "Ten Thousand Miles," "In Love," "I'll Always Be In Love With You" and "Stairway Of Love."

Since his first release, "The Yellow Rose Of Texas," Columbia has issued 31 singles, 5 albums and 17 EPs of Mike's.

New Musical Express 1963

THE COLOUR SECTION

This is a great day for The Sunday Times. Its Colour Section, something new in national journalism, makes its bow.

It seems to me that, with this 40-page addition to the two existing parts of the paper, The Sunday Times takes a great stride forward.

Today, however, is only the beginning. When we realise, as we shall in the weeks to come, the full potentialities of this new section, The Sunday Times will become the complete newspaper for all generations of readers.

Roy Thomson

Sunday Times 1962

MR. PROFUMO RESIGNS: I MISLED THE HOUSE

---◆---

DENIAL OF IMPROPRIETY WITH MODEL NOT TRUE

"GRAVE MISDEMEANOUR" TO PROTECT WIFE AND FAMILY

From Our Political Correspondent

Admitting that he was "guilty of a grave misdemeanour" in deceiving the House of Commons about the nature of his association with the witness who disappeared—Miss Christine Keeler, a model, aged 21—Mr. John Profumo, Secretary of State for War, has resigned his office and his seat in the Commons.

His resignation comes partly as a consequence of representations made to the Prime Minister and the Home Secretary by Dr. Stephen Ward, an osteopath, at whose flat Mr. Profumo met Miss Keeler on several occasions.

On May 7, Dr. Ward had an interview with Mr. T. J. Bligh, the Prime Minister's principal private secretary. Both at this interview, and in a letter sent earlier to the Home Secretary, Dr. Ward alleged that what Mr. Profumo had said in his personal statement to the House of Commons on March 22 was, in certain respects, untrue. This allegation was then put to Mr. Profumo on behalf of the Prime Minister and he adhered to the terms of his statement which included the specific declaration that there was no impropriety in his association with Miss Keeler.

GOVERNMENT SUPPORT

Consequently, the allegation was rejected, just as the allegations made by Labour M.P.s in the Commons on March 21 were rejected, and there was no question of Mr. Profumo being asked to resign. The Government stood by him.

On Tuesday, however, came a dramatic turn of events. In the absence of the Prime Minister in Scotland, and at his own request, Mr. Profumo saw Mr. Redmayne, the Government Chief Whip, and Mr. Bligh at Admiralty House.

It is understood that Mr. Profumo then revealed that what he had said in the Commons about his association with Miss Keeler was not the truth and that he wished accordingly to tender his resignation as a Minister and to apply for the Chiltern Hundreds. Since 1950 he has represented Stratford.

The Times **1963**

THE "SUN" RISES ON 3,500,000 NEWSPAPER READERS

Part of the front page of today's issue of the *Sun*.

The *Sun* has duly risen. Shortly after 10 o'clock last night the button was pressed, the Odhams presses churned, and copies of the first new national daily paper in Britain for 34 years flooded out into Long Acre and the waiting vans.

Today some 3,500,000 readers will have a chance to judge whether the hopes are justified. They will see a paper which at first glance bears obvious signs of its mixed parentage. The old *Herald* is there in the style of the headline type and a rash of familiar by-lines. The *Mirror*, the only parent still living, betrays its paternity in the huge pictures, the brash style of attack, and the horizontal emphasis of the make-up.

Superficially, in spite of the compact masthead and the bold declaration of the *Sun*'s aims and policies to the right of the front page, this 24-page paper does not look vastly different. Yet differences are there in the careful admixture of news and features, the spread of women's articles throughout the paper and, most radical of all, the banishment of sport from the back page (except in the northern editions).

FILM STILLS

The *Sun* has used pictures liberally. A child and his pet donkey occupy almost all the news space on page 7, and the centre-spread, for which no plans were reported to have been made, turns out to be covered with stills from the latest James Bond film.

The paper's stated policy of attracting "the growth generation" emerges clearly. The features have an air of

freshness and youth, and a *Herald* stalwart, Mr. James Cameron, contributes a political column which should strike a sympathetic chord with many a young and uncommitted radical. The main editorial, tucked into a corner of page two, is a diatribe against the delayed general election, which is uncompromisingly socialist in tone.

There is no shortage of advertisements, with five half-pages, eight quarter-pages, and three pages of classifieds in this first edition. Demand from newsagents was so great that the print order had to be increased by 500,000 copies, though circulation is expected to fall to a more realistic figure once the novelty appeal has faded.

HIGH STANDARDS

Although there are few signs at present that Mr. Hugh Cudlipp, the editorial director, is aiming at the quality market in newspaper readership. The *Sun* sets out with high principles. In the front-page article announcing its own birth it says: —

"It will set itself the highest journalistic standards. If inadvertently, though in good faith, we ever fall below the objectives of truth and accuracy we have set ourselves the facts will be corrected with frankness and without delay. We want to hear our readers saying, 'you can believe it because it is in the *Sun*'."

If Mr. Cudlipp and his editor, Mr. Sydney Jacobson, really mean what they say, the *Sun* is going to bring something new into British journalism.

The Times **1964**

Noel Coward at the piano during rehearsals for his musical *High Spirits* at the Saville Theatre, September 1964.

The Passing Of TWTWTW

New Daily **1963**

TWTWTW died on Saturday night and in doing so gave irrefutable evidence of what I always suspected—those who ran it never really understood what they were about.

This was shown by the repetition of the vulgar and senseless sketch about a man's fly-buttons being undone, and the re-singing of the Ballad of Camberley Kate.

These were the kind of items which built up the opposition to the programme which finally killed it.

NOBODY that mattered objected to the real satire, even when it was cruel.

Politicians and public men of all kinds could take the exposures of their incompetence and inconsistencies, even when they were malicious. Take them and laugh at them.

What a great many people could not take, and rightly, was the exhibitions of lavatory "humour" which immature producers and compilers insisted on mixing into the programme, and over which even the Director-General apparently had no control.

TWTWTW could have been of tremendous service both to the nation and to the BBC.

It is the measure of stupidity at many levels that a great opportunity has been muffed.

• • •

WARD CONVICTED

He lies in coma, his sentence to come

By Daily Mail Reporters

DR. STEPHEN WARD, his life still threatened by a drug overdose, was last night convicted of living on immoral earnings.

After an absence of 4hr. 36min. the jury at the Old Bailey found him guilty of being kept partly by the prostitution of C h r i s t i n e Keeler and Mandy Rice-Davies.

The jury of 11 men and one woman cleared 50-year-old Ward of three other charges—living off the immoral earnings of Vickie Barrett and being involved in procuring two girls.

The maximum sentence on each count on which Ward was found guilty is seven years. The sentences could be made consecutive, making 14 years' jail, or he could be fined.

We appeal

Last night Ward was still "grievously ill" and deeply unconscious in St. Stephen's Hospital, Chelsea. He will be told the verdict as soon as he recovers.

Daily Mail 1963

CATHEDRAL'S FIRST DAYS

IN the last four days the new Coventry Cathedral has been a setting for a religious experience the like of which has not been seen in this country for a long time.

The Consecration services, with all their splendour, were profound acts of worship. The sequel has been stupendous.

Multitudes of people have surged up to the Cathedral. They have stood in their thousands in long queues waiting to get near it. And those who could not enter because services were in progress have stayed as though they wanted to share in what was going on inside.

The Cathedral has been packed for a succession of services in which the great congregations have joined with a fervour that has been deeply moving. And outside under the high canopy and on the steps leading to the ruins hundreds who could not get in have looked on through the great west window and have joined without any prompting in the singing of the hymns.

Coventry Evening Telegraph 1962

Off to Heartbreak House

CHRISTINE KEELER BEGINS JAIL WITH BREAD AND COCOA

Express Staff Reporter

CHRISTINE KEELER'S high society life of politicians, stately homes, and elegant gowns shrunk last night to the loneliness of a cell in the jail they call "Heartbreak" Holloway.

At long last, the Profumo affair that shook a Government had reached its final scene. And the auburn-haired girl who by the age of 21 achieved a notoriety to match that of some of the great courtesans of history, was just another number in Britain's largest women's jail.

Ahead of her is a nine-month sentence for conspiracy and perjury in the case of Lucky Gordon, her one-time lover.

Daily Express 1963

KATHY KIRBY
Secret love

The Beatles, 1963.

We are in the grip of mania

A "CRAZE" is defined in our dictionary as "a mania, an extravagant idea or enthusiasm, a rage; madness; a flaw, impaired condition."

Could any sensible person deny that much of this definition can be applied to many of the so-called Beeching Plan closures?

Incidentally, let us drop blaming Beeching. This is just what the Tories hoped—that Beeching and the Railways Board would get the backwash of public anger.

All that has happened has been at the injunction of the Tory Government. Public attention was deliberately diverted to Beeching in order to save the Government. We must not fall for this trap. Let's impress upon the people that Beeching is just carrying out what the Tory Government, and especially Harold Macmillan, ordered.

It is true that some of the railway management have played traitor to the great industry they were supposed to serve. Some have been prepared to throw in their lot with the powers that be, even though it has meant carrying out instructions which are ludicrously and pathetically wrong.

When the day of reckoning comes—and it will, after the General Election—there is no doubt some of these crinkles will be squeezed into shape or untwisted.

Railway Review 1964

Prof Dorothy Crowfoot Hodgkin is the third woman to win the Nobel Prize for chemistry. A distinguished X-ray crystallographer, Prof Crowfoot Hodgkin was the first person to determine the structure of any substance solely by X-ray analysis. Her most widely known work was on the establishment of the structure of vitamin B12—after eight years' work by herself and her colleagues. The problem was made the more difficult by the fact that very little was known of the chemistry of the molecule before the X-ray crystallography was commenced. It transpired that the structure of Vitamin B12 was more complex than any which, up to that time, had been solved by X-ray analysis even with more information supplied by chemists.

Previously Prof Crowfoot Hodgkin had settled the structure of penicillin, the work, however, being published later in a post-war volume covering all work on penicillin. After leaving Oxford in the early thirties she joined Prof J. B. Bernal at Cambridge, where she took the first X-ray photographs of a protein-pepsin. She subsequently returned to Oxford where much of her later work was conducted. She is married to Mr Thomas Hodgkin, Director of the Institute of African Studies, University of Ghana.

Chemical Trade Journal 1964

England Reacts To TV Cigarette Ad Ban

By Melita Knowles
Staff Correspondent of The Christian Science Monitor

London

The government's decision to ban advertising of cigarettes on TV screens here has brought quick reaction pro and con.

There is wide approval of the measure insofar as it protects young people from one form of exposure to tobacco advertising. Advertising of pipe tobaccos and cigars is not banned.

Support of the ban has come from the British Medical Association, the Medical Practitioners Union, and many members of Parliament.

A group of MPs wish to see the ban extended to other media. Health Minister Kenneth Robinson in making the announcement, said other forms of advertising—such as posters and press—were "under survey."

Freedom Argued

"The ban does not go far enough," is an expected reaction from the National Society of Nonsmokers.

In asserting that the move represents a "sinister erosion of freedom," the Daily Express speaks for many who say the government has taken away the right of the individual to choose for himself.

On the other hand many sections of the press agree that preserving liberty is no way to justify encouraging children to smoke.

Commenting on the anomalies of the situation, the Guardian notes that the government believes cigarette smoking is dangerous and habit forming.

"Given this conviction the Minister of Health has a plain duty to try to make us give them up, or at least to smoke less," says the newspaper.

Timing Studied

In the context of the ban on TV cigarette advertising the government is charged with being illogical in exempting tobacco from the recent 15 percent tax levied on other imports.

Paul Adorian of Associated Redifussion recalls the commercial television companies' voluntary agreement with advertisers to delay cigarette advertising until after 9 p.m.

According to Health Minister Robinson, however, 20 percent of children between the ages of 11 and 15 are still watching TV at 9 p.m. and 10 percent of the same group are watching it at 10:15 p.m.

The ban, when fully operative, will deprive 14 commercial TV companies of more than £5,000,000 ($14,000,000) a year, or roughly 6 percent of their revenue.

Campaign Conducted

The government will lose about £1,000,000 ($2,800,000) a year in its TV levy on commercials.

The Treasury gets more than £900,000,000 annually in tax from the sale of all forms of tobacco.

The government spends some of this amount on conducting an advertising campaign against cigarette smoking. The Central Office of Information has prepared short films of risks involved in smoking.

The ban at least will ensure that the TV companies showing these films will not also be advertising cigarettes.

Christian Science Monitor 1965

Mr. Gerald Brooke addressing the court during the closing stages of his trial in Moscow yesterday.
RIGHT: Mrs. Konstantinova and her husband, a doctor, in whose flat Mr. Brooke was arrested, giving evidence at the trial.

FIVE YEARS' DETENTION FOR BROOKE

GAOL THEN LABOUR CAMP

JOHN MILLER
Daily Telegraph Staff Correspondent

MOSCOW, Friday.

A RUSSIAN court tonight sentenced Gerald Brooke, 28, the London lecturer, to five years' preventive detention. Brooke, who has been held by security police for three months, had pleaded guilty to anti-Russian activities, including smuggling anti-Communist literature.

He will spend the first year in Vladimir prison, about 100 miles east of Moscow, and the rest in a strict régime labour camp. Such camps, situated in the far north, Siberia and Kazakhstan, are part of the general system of corrective labour colonies.

They are slightly tougher than other colonies in Russia, which accept minor criminals, such as hooligans, drunkards, and petty thieves.

The sentence was announced by Judge Lev Almazov at the end of a two-day trial held in the theatre of a workers' club.

Unlike other trials, the sentence was not met with applause. But the trial had followed a predictable course, although the court was out for three hours 25 minutes, a surprisingly long time.

Daily Telegraph 1965

GREVILLE WYNNE HOME AFTER SPY DEAL

Greville Wynne, the British business man jailed as a spy by the Russians last year, stepped from an R.A.F. plane at Northolt, Middlesex, yesterday a free man.

He had been handed over to British officials at a Berlin checkpoint at dawn in exchange for the Russian master spy, Gordon Lonsdale, who had been serving a 25-year sentence for his part in the Portland Admiralty secrets case. The Foreign Office said the Russians first suggested the exchange on April 7.

Mr Wynne (45) told reporters at the airport: "I am overwhelmed. I want to get back to normal life as soon as possible."

He said he had been told the news of his release on Tuesday, when sitting in his cell in a Moscow prison.

FOOD "VERY DIFFICULT"

He went on: "The Russians treated me according to how they thought about matters." Asked to explain, he added: "I feel as I look, gentlemen."

He said he had lost a considerable amount of weight. He found the food given to him "very difficult, not being accustomed to it."

Mr Wynne then telephoned his wife, who was waiting for him at their home in Upper Cheyne Row, Chelsea, London.

When he drove up to the house later with a police escort, newspapermen—more than 100 of them—and his neighbours cheered. Mrs Wynne ran down the garden path to greet him.

A doctor who visited Mr Wynne later said: "I found him as well as could be expected. He is in very good heart, but he has got to take things quietly."

Reuter reports from Moscow that the only Soviet comment yesterday came from Mr Wynne's Russian lawyer, Mr Nikolai Borovik, who described the exchange as "very nice." Usually reliable sources said the secret negotiations for the exchange had taken some time and an unnamed Polish lawyer acted as middleman.

Mr Wynne's health became a subject of concern to British officials in recent weeks. He was believed to be suffering from stomach trouble after a steady diet of kasha, a rough porridge which is standard fare in Soviet prisons. He was in Soviet custody for 18 months after his arrest in Hungary in November 1962.

Lonsdale (40), is expected to fade into the background after returning to the Soviet Union. At his trial in London in 1961 he was identified as Konon Molody, son of a prominent Soviet scientific writer.

"HUMANITARIAN MOTIVES"

Our Diplomatic Correspondent writes: In London it is being recalled that when Mr Wynne was seized by the Hungarians and the Russians, officials in Whitehall virtually swore on oath that he was not involved in any spying activities.

The fact that he has now been exchanged for a spy of Lonsdale's importance inevitably raises the question whether official statements at the time were entirely accurate. The Foreign Office yesterday said that Mr Wynne's health had been a big factor in the decision to give up Lonsdale. "Humanitarian motives" were cited as the main reason for the exchange.

The Scotsman 1964

Daily Express loses chains

THE Red Crusader, who appears alongside the "Daily Express" title on the front page each day, has lost his chains today after thirteen years.

The late Lord Beaverbrook had the Crusader "chained" on October 15, 1951—presumably in connection with his Empire Crusade.

Why have the chains disappeared? An Express spokesman said last night: "We have no comment."

Daily Mirror 1964

Project Reaches Above The Clouds

WHEN, last Friday, the Prime Minister, the Rt. Hon. Harold Wilson, by lifting a white telephone receiver, inaugurated operations in the giant Post Office Tower, Cleveland-street, W.1, he also thrust the borough of Camden to the forefront of national and global telecommunications. Camden residents in particular among the hundreds of thousands of people who have seen the growth of the Tower from the depths of its foundations to its completion have reason to be proud of this newest addition to the landmarks of their borough.

Camden and Holborn Guardian 1965

NEXT WEEK'S ELECTION

THE first of the three elections this year for voters in Greater London will take place next Thursday. It is the election for the Greater London Council. There are many electors who do not know, or only have a vague idea, what it is all about. They can hardly be blamed. Tell them that the Greater London Council is going to replace the Middlesex and London County Councils, as part of the Government's plan for modernising the local government of Greater London, and they will probably take it in. But go on to tell them that the Middlesex and London County Councils will not go out of business until April next year and that they will exist side by side with the Greater London Council until then, and go on still further to tell them that the representatives they will elect to the Greater London Council—if they vote at all—will be the representatives for boroughs that do not yet exist—tell them this and it's ten to one they won't take it in. Or if they do they will accuse you of making it up. But it's true enough although there are many who regard the new arrangements as all wrong.

Hornsey Journal 1964

Three major Acts given Royal Assent

DAILY TELEGRAPH POLITICAL STAFF

THREE major pieces of legislation passed into law yesterday when a Royal Commission in the Lords justified the Royal Assent to the Murder (Abolition of Death Penalty) Act, the Rent Act and the Race Relations Act.

Each had a long, rough passage to the Statute Book and took large slices of the Parliamentary timetable in the past year. The Royal Commission was followed immediately by the prorogation ceremony ending the old session.

Undoubtedly the most historical of the trio is the no hanging Act. It represents a personal triumph and the fulfilment of a years'-old ambition for its sponsor, Mr. Sydney Silverman, Labour M.P. for Nelson and Colne.

Although technically a private Member's measure, the Bill would never have survived without the generous allocation of Government time.

HANGING OFFENCES

Treason and piracy

Life imprisonment is now the punishment for murder, with judges able to recommend a minimum length for the sentence. The death penalty is retained only for offences of treason, piracy with violence, arson in H.M. dockyards and certain military and naval offences.

The last hanging in Britain was in 1964. Two men are still under sentence of death: David Henry Wardley, 19, sentenced at Stafford Assizes for the murder of Det. Sgt. James Stanford, of Wolverhampton; and David Stephen Chapman, 23, of Scarborough, sentenced at Leeds for the murder of a swimming pool nightwatchman.

The Act will be in force for five years, but politicians expect an automatic renewal at the end of this trial period.

Daily Telegraph 1965

Timothy Evans pardoned

By our own Reporter

Timothy Evans, wrongly executed in 1950 for the murder of his baby daughter Geraldine, has been pardoned 15 years and two inquiries later. The significance of this event, in the view of those who have campaigned for recognition of the error, is that any hope of reviving the practice of hanging when the review period ends in 1970 has also been interred.

'No precedent'

The Home Secretary, Mr Jenkins, wasted no time in pursuing the findings of last week's Brabin report. The Commons resumed yesterday, and a messenger was dispatched to Buckingham Palace. Later, the Home Secretary told the Commons:

"Mr Justice Brabin's conclusion . . . is that it is now impossible to establish the truth beyond doubt, but that it is more probable than not that Evans did not kill his daughter, for whose murder he was tried, convicted and executed.

"In all the circumstances I do not think it would be right to allow Evans's conviction to stand.

"I have, therefore, decided that the proper course is to recommend to her Majesty that she should grant a free pardon, and I am glad to be able to tell the House that the Queen has approved my recommendation and that the free pardon was signed this morning.

"This case has no precedent and will, I hope and believe, have no successor."

The House cheered; and so, no doubt, did all those others, including Evans's mother, who would not accept the coincidence that 10 Rillington Place was occupied by two murderers at the same time and that both killed by strangulation using a ligature."

Guardian 1966

Nuclear horror film still waits for BBC's blessing

SCREENING of "The War Game," a controversial anti-nuclear war film, much of which was shot in and around Tonbridge and Tunbridge Wells, has been delayed because the B.B.C. has not yet approved all the scenes.

Kent and Sussex Courier 1965

The film was to have been shown this week to coincide with the 20th anniversary of the Hiroshima bombing—the first time an atomic bomb was used.

But a spokesman for the producer's office said this week the film would now be shown at the earliest towards the end of September and perhaps in December—"if at all."

The editing has just been completed and final approval is still awaited.

"We had hoped to have it on the screens this week, but we were not ready. It will certainly be six weeks before there is any chance," said the spokesman.

The film, shot during April and May, shows the effect of a nuclear attack on Kent. People's reactions, and their deaths from radiation, fire, thirst or hunger are seen through the lens of a newsreel camera.

Too horrific

It is produced by Mr. Peter Watkins, who was widely acclaimed for his work on the documentary about the battle of Culloden.

"Culloden" was said by some viewers to be too horrific—"The War Game" goes far beyond anything shown then.

Some of the firestorm scenes which were shot in Priory Street, Tonbridge, showed the devastating effect fire could have on the human body when fanned by 200-mile-an-hour gusts.

The realism of the Vietnam jungle scenes, shot at Horsmonden, almost fooled Elstree technicians.

"Realistic enough to be used on the news," was their comment after the first rushes had been seen.

The amateur cast was drawn largely from local people.

EVELYN WAUGH ('THE LOVED ONE') IS DEAD

EVELYN WAUGH, one of Britain's greatest novelists and satirists, died yesterday, a few hours after celebrating Easter Mass at his local church.

His death comes at a time when the film version of one of his most famous novels, 'The Loved One,' has just opened in London.

He was reported as saying that he sold the film rights of the book—a satire on the funeral business in California—for a "small sum."

ACCLAIMED

Mr. Waugh, who was 62, collapsed and died at his home, Coombe Florey House, Taunton, Somerset.

He first achieved literary fame in 1930 with 'Decline and Fall,' which was acclaimed as one of the most humorous novels of the century.

Sun 1966

Imaginative man of action

SIR WINSTON CHURCHILL would have been great if he had never been in parliament; great as a man of action, as an orator, as a man of letters, as a man simply, clothed in his own genius. He was a figure on such a scale that no one institution could contain him. And he himself had moods of impatience with parliamentary routine and detail which caused him to fall short in one limited sense of the ideal of a House of Commons man, yet there was something about the place which was particularly fitted to set him off, and those who were privileged to watch him day after day on the front bench or at the despatch box probably gained as full a sense of his true quality as any but the most intimate observers.

What then were the characteristics in him that we sensed from the gallery of the House of Commons? First and foremost, courage. The rectangular house, with its opposing benches squarely facing each other, is a place of combat. Into this he fitted perfectly. When German bombs destroyed it and it had to be rebuilt, he powerfully influenced the decision to preserve its old form, for reasons which he set forth in a classic statement. He loved the small intimate chamber in which the two sides looked each other straight in the eye, and he himself as Prime Minister sitting on the Treasury Bench at Question Time with head cocked, hands pendant between open knees as he listened for the next question, had unmistakably the air of the old champion in his corner of the ring waiting for the bell. And in this spirit he fought every round until the very last.

Listener 1965

I HEARD of Winston Churchill's death from a shepherd at home. 'The old gentleman's away', he said; and then added: 'He was in every way a man of parts'

Listener 1965

P.c. finds her stabbed to death in fashion shop

MRS. RACHEL HEILPERN, sister-in law of Mr. Geoffrey Heilpern, Q.C., counsel defending Myra Hindley in the moors case, was found murdered shortly before midnight.

Today the news was broken to Mr. Heilpern by the police shortly before he went to court for the second day of the moors murder trial.

Mrs. Heilpern, who was 53, had been stabbed four times in the chest — one of the wounds penetrating her heart.

It was at 11.31 p.m. that a patrolling policeman tried the door of the London Fashion House on Broadstreet, Salford, Lancashire. It was unlocked and inside was Mrs. Heilpern's body.

Grimsby Evening Telegraph 1966

Freddie Mills 'suicide' mystery

DETECTIVES investigating the mystery death of ex-world light-heavyweight champion Freddie Mills were trying to find out yesterday if he had any reason to commit suicide.

Last night — nearly 24 hours after Mills was found shot dead in a car parked behind his Soho night club — his friends talked about the suicide inquiries.

Boxing promoter Jack Solomons said: "I just don't believe that Freddie shot himself.

"He would never take the coward's way out. He had too much guts. He would face the world.

"Freddie had no worries that I knew of, and I'm sure he wasn't being troubled by a protection gang.

"He and his wife, Chrissie, were devoted—real love-birds, whatever anyone else may say."

Sun 1965

HER name is Chi-Chi, which, according to Dr. Desmond Morris, means "mischievous little girl!" in Chinese.

But the London Zoo's problem bachelor girl was looking anything but frisky yesterday as she sat and brooded in her pen.

For Chi-Chi is, as Zoo curator Dr. Morris bluntly explained, just plain sex-starved.

CONFIRMED

The frustrated panda may have looked a deal more cheerful, though, if she had known that her marriage has been arranged.

Come the spring Chi-Chi will fly to Moscow to conduct a wary courtship with An-An, the only other giant panda in captivity outside China. His name, by the way, can mean any one of 130 things.

Yesterday, suitably enough on Valentine's Day, came confirmation that the love match is on after a long courtship.

Sun 1966

It's A Bit Of A Lark For Goldie

GOLDIE, the Zoo's flyaway eagle, was up with the lark this morning on his third day of freedom. And what a lark he appeared to be finding it.

Keepers have been trying to lure him down to earth with a dead rabbit on the end of a rope.

But Goldie seems to be much too cagey to be put behind bars again in a hurry.

The nostalgic memory of the Muscovy duck he killed when he escaped last February still lingers. With only six more shopping days to Christmas, he is already staking his claim to one of the geese on the Regent's Park lake.

Evening News 1965

Hackney Gazette and North London Advertiser 1964

AFTERMATH OF THE BIG BLAZE

TURPIN'S DEATH

" Morning News " Reporter

The violent death of Randolph Turpin, cafe owner, wrestler and one time middleweight champion of the world, gave him the international publicity he had not known for many years.

Within minutes of a Press Association message that he had been found shot dead in a room above his wife's cafe in Russell Street, Leamington police were inundated with Press enquiries from many parts of the world—including New York.

Near the 37-year-old ex-champion's body lay his 17-month-old daughter, Carmen, youngest of his four children, critically ill with a bullet in her head.

FOUND BY WIFE

It was about four o'clock on Tuesday afternoon that Turpin's wife Gwyneth, whom he married in 1953, found them.

The baby was rushed to the Warneford Hospital and a message flashed to Leamington Police Station.

Detectives rushed to the cafe and found Turpin's body in an upstairs room. They took away a revolver.

POLICE GUARD

A police guard was put on the cafe and baby Carmen was transferred to Birmingham Accident Hospital.

At 8-15 p.m., Detective Chief Inspector Frederick Bunting, head of the Mid-Warwickshire C.I.D., gave a short Press conference to a crowd of national newspaper reporters waiting at the High Street Police Station.

He declined to comment on the possibility of foul play and said police enquiries were continuing.

After he quit the ring Randy, greatest of the " fighting Turpins," became boxing's forgotten champ. He became a wrestler—always topping the bill—but it did not bring the fame or fortune his fists had won him in his boxing heyday.

The "Leamington Licker", who pulled on his first pair of gloves in Leamington Boys' Club gym, had his greatest moment on July 10, 1951, when he took the world middleweight crown from Sugar Ray Robinson.

But 64 days later the " invincible " Robinson k.o'd him in the 10th round of the return contest in New York.

Leamington, Warwick, Kenilworth and District Morning News 1966

INQUESTS on the two Customs men who died in Saturday's multi-million pound blaze, which wrecked Bishopsgate goods station, will be held tomorrow at St. Pancras Coroner's Court. Firemen risked their own lives to search for them in the blaze, which was described by onlookers as the worst since the blitz.

The bodies were recovered from among tons of debris near their office, which had been crushed under falling masonry and steel girders.

Victims were Mr. George Humphrey, 62, of 120 Connington-crescent, Chingford, and Mr. Thomas Tanner, 44, of 28 Philip-avenue, Rush Green, Romford.

300 firemen called out

Nearly 300 firemen, including volunteer firemen, fought the fire. Many families were told to evacuate their homes as whisky and other spirits in the goods store blew up in a barrage of explosions. Mrs. Emily Johnson, licensee of The Norfolk publichouse, opposite the goods depot, told a *Gazette* reporter: " I was wakened by the explosions . . . within no time the fire spread as if the building was made of matchwood. It was as if a lot of incendiary bombs had exploded. I've experienced nothing like it since the blitz."

Another onlooker described the explosions as "sounding just like ack-ack firing."

Huge piles of export goods as well as new imports were completely destroyed. Yesterday assessors estimated the cost of the blaze as likely to run into millions.

Substantial Find Claim By Gas Council Group

INDICATIONS that a substantial commercial find had been made were announced on Monday by the Gas Council-Amoco group following initial testing of their North Sea well in block 49/18, 60 miles north-east of Great Yarmouth. The discovery was made by the rig "Mr. Louie" and first announced on May 18.

The well has flowed gas at various rates up to 25 m.c.f.d. on restricted chokes (this term relates to the diameter of the pipe through which the gas is allowed to flow).

Additional wells will, however, be required to determine the size of the field. In the meantime, it has been decided to move "Mr. Louie" 25 miles south-west to block 49/27—the next block to that in which Shell-Esso have already discovered gas.

Earlier, the Phillips Petroleum group had claimed for their own well the highest gas flow so far reported in the North Sea, at 17 m.c.f.d. All data had to be processed and full details would not be available for a week or more. Design work had started on two large drilling and producing platforms and consideration was being given to the pipeline to connect with the English coast.

Gas World 1966

Nova 1965

Ask a silly question and you get a silly answer. As this one is addressed to politicians and concerns a topic that raises temperatures in Parliament (if nowhere else), the silly answer seems a fair bet. Just possibly, though, it's not such a silly question. For whatever becomes of the steel business this summer, we're stuck with plenty of other attempts to run industries in our name. The received phrase for it now is 'public ownership'. But no matter what you call it the question remains: Why doesn't it deliver? We who queue at the Post Office counter . . . we who live in smokeless zones and can't get smokeless fuel . . . we who are still waiting for the promised cheap nuclear energy . . . would like to know.

It's the one aspect politicians don't seem to explore, and it's the only one that matters to us on the receiving end. After all, we have to pay the gas bills and the electricity bills and the railway (sorry, rail) fares—and they never get cheaper. Which was once supposed to be the whole attraction—we were going to benefit because they wouldn't be distracted by any need for profits. That was a long time ago, but must all attempt to deliver be abandoned? Isn't it conceivable that there might be ways of de-bureaucratizing the gas board so that when your new cooker arrives so does somebody to connect it? In fact couldn't these basic services we have all to rely on do better than private firms instead of crowing when they do as well? This is where the party-liners start composing indignant letters. Spare us the daft statistics, please. We've all read about the new pithead baths, and the GPO's STD, and the year BOAC made a profit. This isn't an attack on Labour Party Policy. The Tories are in it too. They had 13 years to do something imaginative about these great national businesses, and it was right at the tail end that they got around to trying a Beeching.

It's become a commonplace that whatever the State runs is a disappointment to the customer. This applies, not just here but everywhere. Post offices aren't marvellous in any country. Telephones are poor in Britain, but even worse in most parts of the Continent. They're outstandingly better in America, but there the State doesn't run them (it does run the post offices and they're terrible). Britons take it as normal that thousands should languish on a waiting-list for phones, but you don't hear of waiting-lists for washing machines. Same with State electricity, always unable to keep up with demand. Nuclear power, State-run since the start, and so little to show for its 20 years' effort that you wouldn't know it's there. Meanwhile the oil industry has come up from nowhere and moved in.

Here and there you do find the odd State business that keeps its end up, like France's Renault cars. But that's as far as it goes. The normal picture is more like the Forces, as so many who served in or alongside them can attest: organized chaos.

Which brings us back to the silly question: Why?

Because nobody cares when it isn't their money? Because politicians can't keep their ham hands off? Because retired generals and civil servants don't make business men? There could be a lot of reasons, but nobody seems to know—and nobody seems to be finding out. Somebody should be. There ought to be a way to give a State business some built-in momentum, just as competition and profits keep private firms clicking. Looking for it would be a more constructive way to spend the summer than wrangling over steel.

The first North Sea oil

In renewed tests last month the Burmah North Sea group's well in block 48/22, 15 miles north of Cromer, again produced oil, and plans for further work in the area are under consideration. During tests of the Magnesian Limestone range between 6 739-6 783 ft the well produced a total of about 4 000 barrels of crude oil in four days. Owing to limitations of storage capacity on the rig " Ocean Prince " and to the prevailing weather conditions, the crude oil produced in the successive tests had to be burnt at a flare. The " Ocean Prince " is being moved from the location to Norway for overhaul. Meanwhile arrangements are being made to cap the well on the sea-bed in such a way that it can be re-entered later.

Petroleum Times 1966

Shepherds Bush Gazette and Hammersmith Post 1966

WOMAN IN BRAYBROOK STREET ROBERTS' LIFE SPEAKS

A WOMAN who knew and lived with Harry Roberts — wanted all over the country for questioning about the Q car killings — told the West London magistrate on Friday of his friendship with Jack Witney and John Duddy.

Mrs. Lilian Margaret Perry, of Filton-grove, Bristol, said she first met Roberts in Bristol three years ago and came to London with him around June this year.

While she was living with him at the address of a Mrs. Howard in Wymering Mansions, Paddington, she met some of his friends.

"I met John Duddy and Jack Witney," she said, and identified the two men in the dock.

Witney, 36, an unemployed man, of Fernhead-road, Paddington, and Duddy, a 37-year-old driver, of Treverton-street, North Kensington, are charged with the murders of Det.-sgt. Christopher Head, Temp. Det.-con. David Wombwell and P.c. Geoffrey Fox in Braybrook-street, Shepherds Bush, on August 12.

Hanratty

Sunday Times 1967

IN THE House of Lords tomorrow Lord Russell of Liverpool will ask the Government "whether they are now in a position to make an announcement about the holding of a public independent inquiry into the A6 murder, having regard to the further detailed confession made by Peter Louis Alphon and other important new evidence about the Rhyl alibi, particulars of which have been given to the Home Secretary."

Lord Russell's stubborn persistence in demanding an inquiry into the A6 murder, for which James Hanratty was hanged in 1962, has already irritated the Home Office. Ten days ago he received a waspish note from the Home Secretary, Mr Roy Jenkins, bluntly refusing a meeting to discuss the case. Tomorrow's question will add to the embarrassment.

The "further confession" of Alphon refers to the latter's Press conference in Paris, details of which were published in the Sunday Times on May 14. The "new evidence about the Rhyl alibi" reached the Home Secretary's desk only last week.

Doubts about Hanratty's "Rhyl alibi" have persisted since last November when, in a "Panorama" programme on BBC TV, a Rhyl paperseller, Charles Jones, claimed to have directed Hanratty to lodgings in Rhyl on the night of the crime. Jones later agreed that he could not be sure of the date, but Press inquiries uncovered other Rhyl inhabitants who claimed to have seen Hanratty on the night of the murder.

Accordingly, on January 30, Mr Jenkins set up a police inquiry into the alleged alibi. It was conducted by Chief Superintendent Douglas Nimmo of Manchester CID. His report was presented to the Home Office on March 22 and a statement on it was promised "shortly after the Easter recess." It is still awaited.

POP SCENE

By NIK COHN

The current influx of hippiedom – the English counterpart of the San Francisco flower children – on to the London scene has meant, among other things, a period of maximum own-up for Nik Cohn. This is the first time that a major pop movement has been directed at an audience appreciably younger than myself and, at twenty-one, it really hurts to find out that I've had it. Because of this, I find it almost impossible to be fair, and spend much of my time dreaming black dreams of disaster for the whole hippy bandwagon. It's got to the stage when the next kid to hand me a flower gets his eye blacked regardless and so much for flower power.

Still, hanging miserably round the fringes of the hippy scene these last weeks, I have had to admit that the beautiful people aren't quite as sick as they might be. It's true that they're arrogant, naive and ridiculous but all of these faults are more than cancelled out by their peacefulness. For the first time that I can remember punch-ups have stopped being an essential part of teenage lore. Instead, the hippies have played to their strength and introduced the black arts of the snicker, the sneer and the snide aside. None of this is very improving for my own old-fashioned and physical temper but it is quite marvellous for my health and I welcome it without reservation.

The reason for this sudden reticence is only partly that hippies use drugs rather than alcohol and that drugs are mostly too dreamy for fighting on. Beyond that, the real explanation is that hippies are overwhelmingly smug and, therefore, don't have to purge their insecurities by brawling. Calm behind their granny glasses, safe in wild but financially secure anarchy, they can afford to be cool and they are. And the only sad thing is that this same smugness which makes them civilised also makes them boring.

Queen 1967

Why Premier and Chancellor did devaluation somersault

By Our Political Correspondent

FAILURE to get the balance of payments surplus expected from the deflationary measures of July 20 last year prompted the decision to devalue.

From this reverse for Government policy arose the wave of speculation which caused Mr. James Callaghan, the Chancellor of the Exchequer, to change his mind.

Policies which led to a large rise in unemployment, and refusal to tackle the basic questions of wasteful overseas military expenditure, have had their fatal consequences.

The decision for the package deflationary measures and devaluation, eventually taken at Thursday's Cabinet, is said to have been unanimous.

Mr. Callaghan consulted Mr. Wilson some three weeks ago about the situation.

Morning Star 1967

JOE ORTON, the bed-sitter playwright who became obsessed by death and made a fortune writing about it, died violently yesterday.

The 34-year-old author of the West End hit play *Loot* was found battered to death in his top-floor flat in Noel Road, Islington, London, N. Later police took away a hammer.

Near him was the body of his close friend, 41-year-old Kenneth Halliwell. He is believed to have died from a drug overdose. The two men shared the flat for six years.

Daily Mail 1967

"Pop" Studio Deaths Inquest Adjourned

EVIDENCE of identification only was given at the inquests opened at the St. Pancras Coroner's Court on Wednesday morning into the death from shotgun wounds of two people, one of them a famous recording manager, at a Holloway "pop" studio.

The combined inquests were on Mr. Robert Meek, aged about 36, who was found dead in his studio flat in Holloway-road, Islington, N.7, on February 3, and that on Mrs. Violet Shenton, aged 54, who was dead on arrival at the Royal Northern Hospital, Holloway-road, N.7.

The Deputy St. Pancras Coroner (Dr. John Burton) adjourned the inquest until March 9, with the remark: "There is a further amount of investigations and inquiries to be made in this matter."

FOUND BODY

Evidence of identification of Mrs. Shenton was given by her husband, Mr. Albert Shenton, of Twyford-avenue, East Finchley, N.2, who said that his wife worked with him at their leather shop below Mr. Meek's premises.

Det. Cons. Corner, attached to Holloway police station, told the Coroner that he found Mr. Meek's body.

Mr. Meek, who discovered the Tornadoes and wrote for them the "hit" tune "Telstar", was dead from shotgun wounds in the head.

Mrs. Shenton was lying on the stairs connecting the shop with the studio, dying from wounds in the back.

It is believed that both wounds were inflicted by a 12 bore shotgun.

Mr. Meek rented his studio from the Shentons.

Camden and St Pancras Chronicle 1967

Blake's escape to Berlin said to have cost £5,000

Bonn, November 21

The West German news magazine "Der Spiegel" stated today that George Blake, the spy, was taken out of Wormwood Scrubs and across Germany to East Europe in an operation which cost £5,000 and was executed on military lines.

The article quoted informed Czech quarters as saying there was no doubt that Blake was now in East Berlin and that he intended to stay there some time.

Officials here would say nothing about an investigation into the validity of the report. The magazine's offices in Hamburg were non-committal about the author of the article, which appeared under the name of Michael Rand. "Der Spiegel" said this was a pseudonym of a Fleet Street journalist.

British passport

Rand, who quoted Communist sources for his information, said Blake was on his way by air to Frankfurt within eighty minutes of his escape. He used a British passport and was met at Frankfurt by two Czechs.

The Czechs had even prepared for the unlikely event of anyone recognising Blake, who wore dark glasses, a new suit, and a new raincoat. One of the Czechs carried an official document which said Czechoslovakia would give Blake political asylum.

Blake was driven to Nuremberg and handed over to members of the Czechoslovakian military mission in Berlin. They drove him 80 miles to Waldsassen, in Northern Bavaria, and there he changed cars again. But two cars left Waldsassen—one of them carrying Blake, the other an unnamed Briton—and crossed into Czechoslovakia at two different points normally closed to foreigners.

The passengers of both cars put up at hotels in the small towns of Krasnice and Sokolov, where they were awaited in the early hours of Sunday morning, the day after Blake's escape. The two Britons met again on Sunday evening in the International Hotel in Prague, where they occupied the fourth floor.

The unnamed Briton left for East Berlin on Tuesday, and Blake left for the Czech resort of Marienbad on Wednesday, October 26, in a convoy of seven cars. There, the members of Blake's group put up at the Praha Hotel, opened specially for their stay.

Helicopter flight

Also in the hotel were several Soviet and East German security service officials. They did not leave until November 3, when most of the party returned to Prague.

Blake and three East Germans drove to Karlsbad airport and took off in a helicopter for Karl-marxstadt, in East Germany.

Rand, described by "Der Spiegel" as a former diplomatist and expert on East European secret services, said that in informed Czech quarters there was no doubt that Blake was now in East Berlin. All his former Soviet contacts lived there. "East Berlin is also the headquarters of the Warsaw Pact counter espionage service, which is mainly staffed with Russians, East Germans, Poles, and Czechs.

It was stated in the article that the East European embassies in London did not take a direct hand in Blake's escape, but provided money for middle men. "The rest they left to the prisoners who were serving out small sentences in Wormwood Scrubs."—Reuter.

Guardian 1966

WILSON, SMITH TALK ON

BRITISH cruiser H.M.S. Tiger returned to Gibraltar last night with Prime Ministers Harold Wilson of Britain and Ian Smith of Rhodesia still aboard.

Mr. Wilson was expected to fly back to London today and unofficial reports said Mr. Smith may leave for Rhodesia during the night.

There has been no hint so far of the progress of the seaborne talks to seek a solution to the Rhodesian Independence crisis.

In Salisbury yesterday it was announced that Mr. Smith's Rhodesian Ministers had been called for a special cabinet meeting, but it never took place.

The Tiger is due to arrive at Devonport on Friday to be paid off. It is planned to turn her into a helicopter ship.

Plymouth Independent 1966

Friday, April 14th, 1967

The truth about the oil

Those who have been actively concerned with the problems arising from the grounding of the Torrey Canyon have received more criticism than praise. The Government, local authorities in West Cornwall, and the Press, radio and TV have all been told by people blessed with both omniscience and hindsight how they should have done their jobs. Political capital local and national, has been the object of some of the talkative experts who knew exactly how to prevent 100,000 tons of crude oil from a holed tanker doing any damage, and just how to make hundreds of tons of oil disappear at short notice from a sandy beach.

VIOLENT ATTACKS

The Press and TV have come in for violent attacks, most of which have been quite unfounded and based on a few out of hundreds of headlines, and the rare silly story like the report about people praying in the streets of Penzance.

Generally, the reporting of the disaster in the national and provincial Press and on radio and TV has been responsible, accurate and restrained. But lately as a result of protests about exaggerated reporting, some newspapers have been unjustifiably minimising the disaster.

It is the duty of the Press and the news services of radio and TV to tell the truth. Reporters from national and provincial newspapers saw a lot more of the effects of the wreck of the Torrey Canyon than those who criticised their reporting.

St Ives Times and Echo 1967

BUSINESS VIEWPOINT
Where to start on tax
KENNETH BAKER, MP

Kenneth Baker is managing director of three companies in the Minster Trust Group. He won Acton for the Conservatives in the by-election last March.

Tax reform is urgent and necessary. If you do not believe this, then read no further. If, on the other hand, you agree that our tax system is archaic, incomprehensible and discouraging, then you will welcome its reform.

It is a product of our history and, like many of our institutions, it has been shaped by the conditions of the past rather than the needs of the present. Moreover, it has now become so complicated that a third of the Finance Act of 1968 was devoted to plugging loopholes.

A new system should be based on three principles—simplicity, fairness and the removal of obstacles to growth. First, it must be simple. Few people can claim that they understand their annual tax returns and when it comes to surtax an accountant is necessary. In a survey carried out in Glasgow in 1967, not one of the workers and only 6 per cent of the executives questioned knew that their marginal rate of income tax—that is the tax they would pay on any increase they may get—was 6s 5d in the £. They cannot be blamed for this ignorance, but in the long run if taxes are not understood by ordinary citizens, they will not be paid.

Secondly, the system must be fair. In many respects ours is not. Without doubt it is just that those who earn more, who acquire more or who own more should pay more than those less fortunate. It is over the question of how much more they should pay that injustice creeps in. For example, from £1,000 a year upwards, the marginal rate of tax for a married man with two children is substantially higher than in Germany, America or France, which is bad enough, but from £5,000 a year upwards the British rate rises so steeply that it leaves all the others well behind and puts the man earning more than £10,000 a year in the most highly taxed class in the world. There are other examples of unfairness. One is the aggregation of the incomes of husbands and wives, a practice dating from the Napoleonic Wars.

Thirdly, the system should not create obstacles to growth or hinder the production of wealth. Taxes are still regarded by many of the older-fashioned socialists as a means of destroying wealth. This is the reason why so little encouragement is given to positive measures to increase savings of all income groups. This is why the present Government has done away with stock options and thereby made it impossible for either worker or executive to build up his own stake in the company he works for. This is why all major reforms of estate duty have been rejected. Yet this duty is one of the most counter-productive of all taxes, since the high tax payer is encouraged by it to invest in such unproductive though delightful things as

Old Masters and French commodes. If estate duty were replaced by a legacy duty, which would be levied on the various legacies left rather than the whole of the estate, then wealth would be preserved in private hands but at the same time it would be distributed more widely.

None of these things will be put right until there is a real change in how capital as such is regarded in our society. Capital is no longer the means whereby the very rich can insulate themselves from unpleasant social and economic changes, it is instead the very sap of our industrial life and the expansion of our industries—the better factories, the better machines that we all want will only come from the modest capital savings of quite ordinary people. Unearned income is really savings income and should be so called.

Any reforms in our tax system should incorporate these three principles of simplicity, fairness and the creation of incentives. Many suggestions of reform have been made over the last few years. At one extreme Professor Merrett has argued that all our direct and indirect taxes could be replaced by an overall sales tax at about 28 per cent. This would have to be accompanied by a substantial revision of Social Security payments to cushion the effect of this on the poorest. Such a complete change has the advantages of extreme simplicity, major administrative savings and the increase of incentive through switching taxes from earning to spending, but it lacks any gradation of tax according to income, which I think is a major weakness. None the less, reform should take us some way along the road indicated by Professor Merrett.

The first step is to make a clear shift from direct to indirect taxation. It is commonly supposed that the 1968 Budget made this shift, but in fact the proportion of revenue collected from direct taxes in 1968 is higher than it was in 1964. So the present Government, in spite of this Budget, has followed all Socialist administrations by taxing earnings more highly. I would favour, and I understand that thought in the Tory party is also turning the same way, a *Sales Tax* of an added value type replacing purchase tax and excise duties and extended to cover a range of services, though certain essentials such as food should be exempted.

The Spectator 1968

Now you can join in The Award Game. Vote for your candidate in each category listed on the Voting Form by circling a, b or c: or, if you have a better candidate, write his, her or its name alongside d. You don't have to use the voting form; you can write your entry on a separate piece of paper. Send your entry to

Queen's Awards, QUEEN, 52/53 Fetter Lane, London EC4

A prize of 5 gns – plus a year's subscription to the MAGAZINE OF THE YEAR – will be awarded to the sender of the most perceptive entry received by us before midnight on 6th January 1968. The winning entry will be published in our 17th January issue. The Editor's decision is final.

MYSTERY OF THE YEAR
a What *is* happening in China?
b Were those flying saucers over England?
c Why do we persist in trying to get into the Common Market?
d

MOST OBNOXIOUS TELEVISION PROGRAMME OF THE YEAR
a It's A Knock-Out!
b The Golden Shot
c Any party political broadcast
d

BREAK-UP OF THE YEAR
a Elsie Tanner and Sgt Tanner
b Mia Farrow and Frank Sinatra
c John Collier and Montague Burton

SOLDIER OF THE YEAR
a General Moshe Dayan, Commander of the Israeli forces
b General Nguyen Cao Ky, Commander of the South Vietnamese forces
c Private Charles Wood, author of *How I Won The War* and *Dingo*

SPORTSMAN OF THE YEAR
a Peterborough United, banished to the bottom division of the Football League for illegal bonuses and signing-on fees to players
b Celtic, who turned the final of football's World Club Championship into a boxing match
c *Foinavon*, who won the Grand National only because he was too far behind to fall at the twenty-third fence with all the other horses
d

CON OF THE YEAR
a Antique markets, for commercialising tat
b The Maharishi Mahesh, for commercialising yoga
c Engelbert Humperdinck, for proving that a rose by any other name can smell as sickly

BRIDE OF THE YEAR
a Peggy Rusk, who married a Negro
b Hoki Tokuda, twenty-nine, who married Henry Miller, seventy-five
c Elsie Tanner, who got more presents than either of them
d

MOST UNFORGETTABLE FORGETTABLE SONG OF THE YEAR
a A Whiter Shade Of Pale
b Puppet On A String
c A Pinta Per Person Per Day

SACKING OF THE YEAR
a Colonel Sammy Lohan by the Prime Minister
b John Neville by Nottingham Playhouse
c Rediffusion by the ITA

BUTTON OF THE YEAR
a God IS Alive—He Just Doesn't Want To Get Involved
b To Go Together Is Blessed, To Come Together Divine
c Lee Harvey Oswald, Where Are You Now That We Need You?

MOST INFURIATING SLOGAN OF THE YEAR
a Schhhhhhhh, You Know Who
b Beanz Meanz Heinz
c Support The Stones
d

REVELATION OF THE YEAR
a That *Encounter* was subsidised by the CIA
b That Churchill didn't kill Sikorski
c Hayley Mills
d

MOST MEANINGLESS PHRASE OF THE YEAR
a 'Swinging London'
b 'The electronic village'
c 'Tune in, turn on, drop out'
d

Queen 1967

Chance meeting
My teenage daughter wrote on the identity card inside her new purse: *In case of accident please notify Adam Faith.* "That's the only way I will ever meet him," she sighed.—MRS. M. B., CHRISTCHURCH, HAMPSHIRE.

Woman's Realm 1966

BEFORE THE TURMOIL— THE MAN WHO KNELT TO PRAY

BY WILLIAM RAYMOND

HOURS before the start of the anti-Vietnam war demonstration and march on Sunday policemen specially handpicked to stop any trouble in Downing Street were approached by an elderly man who quietly asked permission to enter the street.

This was no stranger or demonstrator. It was Major Albert Roche, of Claverton Street, Pimlico, who daily in the early morning kneels opposite No. 10 and says a prayer for the Government of the day.

The police, who know Major Roche well as a friend, let him pass into Downing Street where he knelt in the roadway as he is accustomed to do, said his prayer and left quietly.

There was a striking contrast to this hours later, at about 3.30 p.m., when the demonstrators shouting slogans and dancing up and down in the air, right across Whitehall with arms linked tried to force a way over the strong metal barrier and rows of stolid looking uniformed policemen at Downing Street.

One man did climb the barrier, but was pushed back.

Tariq Ali, who had led the marchers, down Whitehall was allowed through the barriers to deliver a note to No. 10.

At the Cenotaph the demonstrators destroyed wreaths.

As the demonstrators passed along Victoria Street, the chanting stopped, which allowed one objector to the demonstrators to shout, "How much are they paying you, Ali?"

Westminster and Pimlico News **1968**

It's Simon Dee

The show's the same, but the day and the place are different— when Simon introduces his guests tonight from London

ON BBC-1 AT 6.15

Radio Times **1967**

HE SAYS "NO" YET AGAIN

To support his rejection of British membership President de Gaulle made these points:—

● France cannot at present enter any negotiations with Britain and its associate countries which would lead to the destruction of the community to which it (France) belongs.

● Britain must modify its own character before it can join the Common Market, and any attempt to impose British membership in spite of everything would lead to the break-up of the Community.

● The report drawn up by the EEC Commission has clearly shown that the Common Market as it is at present is incompatible with the British economy as it now is.

● It was difficult to admit Britain, in view of the pound and its difficulties, into a Community of countries with solid currencies like the franc, the lira, the mark and the Benelux monies.

● Britain's food supplies system, too, would prevent her from accepting the levies provided for in the Common Market's financial settlement for agriculture.

● The British Isles, in fact, would have to go through a considerable evolution, not only economically but also socially and politically, before they could fit into the Common Market without dismantling it.

The privileges of gold

On the position of gold the President said:

● The present squalls in the international monetary system might end up with the re-establishment of a monetary system based on the universality, immutability and impartiality which are the privileges of gold.

Financial Times **1967**

PRAGUE TELLS RUSSIANS 'GO HOME'

President on 'free radio' Civilians resisting

FIRES raged in Prague last night as the Russian invaders tried to stamp out pockets of Czechoslovak resistance. At least 25 people were killed and hundreds injured throughout the country as Czech civilians took to the streets, most to shout abuse and to plead with the invaders to leave, but some to fight back with stones and Molotov cocktails.

Mr. Dubcek and several other liberal Communist leaders were arrested by Soviet troops yesterday. The tape-recorded voice of President Svoboda, also reported to have been arrested, was broadcast last night by clandestine radio stations set up after the Russians closed down official stations.

The President said: "We are living through an exceptionally grave moment in the life of our nation." Russian and Warsaw Pact forces had "entered our territory without the consent of the constitutional authorities of our state."

Daily Telegraph 1968

□ It is always a tragic moment when an able man leaves the arena of civilised politics. Sir Oswald Mosley had plenty of admirers in all parties who must have watched in growing horror as he marched steadily into the night. I hope it is not too late to bring Enoch Powell back. He has made a foolish and wicked speech, and has rightly been dismissed from his post; but I suspect there is more folly than wickedness in his conduct. He is a very odd man indeed, powerfully gifted but with curious *lacunae* in his mind. For someone like Powell, who I suspect has a solitary nature and is not inclined to commune deeply with colleagues, to choose the path of unreason, if only on one occasion, can be a fatal error. Naturally he receives thousands of letters and telegrams of support – there are plenty of dark minds around – and this illusion of public approbation makes the hostility of the educated seem incomprehensible, even deliberately malicious. For a highly intelligent person such an experience can be devastating and send him hurtling along a path he would not otherwise choose. There is no one so dangerous as an intellectual banished from his tribe.

New Statesman 1968

THE QUEEN smiled. The Duchess of Windsor bowed slightly from the waist. The Duke of Windsor stood erect, looking slightly tired, but happy.

This was the moment when the Queen met the Duke and Duchess in public for the first time since the abdication just over 30 years ago.

The occasion was the unveiling of a plaque to the memory of Queen Mary — the Duke's mother, the Queen's grandmother.

When the curtains slid apart and the plaque was revealed on the wall of Marlborough House, the face of Queen Mary—who was born 100 years ago—looked out on this nostalgic royal reunion wearing the slightly hard, enigmatic smile that Britain knew so well.

The ceremony over, the Duchess of Windsor, wearing a little blue pillbox hat, and a white mink stole over a blue silk coat, chatted for a while with Princess Marina and then, a little longer, with the Queen Mother,

And then it was all over. The Queen and Prince Philip were driven away down the Mall, followed by other members of the Royal Family, including the Duke and Duchess of Gloucester, the Duke and Duchess of Kent, and Lord Harewood.

The Windsors stepped into their official Buckingham Palace car and followed.

The Queen was off to Epsom for the Derby. The Duke and Duchess of Windsor were heading back to Paris in an aircraft of the Queen's Flight.

But the crowd remained, savouring those fleeting minutes when they saw a family reunited.

Daily Mail 1967

Sailing from Southampton on 17 February 1967, 2360 emigrants take advantage of the Australian government's £10 assisted passage scheme, joining 1.4 million emigrants already settled in Australia since the end of the war.

Sunday, October 13—Trinity 18

CHRISTIAN ACTION

Whatever may be the ultimate outcome of events in Londonderry on Saturday it will be long before their imprint is erased from the minds of Irishmen of peace and goodwill. No doubt the rights and wrongs of the affair will be debated on every side and through every medium of communication. In the nature of things, it is hardly to be expected that the arguments will be without bias. It is not our purpose here to add to acrimony.

But something has happened in this country that should not have happened. What we have seen on the television screen and in newspaper photograph is far too reminiscent of what we have become only too accustomed to seeing as the evidence of violence in places where violence is part of life. Whatever claim we may make to be a Christian country is immeasurably weakened. Especially if it is admitted that there is a "religious" background to the events of Saturday.

Church of England Gazette **1968**

DEMOS & MEETINGS

16 Oct Annual Convention of CARD (Campaign Against Racial Discriminatic the Conway Hall, Red Lion Sq., WC2 (242 8032). Open to visitors.

19 Oct Punjabi Social at the Conway Hall.

18 Oct Cartoon Archetypical Slogan Theatre (CAST) are putting on 2 plays in conjunction with the Vietnam Solidarity Campaign at Aston University.

19 Oct Children's Rights, a conference sponsored by NCCL, Council for Children's Welfare, and the Child Poverty Action Group. All day. Mary Ward Hall, 5 Tavistock Place, WC1. Further details from NCCL, 4 Camden High St. NW1 (EUS 2544).

20 Oct The Restoration Of Civil Rights For N. Ireland. Demonstration to assemble at Speakers Corner at 3pm, then march to Trafalgar Square. This is the first demonstration for 50 years on Ireland iniated by the Labour movement of Britain.

27 Oct Folk Concert at the Unity Theatre to coincide with this important day

27 Oct is National Anti Vietnam War Day! Violence on this day will only alienate people from the anti Vietnam war cause. They will see only the violence and not the motives which drive people to it. To make it effective please make it peaceful.

'War A New Perspective'. Anyone who still thinks the American action in Vietnam is justifiable should read an unbiased scientific book called 'War A New Perspective', which gives an account of the chemical and biological warfare in Vietnam. Quote from General Rothschild 'A war like this can only be fought on land dispensible to both parties............' It costs 6/6, available from TIME OUT.

Time Out **1968**

MALCOLM Muggeridge is not my personal guru, nor do I find spiritual peace in his utterances. But I am sorry he has been so badly treated. "It was done deliberately," says Anna Coote, editor of 'Student'. "We didn't want Muggeridge, so we used the pill to get rid of him." Was she surprised when the Rt. Hon. Quintin Hogg, QC, announced in the dailies that the public cannot be expected to continue to support promiscuity? (But is it costing anyone anything? The best things in life are free).

Varsity **1968**

Daily Express 1970

Leila: Last six free

By SQUIRE BARRACLOUGH

THE way is open for Britain to free hijack girl Leila Khaled. The last hostages have been released.

The remaining six held by the Palestinian guerrillas finally turned up in Amman.

The British and other Governments facing hostage demands agreed that their guerrilla captives could be released only when the last of the hostages was in safe hands outside Jordan.

The Red Cross was expected to fly the six—all Americans—to Nicosia today. Apart from grenade girl Leila, six guerrillas are held—in West Germany and Switzerland.

It was reported in Bonn that Leila and the others might be released today to Amman or Cairo.

And as the mass hijacking which began on September 8 seemed to be drawing to its last chapter, President Nixon in the Mediterranean saw the last chances of his Middle East peace plan sliding away.

The unexpected death of President Nasser ended the peace hopes just as suddenly as those hijackings began, according to White House aides.

President Nixon would now give up efforts to get Israeli and Arab leaders to the conference table—at least for now—because no new Cairo leader can expect to announce peace with Israel as his first act.

ROSS MARK writes: The President will now look to President Tito of Yugoslavia.

The U.S. President will plead urgently with President Tito today to use his influence as a third world leader to persuade the Arabs to extend the 90-day cease-fire beyond expiry date November 5.

Mr. Elliot Richardson, American Secretary of Health, will head the U.S. delegation at Nasser's funeral.

IN CAIRO the nation was put on a full emergency with troops on the alert along the Suez Canal.

In Beirut, an Arab committee supervising settlement of the civil war in Jordan announced that fighting had ended and life in Amman and elsewhere was returning to normal.

Shell-Esso sea strike

By CLIVE CALLOW

The Shell-Esso group has found traces of oil in the North Sea off Scotland. This explains why the group has been persistently drilling in this area for more than two years now and is bound to encourage bidding for the new exploration concessions to be granted in these waters by the Ministry of Power early next year.

Shell, as operator for the partnership, has put down five wells off Scotland with its specially built rig, Staflo, and is currently drilling in block 29/3, about 150 miles east of Aberdeen.

Company officials are very cautious about making any predictions for the area

The Times 1969

Judy in Chelsea: the happier times

BY WILLIAM RAYMOND

JULY GARLAND, film idol of the generation who remember her best for her performance in the 1939 film, "The Wizard of Oz," who was found dead in her Chelsea home on Sunday morning, was no stranger to Chelsea.

In November, 1960, she lived for a time in the house owned by Sir Carol Reed in King's Road. It had had as previous owners or residents Ellen Terry, Gwen Farrar and Peter Ustinov.

Living with her there were her three children: Joe, then aged five; Lorne, aged eight; and Lisa, aged 14.

Chelsea News and West London Press 1969

Methodists vote for women ministers

BRITAIN'S Methodists gave an overwhelming vote in favour of having women ministers, on Monday.

The Methodist Conference ignored a warning that to admit women ministers might wreck chances of a reunion with the Anglican Church.

Rather, Conference declared that it was "practicable, desirable and timely" for women to be ordained.

Conference this year did not question the principle of women ministers. Theological clearance was settled some years ago.

A past-president of Conference, the Rev. D. W. Thompson, said it was not possible to fight history — the whole trend was for the co-operation of men and women in equal partnership in the ministry.

Another past-president, Dr. I. Packer, pleading with Conference to vote against women being accepted as ministers, said such a step would introduce an almost insurmountable stumbling block between the Methodist and Anglican Churches.

Baptist Times 1970

THREE NUCLEAR POWERS SIGN TREATY TODAY

By Our Diplomatic Staff

Britain, the United States, and Russia today will lead more than 50 non-nuclear nations in signing the long-sought treaty to stop the spread of nuclear weapons. Ceremonies will be held in London, Washington and Moscow.

The treaty is a result of five years' negotiations in Geneva begun with the signing of the partial test-ban treaty. The new pact comes into force after ratification by the depositary States and at least 40 other signatories.

France refused to support the treaty when it was endorsed by 95 countries in the United Nations General Assembly last month, but has promised to behave as a signatory.

Daily Telegraph 1968

Six may offer U.K. five-year transition period

A COMPROMISE plan offering Britain five years' grace to adjust to Common Market rules and a choice of two methods of budget contributions during the transition period has been proposed by the E.E.C. executive commission.

The proposals, contained in a secret document approved by the Community's civil service in Strasbourg, yesterday, represented an alternative to overcome a major stumbling block in British entry negotiations, informed sources said in Brussels today.

Under proposals to be put initially to the Six before being presented to Britain as the Community's negotiating position, the Commission says Britain could contribute £358-million to the E.E.C. budget in 1973—the start of a five-year transition period.

The Commission suggested Britain could start easing into the Common Market's complex financial framework over five years by paying 21.5 per cent of the £1,666-million of an enlarged ten-nation community.

Britain has repeatedly said the question of budget contributions was major difficulty in the negotiations, saying that her share would be far above that of any other country.

As expected, the Commission suggested the British economy be adjusted to E.E.C. membership over five years from January 1, 1973.

Sunderland Echo 1970

A PROUD WARRIOR WHO FOUGHT TO THE BITTER END . . .

The Times 1969

FOR a moment last week the election, the Derby, the World Cup and all the other preoccupations of an English June seemed unimportant. A single four-word news announcement put them abruptly in perspective—and sent a stab of almost personal bereavement through who knows how many million hearts.

"The end of Arkle," the radio said, and, as the voice droned on, laconic, uninvolved, the rest of its sad message was drowned in a flood of memories.

With them, at first, came bitterness—anger at the cruel fate which has cut short the happy retirement Arkle so richly deserved. For he was only 13 years old—and might fairly have looked forward to another decade of sweet grass, warm beds and careless ease.

INTELLIGENCE

He was far too intelligent to be one of those horses who pines when his active life is over and, after all, if from time to time he wanted to hear the roar of the crowd again what racecourse or showground in the world would not have been proud to receive him?

So it is cruel—to Arkle himself and perhaps even more to those who loved him best. Almost everyone who owns a domestic animal has to face, sooner or later, the dreadful decision Anne Duchess of Westminster faced last week.

Once it was clear that the pain in Arkle's feet could not be cured and would get worse there could only be the one decision. But only one person could take it and this great horse, unlike so many others, was lucky enough to have an owner who both deserved and appreciated the gift from the gods that he was.

But to set against his sad, untimely ending, Arkle was lucky in other ways as well. Throughout his life, in a world it takes all sorts to make, his selection of human beings was as unerring as his jumping.

Horse and Hound 1970

PREMIER 'REGRETS' BOMBING OF HANOI

THE Prime Minister, in a statement from 10, Downing-street this afternoon "notes with regret" the bombing earlier today of populated areas of Hanoi and Haiphong by U.S. aircraft.

"We have made it clear on many occasions that we cannot support an extension of the bombing in such areas," he said.

Mr. Wilson says that President Johnson informed him that the U.S. Government judged it necessary to attack targets touching on populated areas.

While naturally accepting the resident's assurance that the attacks would be directed specifically against oil installations, "we should nevertheless feel bound to reaffirm that we must dissociate ourselves from an action of this kind."

New Statesman 1970

Bertrand Russell

May 17th 1872 – Feb. 2nd 1970

His books:
THE ABC OF RELATIVITY
THE ANALYSIS OF MATTER
THE ANALYSIS OF MIND
AUTHORITY AND THE INDIVIDUAL
THE AUTOBIOGRAPHY OF BERTRAND RUSSELL VOLUMES I, II AND III
THE BASIC WRITINGS OF BERTRAND RUSSELL
BERTRAND RUSSELL'S BEST: SILHOUETTES IN SATIRE
COMMON SENSE AND NUCLEAR WARFARE
THE CONQUEST OF HAPPINESS
DEAR BERTRAND RUSSELL
EDUCATION AND THE SOCIAL ORDER
FACT AND FICTION
FREEDOM AND ORGANIZATION 1814-1914
FREEDOM VERSUS ORGANIZATION 1776-1914
GERMAN SOCIAL DEMOCRACY
HAS MAN A FUTURE?
A HISTORY OF WESTERN PHILOSOPHY
HUMAN KNOWLEDGE: ITS SCOPE AND LIMITS
HUMAN SOCIETY IN ETHICS AND POLITICS
THE IMPACT OF SCIENCE ON SOCIETY
IN PRAISE OF IDLENESS AND OTHER ESSAYS
AN INQUIRY INTO MEANING AND TRUTH
AN INTRODUCTION TO MATHEMATICAL PHILOSOPHY
LEGITIMACY VERSUS INDUSTRIALISM 1814-1848
LOGIC AND KNOWLEDGE: ESSAYS 1901-1950
MARRIAGE AND MORALS
MY PHILOSOPHICAL DEVELOPMENT
MYSTICISM AND LOGIC
NEW HOPES FOR A CHANGING WORLD
NIGHTMARES OF EMINENT PERSONS
ON EDUCATION: ESPECIALLY IN EARLY CHILDHOOD
OUR KNOWLEDGE OF THE EXTERNAL WORLD
AN OUTLINE OF PHILOSOPHY
PHILOSOPHICAL ESSAYS
THE PHILOSOPHY OF LEIBNIZ
POLITICAL IDEALS
PORTRAITS FROM MEMORY AND OTHER ESSAYS
POWER A NEW SOCIAL ANALYSIS
THE PRACTICE AND THEORY OF BOLSHEVISM
THE PRINCIPLES OF MATHEMATICS
PRINCIPLES OF SOCIAL RECONSTRUCTION
THE PROBLEMS OF CHINA
PROSPECTS OF INDUSTRIAL CIVILISATION
ROADS TO FREEDOM: SOCIALISM, ANARCHISM AND SYNDICALISM
SCEPTICAL ESSAYS
THE SCIENTIFIC OUTLOOK
UNARMED VICTORY
UNPOPULAR ESSAYS
WAR CRIMES IN VIETNAM
WHY I AM NOT A CHRISTIAN

Allen & Unwin

Grimsby Evening Telegraph 1966

"Sir! Sir! The Accounts Department's on fire—and here are your matches back!"

Punch 1968

Belfast peace line must go, Craig says

From JOHN CLARE

Belfast, Sept. 28

Mr. William Craig, former Northern Ireland Minister for Home Affairs, today accused the Stormont Government of being careless in its approach to law and order.

He demanded the immediate dismantling of the Army peace fence that separates Protestant and Roman Catholic Belfast along a mile-and-a-half front and called for high density patrols in all trouble areas by joint forces of troops and police.

Mr. Craig said that what frightened him about this weekend's rioting was its apparent spontaneity. Such ugly incidents would recur so long as the peace fence remained and the police were denied access to the Catholic areas. The time had come to get tough with the troublemakers.

He asked why no arrests had been made. The law had to be enforced and the law breakers brought to justice. It was the only alternative to anarchy.

He said it should be made plain that the Hunt committee, which is examining the structure of the Royal Ulster Constabulary and the B Specials, is empowered only to make recommendations. Stormont alone should decide how the two forces should be reorganized.

Mr. Craig made it clear that he would not be prepared to stomach any weakening of the Royal Ulster Constabulary, such as the gradual disarming proposed by the police representative body. He wanted the force to be greatly strengthened and the B Specials to be better trained and equipped, not disbanded or reduced in number.

He warned the Government that it could expect trouble from him and the right wing of the Unionist Party if it attempted to make any gesture of appeasement towards critics of the police.

Westminster's interference in Northern Ireland is the second front on which Mr. Craig is preparing to fight when Stormont reassembles on Tuesday. Last night he brought 2,000 members of the Ulster Loyalist Association to their feet when he said that the suspension of Stormont or interference with its powers was the one thing he would not tolerate.

The audience, all Unionists or members of the Orange Order, gave him a standing ovation when he declared: "Let it be known that we are masters in our own house."

Mr. Craig described the Government's package of reforms to be presented, in the forthcoming session as largely irrelevant. The timing of the reforms was wrong because it looked as if the package had been won by rioting and disorder. Stability and the reestablishment of law and order should have had the first priority.

NIGERIA

Must Biafra starve?

NICHOLAS STACEY

The Rev Nicholas Stacey is deputy director of Oxfam.

The tragedy of the Nigerian civil war escalates daily. The Swiss Red Cross representative in Biafra, Mr Jaggi, puts 3,000 children dying a day as a cautious and conservative estimate. When the Irish Roman Catholic Bishop of Oweri, Bishop Wheelan, whose diocese is in Biafra, told a press conference called by Oxfam four weeks ago that a million Ibos were likely to die between now and the end of August, some thought that he was over-emotionally involved in the agony of his people, and was exaggerating. Today all reports confirm the horrifying accuracy of his prediction. And still nothing effective is being done to bring relief to the starving. Not since I was a seventeen year old midshipman standing amid the ruins of Hiroshima a few weeks after the atomic bomb was dropped in 1945 have I experienced such agony of heart and mind as during the last weeks when my colleagues and I in Oxfam have been struggling to find ways of getting emergency supplies into Biafra.

The Spectator 1968